T0402466

Water Politics and Spiritual Ecology

As water resources diminish with increasing population and economic pressures as well as global climate change, this book addresses a subject of ever increasing local and global importance. In many areas water is not only a vital resource but is also endowed with an agency and power that connects people, spirit beings, place and space.

The culmination of a decade of ethnographic research in Timor Leste, this book gives a critical account of the complex social and ecological specificities of a water-focused society in one of the world's newest nations. Comparatively framed by international examples from Asia, South America and Africa that reveal the need to incorporate and foreground cultural diversity in water governance, it provides deep insight into the global challenge of combining customary and modern water governance regimes. In doing so it addresses a need for sustained critical ecological inquiry into the social issues of water governance.

Focusing on the eastern region of Timor Leste, the book explores local uses, beliefs and rituals associated with water. It identifies the ritual ecological practices, contexts and scales through which the use, negotiation over and sharing of water occurs and its influence on the entire socio-cultural system. Building on these findings, the book proposes effective conceptual and methodological tools for advancing community engagement and draws out lessons for more integrated and sustainable water governance approaches that can be applied elsewhere.

This book will be of great interest to students and researchers in environmental studies, environmental policy and governance.

Lisa Palmer is Senior Lecturer in Geography at the University of Melbourne, Australia.

Routledge explorations in environmental studies

Nuclear Waste Management and Legitimacy
Nihilism and responsibility
Mats Andrén

Nuclear Power, Economic Development Discourse and the Environment
The case of India
Manu V. Mathai

Federalism of Wetlands
Ryan W. Taylor

Governing Sustainable Urban Renewal
Partnerships in action
Rory Shand

Employee Engagement with Sustainable Business
How to change the world whilst keeping your day job
Nadine Exter

The Political Economy of Global Warming
The terminal crisis
Del Weston

Communicating Environmental Patriotism
A rhetorical history of the American environmental movement
Anne Marie Todd

Environmental Justice in Developing Countries
Perspectives from Africa and Asia-Pacific
Rhuks Temitope Ako

Climate Change and Cultural Heritage
A race against time
Peter F. Smith

A Global Environmental Right
Stephen Turner

The Coming of Age of the Green Community
My neighbourhood, my planet
Erik Bichard

Fairness and Justice in Environmental Decision Making
Water under the bridge
Catherine Gross

Carbon Politics and the Failure of the Kyoto Protocol
Gerald Kutney

Trade, Health and the Environment
The European Union put to the test
Marjolein B.A. van Asselt, Michelle Everson and Ellen Vos

Conflict, Negotiations and Natural Resource Management
A legal pluralism perspective from India
Edited by Maarten Bavinck and Amalendu Jyotishi

Philosophy of Nature
Rethinking naturalness
Svein Anders Noer Lie

Urban Environmental Stewardship and Civic Engagement
How planting trees strengthens the roots of democracy
Dana R. Fisher, Erika S. Svendsen and James J.T. Connolly

Disaster Risk Reduction for Economic Growth and Livelihood
Investing in Resilience and Development
Edited by Ian Davis, Kae Yanagisawa and Kristalina Georgieva

Energy Security Cooperation in Northeast Asia
Edited by Bo Kong and Jae Ku

Water Politics and Spiritual Ecology
Custom, environmental governance and development
Lisa Palmer

The Politics of Ecosocialism
Transforming welfare
Edited by Kajsa Borgnäs, Teppo Eskelinen, Johanna Perkiö and Rikard Warlenius

'With great clarity and style, Palmer uncovers an unsuspected universe of intricate connections between society and nature created by the flow of water on the island of Timor. Like all great ethnographies, this book is a revelation.'

J. Stephen Lansing, *Asian School of the Environment, Nanyang Technological University, Singapore*

'This book is about more than cultural conceptions of water in Timor Leste. It's an incitement to recognise the parochialism of the Western paradigm of "environmental management". Lisa Palmer's ethnography suggests it might not be too late to learn from other ways of interacting with what Westerners call "nature".'

Noel Castree, *Professor of Geography, University of Wollongong, Australia*

'This *tour de force* is an outstanding addition to the theory and ethnography of water as a material substance and as a component of social, ritual, and cosmological relationships; its geographical frame of reference is the small nation-state of Timor Leste but the lessons it teaches apply to the developing world in general.

Based upon intensive and extensive fieldwork, complemented by widely-ranging sources, *Water Politics and Spiritual Ecology* is a major addition to the published ethnography of Timor Leste and will appeal to scholars and policy-makers interested in the social, ritual, and mythological ramifications of water in that post-colonial nation-state.

This superb study of water, kinship, affinity, ritual, and narrative seamlessly brings together Timor Leste's past and present and provides an original perspective on this post-colonial nation-state. It is indispensable reading for scholars and policy-makers concerned with the problematic relationship between local communities and national policies.'

David Hicks, *Professor of Anthropology at Stony Brook University, USA, and life member of Clare Hall, University of Cambridge, UK*

'Examining hydro-social cycles in East Timor, Palmer demonstrates the benefits of in-depth ethnographic research in contributing to debates about agency and materiality. Through a rich and enjoyable account of Timorese beliefs and practices, her book illuminates the complex ways in which, over time and space, people and water interconnect and act upon each other.'

Veronica Strang, *Institute of Advanced Study, Durham University, UK*

'In *Water Politics and Spiritual Ecology* Lisa Palmer helps us to appreciate the agency of gushing waters inhabiting the underworld of East Timor's drylands. She alerts us to an underground economy of debt, reciprocity, connection and disconnection that the sacred springs of the Baucau Plateau continue to mobilize. We learn how past and present, upland and coastal people, pre-colonial, colonial and post-colonial modes of water governance are entangled in a lively mesh of relationality. Most importantly, we are given tantalizing insights into living together with the non-human world differently.'

J.K. Gibson-Graham, *Institute for Culture and Society,*
University of Western Sydney, Australia

'Palmer's extraordinary account of the ritual ecology of water in Timor Leste alerts us to a worldview that accords water a powerful agency and influence on not just the natural world, but also the human and supranatural. This book is a first in its intellectual engagement with a matter of global importance – human relations with water – and a welcome contribution to anthropology in complex postcolonial conditions.'

Marcia Langton, *Chair of Australian Indigenous Studies,*
The University of Melbourne, Australia

Water Politics and Spiritual Ecology

Custom, environmental governance and development

Lisa Palmer

LONDON AND NEW YORK

First published 2015
by Routledge
2 Park Square, Milton Park, Abingdon, Oxon OX14 4RN

and by Routledge
711 Third Avenue, New York, NY 10017

Routledge is an imprint of the Taylor & Francis Group, an informa business

© 2015 Lisa Palmer

The right of Lisa Palmer to be identified as author of this work has been asserted by her in accordance with sections 77 and 78 of the Copyright, Designs and Patents Act 1988.

All rights reserved. No part of this book may be reprinted or reproduced or utilized in any form or by any electronic, mechanical, or other means, now known or hereafter invented, including photocopying and recording, or in any information storage or retrieval system, without permission in writing from the publishers.

Trademark notice: Product or corporate names may be trademarks or registered trademarks, and are used only for identification and explanation without intent to infringe.

British Library Cataloguing-in-Publication Data
A catalogue record for this book is available from the British Library

Library of Congress Cataloging-in-Publication Data
A catalog record for this book has been requested

ISBN: 978-0-415-71351-1 (hbk)
ISBN: 978-1-315-88325-0 (ebk)

Typeset in Goudy
by Wearset Ltd, Boldon, Tyne and Wear

Printed and bound by CPI Group (UK) Ltd, Croydon, CR0 4YY

For Jose Maria Mok Kingsang and his many grandchildren

Contents

List of figures	xiv
List of maps	xvi
Preface	xvii
Acknowledgements	xx

1 Introduction   1

Modernizing water governance and the place of custom 5
The spiritual ecology of water and the eastern archipelago 8
Agency and the hydrosocial cycle 17
Ontological frictions 19
Inclusive sociality and ecologies of spirit 20
'Coming-into-being': customary renewal and transition 23
The ethnography 25

2 Water cosmologies   39

People and their dai 42
The hydrosocial cycle 45
The spiritual ecology of spring water in Baucau 49
The hydrosocial cycle and the ritual centre of Luca 51
Discussion 56

3 Watery histories   61

The emergence of the world 63
The speculations of historical linguistics 68
The returnees 71
Baucau and the origins of irrigated rice production 73
Kisar and respectful relations 76
Discussion 78

xii *Contents*

4 Water pathways   83
The descent: the story of Wani Uma and their water 84
The expansionary presence of Luca 88
Emergence and division: the house of Loi Leki 91
The making of relationships: the story of Wai Lia 92
Custodians of the savanna: Wai Lia Bere and Wai Lia Mata 96
Complicating things: Wai Lili-Wai Wa and Wai Husu-Wai Lewa 99
The exodus: the movement to Caisidu 101
Discussion 102

5 Challenging the moral order: water, kinship and war   106
The excesses of Joao Lere 109
The fall of Luca and the rise of Vemasse 115
Dom Boa Ventura and the waters of Baucau 117
Nai Leki's triumph 122
Discussion 125

**6 Water relations: the embodied politics of ritual and irrigated
rice production**   129
The mixed agricultural economy 131
The springs of Loi Hunu 133
Irrigated rice production in Baucau 137
Traditional irrigation co-operatives 143
Ritual politics, ancestral names and bodies 145
Discussion 147

7 Independence and the (re)negotiation of customary relations   153
Late colonial development in Baucau 154
Catholic syncretism 157
Independence-era water supply in Baucau town 161
Groundwater research and policy development 163
Community managed water supply systems 166
Ritual dynamism 167
Springs and national politics 170
Discussion 172

Conclusion   181
The hydrosocial cycle revisited 182
Bodily ontology 186

Contents xiii

Appendix 1: Key research participants 195

Appendix 2: Luca and We Hali 198

Appendix 3: The custodian of the *tais* 203

**Glossary of selected Tetum, Waima'a (W) and
Makasae (M) terms** 204

Index 205

Figures

I.1	*Wai Benu* ceremony at Wai Daba spring, Berecoli	xix
1.1	Interview with elders at the houses of Wani Uma Chefe Sau Rai	27
1.2	Major Ko'o Raku (Antonio da Costa Gusmao), Bahu *lia na'in* wearing ritual regalia	28
2.1	Mundo Perdido (Watu Nete Watu Ba'i) rocky outcrops and *tara bandu* (ritual prohibition) pole, Ossu de Cima	41
2.2	Major Ko'o Raku carrying out a healing divination, Ono Seri, Buruma	44
2.3	Wai Kinari spring, Caibada Makasae	48
2.4	David Amaral, Luca *lia na'in* (right) and apprentice	53
2.5	Water blessing for new arrivals (Gari Modo, water custodian for Mau Pula spring, Seu Baru, Mundo Perdido)	55
3.1	View of Mount Matebian from Berecoli ricefields	72
3.2	Wai Mata Me hillock and coastal irrigation channels, Baucau	75
3.3	Mau Ba'i beach and coastal features, Baucau	76
3.4	Laga coast and ricefields	79
4.1	Wani Uma sacred house complex, Baucau	86
4.2	Wailili spring, irrigation channel and spring grove	88
4.3	Boile Komu sacred house renovation, Bahu (January 2012)	91
4.4	Water custodian of Wai Lia Bere (Wono Loi, left) at Ledatame Ikun sacred house, Darasula with Major Ko'o Raku (right)	97
4.5	'Closing the door' (*taka odamatan*) ceremony at Wai Lia Bere	98
4.6	Buffalo and herder, Baucau plateau (with central ranges in background)	99
5.1	Re-construction of Wani Uma *umo oe* (W: ruling political house), October 2013	110
5.2	Watu Tege (Joao Lere's basket) and Bundura coastline	113
5.3	Old Baucau market and irrigation channel feature, built during the colonial administration of Armando Pinto Correia (circa 1930s)	123
6.1	Community spring water and agricultural fertility ritual, Lekitehi, Maubisse	130

Figures xv

6.2	Roadside vegetable stalls and sellers, Logo Bere spring, Mundo Perdido	132
6.3	Annual irrigation channel repairs overseen by the *kabu bee* (water controllers) from Bahu and Caibada (Jose da Costa (right) and Enrici da Costa)	144
7.1	Wai Lia pump station and Wai Lewa spring and grave, Baucau	155
7.2	Procession of Santu Antonio, Baucau	158
7.3	Baucau's Wai Lia spring and cave with unfinished Nossa Senora project at rear and author in foreground	160
7.4	Escarpment edge houses and water pipes on the way from Wai Lia to Baucau's new town	162
7.5	A privately owned water truck refilling at Wai Lua spring, Baucau	163
7.6	Rally for Fretilin's 2012 presidential candidate in main street of old Baucau town near Wai Lia	171

Maps

1.1	Baucau Viqueque zone of Timor Leste	2
1.2	Hydrogeology of Baucau Viqueque zone	4
1.3	Timor Leste and the eastern archipelago	11
2.1	Topography of Baucau Viqueque zone	40
3.1	Hypothesized migration pathways and influences on Kawamina and Makasae languages	69
4.1	Baucau sub-district map (with key villages and springs from text)	85
4.2	Locally asserted underground flows from Wai Lia Bere	96
5.1	Timor Leste district map (with key towns, mountains and other places from text)	108

Preface

When I first went to a liberated Timor Leste (East Timor) in the year 2000 the country was still recovering from the aftermath of the 1999 emergency and violent withdrawal of Indonesian troops. Yet from the ashes of this scorched earth retreat, new life was already emerging, literally out of the earth. In the country's second city, Baucau, a locally famous spring called Wai Lia had once more gushed forth, feeding the town's depleted water supply and channelling irrigation waters to the terraced fields below. I was told that this spring, which had been near dry for many years, had spontaneously gushed forth as the Indonesian military departed the town, as though it too was celebrating a victory. While years later I was to hear many stories about this spring and its temperamental flow, there remained a constant refrain: the water had its own agency. It was also made clear to me that the agency of this spring was linked to this unlikely Timorese victory. Like other springs, it was said to have given spiritual assistance and power to the people in their resistance activities.

In this first visit to Baucau in 2000 I stayed at the home of Jose Maria Mok Kingsang, an ex-resistance leader (*nom de guerre*: Mautodo) and the son of a Chinese immigrant jeweller from Macau and a Waima'a-speaking woman from Berecoli in Baucau's hinterland. Jose had grown up in the town of Baucau in the 1930s, living amongst the Chinese shop houses which had sprung up in the vicinity of Wai Lia. As a boy he was known locally as Ano Wai Lia (the boy of Wai Lia), and much later still he named his small construction business Wai Lia and his restaurant Café Vitoria (Victory) in honour of his nation's remarkable victory. By twist of fate, when I next met Jose in 2004 I was returning to his home as his daughter-in-law, having married his fifth son Quintiliano who was living in Australia.

This book is dedicated to the memory of Jose Maria Mok Kingsang (1932–2013). He was the first person to tell me the story of Wai Lia and it was his connection to this spring that enabled me to trace the watery paths leading from it to the world beyond. As I came to know more about this interconnected world, I also slowly began to understand the profound connection of water to local histories, politics and rituals of life and death.

In 2013 Jose died in tragic circumstances. His funeral was, like many such events, a catalyst for endings and also renewal. It was a time for the elders from

xviii *Preface*

associated lineage houses to come together and sort out the unfinished business of marriage and life cycle exchange obligations. These familial interconnections had commenced in some cases over sixty years earlier and while Jose had also been a central player in most of them, his Timorese Chinese heritage had enabled a degree of ambiguity to surround his actual relationships with extended kin and affines.

On the day of his burial, as Catholic priests converged on the house for a pre-burial mass, elsewhere on the family property these 'house' negotiations were reaching a climax. An elaborate oratory exchange between the elders of two houses was trying to determine which origin house would now 'shade' and protect these Timorese-Chinese children, a lineage which now stretched to include many grandchildren. As Jose's sons sat quietly listening and waiting to bury their father, they also anxiously awaited an indication about their own children's long-term wellbeing. While, as is usually the case, these complex negotiations could not be concluded on that day, in order that the burial might proceed an interim agreement was reached on one critical point. The matter of the primary house (known as the *hun* or *uma fukun* = trunk house) to which Jose's sons and unmarried daughters belonged was, after many years of uncertainty, coming to a resolution. The Makasae-speaking lineage house of their long deceased mother had agreed to accept and participate in the outstanding 'path clearing' and exchange of marriage gifts and counter-gifts (*barlake*) between it and the house of Wai Daba in Berecoli. If these exchanges were concluded over coming years then it appeared that the house of Wai Daba, the house of Jose's own Timorese mother and the Waima'a-speaking founding house of another well-known regional spring, would be the family's *hun* (trunk), the source of its primary 'shade' and protection.[1]

A week after the burial took place, my husband and his brothers were called to participate in a ceremony at the spring of Wai Daba. Here they participated for the first time in their lives in the annual new rice consecration ceremony (W: *wai benu*) where their 'fathers' in the Wai Daba house implored the human and non-human ancestral spirits of the spring to bless the entire lineage, ensure their good health and prosperity as well as that of their surrounding rice fields (see Figure i.1). The ritual included prayers and the sacrifice of seven chickens, the offering of seven bundles of areca nuts and betel leaves from the spring grove, and the collective consumption of the newly consecrated rice. Following this, the dozen or so men present concluded the ritual by imbibing sacred spring water contained in a freshly cut bamboo length. As they took their leave, Jose's sons were each given a small number of the remaining leaves and nuts and instructed to rub them briefly over the bodies of their children when they returned home. This would ensure that they too would receive the life-giving blessings of the ancestral waters of the Wai Daba spring.

This way of being and communicating with water is the subject of this book.

Figure I.1 Wai Benu ceremony at Wai Daba spring, Berecoli.

Note

1 At the time of writing this process was still under negotiation between the houses of Wai Daba and Lalabu.

Acknowledgements

My acknowledgements start from where this particular journey began back in the year 2000. I must thank Hilario Goncalves for inviting me to visit his homeland from Darwin, Filomena Moc for taking me to Baucau and Marcia Langton for being a part of it, in more ways than one.

In the fourteen years that followed I made many journeys to Timor Leste and I am indebted to the Mok family of Baucau and Dili, and all of the associated families across the region, for their hospitality and assistance with this research. In particular I would like to acknowledge and thank the late Jose Maria Mok Kingsang and his son (and my husband) Quintiliano Mok who was my constant (and unpaid!) field assistant and cameraman. It was Quin who encouraged me to write this book and who, in many ways, enabled me 'access' to document its stories. I would also like to thank my brother and sister-in-law Rogerio Mok and Louisa Freitas for their patience as I grappled with learning Tetum and for their willingness to discuss all matters cultural. For their hospitality and endlessly varied assistance, I am also indebted to Fatima Mok and Jose Smith, Domingos, Jose and Januario Mok, Ireni Gustavo Rego, Carolina and Angelo do Rosario, and Kiku.

Others family members and colleagues in Baucau require special mention as research facilitators. In particular, I am indebted to Cesaltinu Da Silva Freitas for many illuminating conversations, for his research assistance and for his outstanding Makasae, Waima'a, Midiki and Kairui language translation skills. I was also assisted in the translation of Makasae by Domingos Freitas and Louisa Freitas and of Waima'a by Mauricio Belo. Antonio Vicente Marques Soares was a constant source of knowledge and advice and frequently enabled my research to remote regions, particularly in the Viqueque district. Others who facilitated my research in the villages around Baucau and Viqueque included Jose da Costa (Kabu Bee Boile), Julio da Costa (Ocadaba), Alceda, Father Mario da Costa Melo Cabral, Armindo Ornai, Placidio Rosario, Elijio de Cha, Father Basilio Ximenes, Chefe Helioterio Boavida (Bahu), Chefe Julio da Silva Baptista (Bahu), Alberto Ribiero, Bernadino Sarmento Ornai, Raimundo Sarmento Freitas, Chefe Justino Ruas (Builale), Jose Andre dos Santos, Father Abel Soares Alves, Edmundo da Silva and Manuel da Silva.

For sharing their stories with me I am indebted to many *bee na'in* ('custodians of the waters') and *lia na'in* ('custodians of the words') from the Baucau and

Viqueque districts. Given their large number, the names of these people are listed in Appendix 1. In particular, I acknowledge and thank Major Ko'o Raku (Antonio da Costa Gusmao).

From the government and non-government sector in Timor I acknowledge the assistance, both large and small, of Demetrio do Amaral de Carvalho, Santina Amaral Fernandes and all the committed staff at the Haburas Foundation, Lindsay Furness, Joaquin da Costa Ximenes, Craig McVeigh, Kerryn Clarke, Giacomo Mencari, Filomeno Bruno Soares, Father Elijio Locateli, Father Rolando Fernandez, Nuno Oliveira, Leo Belarmino, Anor Sihombing, Fransisco do Castro, Luciano Periera, Cecilia Fraga, the Office of the District Administrator of Baucau, the Office of the Sub-District Administrator of Baucau, and Bishop Dom Basilio do Nascimento.

Outside of Timor I greatly benefited from the support, advice, assistance and commentary on various parts of this manuscript (or its earlier versions) which was provided by Balthasar Kehi, Salustiano Freitas, Andrew McWilliam, Sue Jackson, Susana Barnes, David Hicks, Christopher Shepherd, Stephen Lansing, Thomas Reuter, Marcia Langton and Simon Batterbury. I also acknowledge the contributions of Lia Kent, Sara Niner, Jon Barnett, Pyonne Myat Thu, James Fox, Alexander Cullen, Gillian Tan, Veronica Strang and Katherine Gibson.

Valuable technical advice was provided at various stages by Seth Keen, Susan and Nick White, Brian Finlayson, Russell Drysdale, Ian Glover, Geoffrey Gunn, Sue O'Connor, Ian Thomas, John Hajek and Barbara Downes.

In Australia, language translations of Portuguese historical texts were carried out by Christopher Shepherd, who also generously made available to me his own archival copies of early twentieth-century Timorese agricultural bulletins. Salustiano Freitas provided assistance with the interpretation of other Portuguese texts, as did Balthasar Kehi who also translated the Eastern Tetum ritual verse from Luca (Appendix 2). Detailed cartographic assistance was provided at the University of Melbourne by Chandra Jayasuriya (School of Geography), with assistance from Glen MacClaren and Stephen Wealands (Environmental Systems Solutions) and Luke Wallace and David Arnold (Geosciences Australia). Lily O'Neil provided bibliographic research assistance.

I would like to thank the editorial and production team at Routledge, in particular Khanam Virjee and Bethany Wright for their enthusiasm, consideration and efficiency. I also acknowledge the Australian Research Council whose support in the form of two grants (LP0561857 [2005–2008] and DP1095131 [2009–2012]) provided the necessary funds to carry out this long-term field research. For their ongoing support, I thank the faculty of the School of Geography at the University of Melbourne.

I am indebted to the support of my parents and other family and friends in Australia. Most of all, I thank my husband, Quintiliano, and our children, Madalena and Zeca, who were with me nearly every day of this book's journey.

1 Introduction

Water, as we know, dissolves more substances than any other liquid, known as the 'universal solvent', wherever it flows 'it carries substances along with it' (Altman 2002: 10). This analogy is particularly poignant in the Baucau Viqueque region of Timor Leste, which like much of the rest of the island, is underlain by karst formations. In such environments the topography is formed chiefly by the dissolving of rock by water and complex and changing surface and subsurface water pathways are always in the process of ending or becoming. Earthly substances are always on the move.

In the course of carrying out research for this book, I slowly came to understand another reality: that in this particular karstic landscape the subsurface waterworld carries with it and is inspirited by aspects of a sacred and animate cosmos. In the material reality of this society, such water is the life-nourishing milk and blood of the earth and a key medium of communication between the visible and invisible worlds, the worlds of light and dark. Emerging from springs into the light of the surface world, karst water carries with it, mediates and transforms the spiritual essences of both life and death.

Drawing on primary ethnographic research carried out between 2004 and 2014 in the eastern districts of Baucau and Viqueque (population 182,000 (NSD and UNFPA 2011); see Map 1.1), this book is an important contribution to the recent resumption of anthropological work in post-independence Timor Leste (McWilliam and Traube 2011). It examines the spiritual ecology and associated hydrosocial cycle of a water focused society, following the trails of water and water associated spirit beings travelling through the karstic landscape from the mountains to the sea. It argues that in this hydrosocial cycle the material reality of water is critical to the ways in which local agricultural communities create and maintain place, to their understandings of space and social relationships and to their particular cosmopolitical configurations of life and being. This supra-social landscape (where the social is not confined to the domain of human beings) was created by and still governed through complex interactions between spirits, humans, animals and other physical objects and forces. Laying out in a 'perspicuous' view (Wittgenstein 1979: 9e) my own ethnographic data and interpretation, this book tries to answer questions about how water is perceived, managed and used in this region of Timor Leste and how local people's own

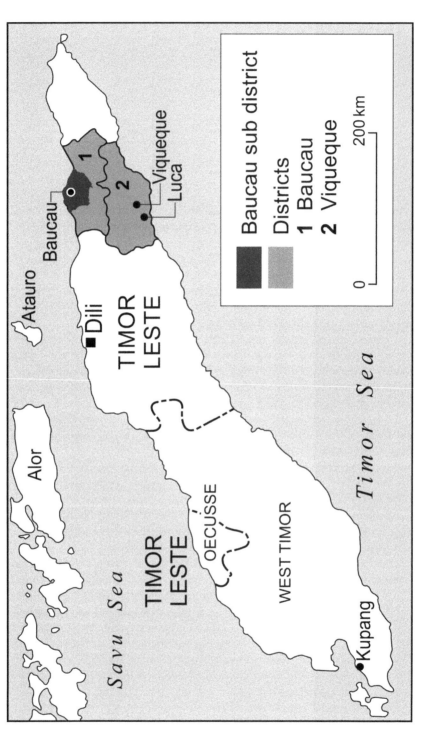

Map 1.1 Baucau Viqueque zone of Timor Leste (copyright Chandra Jayasuriya).

understanding of their past and future trajectories are linked to their particular understandings of the significance of water. It then considers how these local realities engage with and are today co-constituted by modernist technologies of water governance.

The Baucau Viqueque zone is divided in its central region by rugged forested hills and mountains splitting on either side into tracts of savannah and coastal areas replete with limestone terraces, caves, outcrops, sinkholes, depressions, springs, subsurface drainage and subsurface rivers of which, until recently, little was scientifically understood (cf. Metzner 1977). In order to better locate and potentially access these groundwater resources, in the late 2000s hydrogeological research was systematically carried out in Baucau by scientific advisers to the Timorese government (Furness 2011, 2012; Wallace *et al.* 2012a; see Map 1.2). The karst limestone formations of the Baucau Viqueque zone vary greatly in age between the ancient mountains of the central Mundo Perdido range to the much younger Pleistocene raised coral reefs of Baucau plateau and marine terrace zone (Audley-Charles 1968; Wallace *et al.* 2012a).[1] Impermeable clay formation separates these two zones.

Water flowing through the younger karst of the Baucau plateau region does so via a 'two phase flow system' (Furness 2012). After rain water enters the weathered rock and thin soils, water flow is activated initially through the porosity of the limestone. The second phase of flow is through the secondary karst features of sinkholes, dolines, caves and enlarged fractures. While the initial flow through the limestone is diffuse, connected to the secondary porosity features and flows are large springs which are potentially high yielding (Furness 2012: 3; see Map 1.2).[2] While the region has a pronounced wet season, in some springs such as Wai Lia in Baucau, the annual flow cycle is stronger in the dry season (June–October). This is counter-intuitive and suggests a long time lag in the water's underground flow.

While these hydrogeological surveys (2010–2012) produced much important information on the local hydrology, there was no attempt to understand how the karst water flows and landscape was configured in local cosmological and socio-ecological terms. Yet my own research, intensively carried out during roughly the same period, makes it clear that from a local perspective this entire karstic landscape forms a culturally connected web of seepages and deep underground water pathways stretching from the central mountains, to the plateau, marine terrace zone and eventually to the sea.

Located in the heart of the ancient contact and collision zone between the migrating pacific peoples of Melanesia and Austronesian seafarers from southern China, most inhabitants of the Baucau Viqueque zone speak one or more of the Makasae, Kawamina and Tetum languages.[3] In contrast to the Eastern Tetum (Hicks 2004 [1976]), little ethnographic work has been carried out with Austronesian Waima'a (a 'dialect' of the Kawamina language group) and non-Austronesian Makasae speakers.[4] Taking seriously the import of their localized place making histories and social relations with water, as this book unfolds I carefully consider the ways in which this waterscape, associated topography,

4 Introduction

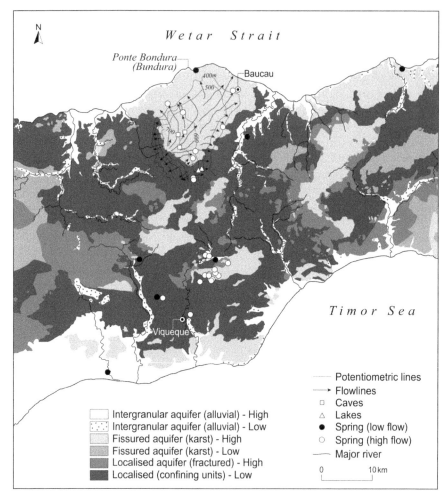

Map 1.2 Hydrogeology of the Baucau Viqueque zone (copyright Chandra Jayasuriya, adapted from *The Hydrogeology of Timor Leste* map, copyright Geoscience Australia (Wallace *et al.* 2012b)).

underground pathways and meteorological phenomena are interpreted and interacted with. I draw out distinctive regional narrative genres relating to house-based origins, settlement and spring water and argue that spring water has, and continues, to play a central role in contestations over power and place. I explore the way narratives told as village and 'house' histories, as well as religious practices carried out at and around springs, continually transform and reverberate across time and space as common myths and practices linked to particular places (which are linked in turn to other places and islands across the region). I argue that taken as a whole, they make clear the all-encompassing meaning and significance of water across the zone and the variables that continue to influence local religious practices and water governance outcomes. In the final chapters I investigate how these localized narratives and associated practices intersect with mainstream colonial and more modern histories of development and exchange across the region.

Understanding that spring water is a critical element through which people relate to one another and the landscape, the book also traces the import of water to the ancient production of wet rice, examining complex social, political, economic and environmental fluidities and continuities across time and space. With the independence era opening up a space for the resurgence and renegotiation of these relations, I argue that despite the neoliberal governance agendas of others, local people continue to foreground and engage with the foundational customary economy under whose auspices water's spiritual agency is activated and local water politics plays out. In these dynamic and opportunistic processes I argue we can locate a new 'politics of possibility' (Gibson-Graham 2006) for alternative modes of environmental governance and economic development.

Modernizing water governance and the place of custom

Coming to its present form in 2002, independent Timor Leste is recognized as one of the most significant contemporary international experiments in building the state from the ground up. With a population and landscape deeply scarred by a tumultuous and complicated colonial history, Timor Leste is a post-conflict state struggling with enormous development challenges. Following centuries of Portuguese missionizing and colonial rule, the often bloody military and bureaucratic occupation of the country by Indonesia from 1975 (Gunn 1999) resulted in the disruption of Timorese land uses and lifestyles through ongoing military surveillance and conflict with Timorese resistance forces (CAVR 2006). During this period the Timorese suffered abuses of human rights, and the widespread loss of life[5] and property (CAVR 2006; Tanter *et al.* 2006; Nevins 2005). Hence independent Timor Leste faces complex social and economic challenges as it attempts to rebuild itself as a modern nation state (Fox 2001; Fox and Babo Soares 2000; Hill and Saldanha 2001; Philpott 2006; Scheiner 2014). Since 1999, numerous United Nations peacekeeping and state-building missions (between the periods of 1999–2002 and 2006–2012) and the independent government of Timor Leste (2002–present) have continued to struggle with enormous development and reconstruction challenges. Timor Leste is one of the five poorest countries in Asia (Pasquale 2011). Some 41 per cent of the population lives below the national poverty line, and adult literacy is only 50 per cent (UNDP 2009). The tiny half island state is characterized by ecological and cultural diversity: a collision zone for an array of little studied (hydro)geological formations and languages[6] and a region of ever changing ecological habitats on which depend multitudes of small-scale livelihood practices and cultures. Most of the million or so Timorese live in rural areas, and they practice traditional

6 *Introduction*

near-subsistence agriculture, and depending on their geographical context, fishing, hunting, gathering and some cash cropping (UNDP 2009).

As quickly as the 1999 violent withdrawal of the Indonesian occupiers destroyed the formal governance systems and infrastructure of the country, it also heralded a large-scale, intensive development intervention by the United Nations, international donors and organizations. The lingering effects of this more than decade long intervention has exerted an unparalleled influence on the nascent nation's development priorities and agenda (Peake 2013). Nowhere is this more evident than in the realm of water governance (see Jackson and Palmer 2012). In the post-independence era, with water and sanitation services either non-existent or in critical disrepair across much of the country, the Timorese state and its international advisers began the long process of developing much needed national water laws and policies. From the outset, the new Timorese constitution claimed all water resources as the property of the state, and donor banks and countries supported resource assessments to better understand the characteristics and limits of water resources (Furness 2004; Asian Development Bank 2004; Costin and Powell 2006; Wallace *et al.* 2012a). Developing laws and policy are based on the widely accepted global best practice of Integrated Water Resources Management (IWRM), defined as 'a process which promotes the co-ordinated development and management of water, land and related resources, in order to maximize the resultant economic and social welfare in an equitable manner without compromising the sustainability of vital ecosystems' (UNEP-DHI Centre for Water and Environment 2009). Yet in this flurry of activity and knowledge building, much less was done to understand the critical importance of water within the vibrant and enchanted ecologies of Timorese lifeworlds. Likewise, even as donors despaired at the reality of local water and sanitation projects which seemed to fail almost as quickly as their success had been proclaimed (Schoffel 2006), little interest was shown in understanding why it was that localized water sources remained much as they had always been: wellsprings of community wellbeing and revered sites of emplaced identity and custodial responsibility, as well as key sites of resistance and empowerment in the face of 'outsider' transgressions. The contention of this book is that this critical 'oversight' was and continues to be driven by the failure to engage politically with what I am calling localized spiritual ecologies.

The lessons of this book, drawn against the backdrop of indigenous worlds colliding and enmeshing with new regimes of governance in Timor Leste, resonate across many post-conflict societies, and indeed for modern water governance regimes more generally they are highly topical. The importance of the rights of local and indigenous peoples, and how exactly those rights are configured and formally recognized, remains one of the most vexing questions in state water governance regimes at all stages of modernity (Jackson and Palmer 2012). Across the globe, indigenous peoples, broadly defined, have systematically lower access to water services than non-indigenous peoples (Jiménez *et al.* 2014). Moreover, if we take the question of 'what it means to be and become human today, in dynamic relationship with non-human worlds' (Sullivan 2009: 24) as one of our most pressing problems (Bakker 2010; Latour 2009; Smith 2007), then the task of making visible and legible alternative ways of being in and knowing the world is critical.

In some countries long-standing practices and beliefs around water and its management have survived the colonial and modern period and continue to exert a significant influence over the contemporary management of these localized water systems (Jackson and Palmer 2012; Jackson forthcoming; Bakker 2007). Diverse customary institutions continue to govern the sharing, distribution and consumption of water in many countries (Jackson and Palmer 2012; cf. Madaleno 2007; Lansing 2007 [1991]; Jackson and Altman 2009; Langton 2006; Boelens 2014; Gachenko 2012; Rodriguez 2007). Yet even when they are formally recognized in law, the majority of these laws treat superficially customary rights and interests, relegating them to 'a legal limbo' where they are dealt with by 'basically separating them out of the mainstream "modern" water rights regulated by statute, and by creating a separate legal space for them' (Burchi 2011: 3, cited in Jackson and Palmer 2012). While in the twenty-first century IWRM continues to be championed as international best practice in water governance, this regime has thus far struggled to incorporate less quantifiable values such as local and indigenous peoples' rights and knowledge, often with detrimental medium- to long-term consequences (Jackson and Palmer 2012; Jackson 2008). Meanwhile, the delineated hydro-ecological units and related assumptions of integrated catchment management which underpin modern water governance are challenged in places like Timor Leste where people are bound and connected to water in more complex social, political and cosmological ways (cf. Barber and Jackson 2012).

Building on theories of post-humanism and vital materialism emergent in socio-nature studies, this ethnography challenges us to think through the ways in which alternative (non-capitalist) value fields require more than a recognition space in existing capitalist systems. Rather it focuses on what these values and practices can teach us about the significance and worth of sociality and communicative reciprocity across human and non-human realms (cf. Jackson and Palmer 2014). Drawing together an understanding and analysis of Timorese lifeworlds through their localized water histories, material imaginations, ritual practices and spirit ecologies it challenges us to reconceptualize water governance and what is meant by the concept of both the hydrological cycle and its neologism, the hydrosocial cycle (Bakker 2003; Swyngedouw 2004; Linton 2010). In doing so, it provides unique place-based insights into three critically under-addressed questions in water governance across the globe: the role of water in sustaining diverse forms of socio-cultural life; the varied socio-cultural ways of valuing, managing and using water; and the consequences of these relations for long-term sustainability outcomes (Johnstone et al. 2012: xi–xii). It argues that deepening our knowledge of the imaginative materialities (Anderson and Wylie 2009; see also Bachelard 1983; MacLeod 2013) constituting water, and the consequences of this for our understanding of and engagement with localized hydrosocial cycles, is critical to reappraising approaches to sustainability (cf. Johnstone et al. 2012: xvi).

8 *Introduction*

The spiritual ecology of water and the eastern archipelago

The influence of religion on human ecology and adaptation has come to be called 'spiritual ecology' (Sponsel 2010: 131, 2012).[7] Advocating for further inquiry into what he argues is an emerging field, Sponsel (2010: 138) observes that as '[h]uman ecology can involve the supernatural as well as the natural, and emotion as well as reason ... more needs to be done in trying to test multiple working hypotheses about the ecological salience and efficacy of aspects of religion' (2010: 138). This book follows in a tradition of works which have interpreted the meaning and significance of localized ritual and spiritual ecologies, specifically building on existing studies of water 'management' embedded in religious beliefs and practices (Conklin 1980; Lansing 2007 [1991]; Gelles 2000; Boelens 2009, 2014; Rodriguez 2007; Strang 2004, 2013; Boelens and Dávila 2006).

In his early consideration of the interface between religious practice and ecology, Rappaport's seminal work (1967) among the Tsembaga of Papua New Guinea argued that the local religious ritual practice of *kaiko* was an environmental regulator of pig populations. While his focus in this ethnography was a supposed self-regulating human-ecological system, more recent work on the religion–environmental interface has engaged with more complex dynamic, adaptive systems paying acute attention to the vicissitudes of historical interconnection and contingencies. Similarly in the case of religious practices associated with water management, historical contingencies linking ritual practices to a larger moral economy are always responding to changes both internal and external to its own logics. In her work on the history and present-day practices of traditional hybrid Hispanic and indigenous *acequia* irrigation communities in New Mexico, Rodriguez remarks:

> The principal of water sharing belongs to a larger moral economy that promotes cooperative economic behavior through inculcating the core value of *respeto* [respect] and gendered norms of personal comportment. Religious beliefs and practices sanction these norms, promote *communitas*, and enact a devotional community's relationship to its traditional irrigated land base.
>
> (2007: 116)

If we extend this analysis to include the dynamism of such moral economies, it is clear that water and water-related practices both carry and allow for the adaptation and reinterpretation of these same norms and traditions. In these open and non-linear systems, water can be understood more as a 'topic' than a resource (cf. Latour 2009), a topic forever saturated with agency, relationality and potentiality.

The ethno-historical description and analysis in the chapters that follow resonate in many respects with the metaphysical concepts and politics of hydrosocial cycles described elsewhere. While in the Andean region Boelens (2014) is interested primarily in the technologies of power which permeate ancient and contemporary hydro-cosmological cycles and the colonization of ancient water truths, the religious practices and metaphysical beliefs he documents resonate with aspects of the hydrosocial cycle under discussion in this book. In his and other Andean ethnographic literature it is clear that communicating with and paying tribute or sacrifice to various natural features such as mountains or deities was once a commonplace act of requesting the Earth's water in times of water scarcity (Gelles 2000; Boelens 2009). Indeed in discussing the hydrological connections between divine, human and natural communities, Boelens argues that the role of water has traditionally been one of 'uniting them all' (2014: 241). He quotes Sherbondy (1998: 212) who writes that '[w]ater is the main element of the Andean cosmos: the principle that explains movement, circulation and forces of change, the essence of life itself' (cited in Boelens 2014: 241). As a vital liquid, it is said to 'order the cosmological body' (Boelens 2014: 241), to connect 'the scales of time' (life cycle) to space (particular places) (Boelens 2014: 242), and through the ancestral origin myths associated with water create water access and property rights (Boelens 2014: 243). A waterworld deep beneath the Earth is believed to be the upwardly permeating source of Earth's water (Boelens 2014: 241). While Boelens writes that in his particular ethnographic context, these beliefs are now treated as 'fragments' and 'incidental events' rather than 'complete' mythical systems, the residue of these beliefs is, he says, still a constituting factor in the localised hydrosocial cycle (2014: 241). Meanwhile, beliefs about the central role of snakes in the provisioning of irrigation waters (something we will also encounter in the Timor context) are still vibrant and Boelens notes that in Andean mythology the snake (*amaru*) represents water (2014: 241; cf. Strang 2013; Barber and Jackson 2012 on indigenous Australia). Water rituals and narrative traditions are likewise fundamental to the functioning of the agricultural cycle, and this includes a suite of ritual practices and offerings made by 'traditional' irrigation co-operatives (cf. Gelles 2000).

As we will also see in Timor Leste, in the Andes '[h]istorically [in the pre-Inca period] whenever water left the underground network and surfaced, local humans and animals saw the Sun for the first time and communities were established' creating as well pathways of life and death (Boelens 2014: 243). In this hydro-cosmological cycle, writes Boelens, '[e]verything "returns" periodically but with major qualitative leaps forward' (2014: 243). In times of crisis, these metaphysical beliefs and traditions of pre-Inca mountain cults and their politically reconstructed Incan derivatives resurface in contemporary Andean communities (2014: 243). This includes the strategic repatterning of (previously localized) divine powers as now located in one (Incan) origin source (Lake Titicaca). According to Boelens, this repatterning made local ancestral origin sources the '*secondary* places of creation in the world's hierarchy' (2014: 243) and enabled the appropriation of the hydrosocial cycle for imperial Incan (and subsequently Spanish and nationalistic) purposes.

Elsewhere, in the south-east Asian region, in places such as the Philippines (Conklin 1980) and more recently in Bali (Lansing 2007 [1991]), broadly

10   Introduction

analogous socio-cultural ways of using and managing water in local agricultural lifeworlds have been listed as examples of outstanding world heritage by UNESCO. In contrast to Boelens' (2014) work on appropriated hydro-cosmological cycles these examples point to a more hopeful, perhaps even purposefully naïve, focus on the ways in which, rather than being a part of the problem, societies of the south 'may have many of the solutions' (Meganck 2012: viii). In Bali these relations are configured through the ideology and practices of '*Agama Tirtha*' ('religion of water'). Lansing argues that in the development of the Balinese Hindu inflected religion of *Agama Tirtha* the Sanskrit 'metaphor of water flowing from a sacred source was joined to the ancient Austronesian concept of descent from a sacred origin [and] the island itself became a metonym for a concept of the sacred that drew from both Indic and Austronesian sources' (2006: 52). The 2012 UNESCO recognition of the waterscapes and associated cultures of Bali as World Heritage Cultural Landscapes is a particularly interesting development. Drawing primarily on the decades of research carried out by Lansing and others, the nomination (The Ministry of Culture and Tourism of the Republic of Indonesia and the Government of Bali Province 2010) recognizes not just the material culture of the rice terrace networks but a *subak* (localized irrigation co-operatives) management system whose beliefs and practices are based upon the sacred landscape principles embedded in Balinese cosmology. The successful nomination has led to the formation of a new governance structure whereby each *subak* manages its own system locally but comes together with others to decide on religious-ecological matters which are intimately linked across the *subak* system(s). In the Balinese cosmology, where mountains are sacred and water sources are linked to important temple complexes, a 'balance' is sought between middle, upper and lower worlds (plains, mountains and the sea) (Watson and Lansing 2012). Meanwhile the environmental effect of *subak* irrigation co-ordination and management in the rice terraces is to protect and enhance nutrient run-off through precipitation and downstream flows as well as regulate the impact of pests through simultaneous periods of flood and fallow (Lansing 2007 [1991]). Even in the central mountainous communities of Bali, where there are no irrigated rice fields, Reuter (1996: 129–131) writes that ritual alliances between village communities united through a common ancestral domain (*banua*) led them to carry out similar collective rites at water temples during critical points in the dry land agricultural cycle.

Water in Timor and elsewhere in the eastern archipelago

Across island Timor and the eastern archipelago, indigenous ontologies or ways of being are largely based on an understanding of place as enlivened by an ancestral and nature spirit world (cf. Fox 1997; Hicks 2004 [1976]; see Map 1.3). In Timor Leste, families of particular lineages are organized around origin groups linked to particular sacred houses (*uma lulik*) and local spirit ecologies which embed these families in intimate, intergenerational social, political and

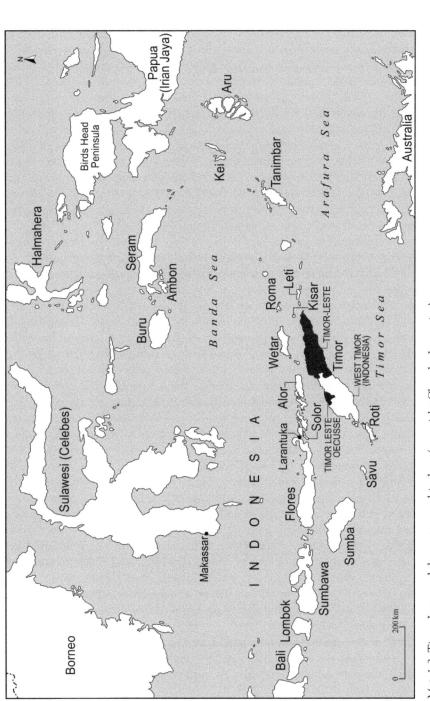

Map 1.3 Timor Leste and the eastern archipelago (copyright Chandra Jayasuriya).

12 Introduction

economic relationships with their extended consanguinal and affinal kin from other sacred houses. Links between these lineages and with the surrounding environment are embedded in a lifeworld of obligation and reciprocity built around socio-cosmic dualisms such as male/female, fertility-giver/fertility-taker, younger sibling/older sibling, indigene/newcomer, political authority/ritual authority, as well as a suite of botanical metaphors such as trunk/tips – the harmonious (or conflictual) relations between which ensure the 'flow of life' (Fox 1980). These sacred house and associated spiritual ecology complexes will often stretch through extended kin networks across ritual domains, including to other islands (cf. Vischer 1992; see also Chapter 3). Frequently springs are the central agents in enabling the movement across and through such domains (Kehi and Palmer 2012; De Josselin de Jong 1937; see Chapter 4) and assist in facilitating interaction and relations between both settlement founders and newcomers (from across both land and sea). As we will see in the chapters that follow there is a close relationship in this vitalist philosophy between the fundamentally generative exchanges between 'houses' linked through marriage and those linked through the life-giving capacities of shared ground and spring water.

In the case of house-based marriage relations, *lia na'in* ('custodians of the words') will negotiate the substance of the exchange of gifts and counter-gifts (glossed in Tetum as *barlake*) between the families of the couple. These gifts will then be exchanged (and re-exchanged outwards) through a series of life cycle events (betrothal or 'path clearing', marriages and deaths) relating to both the couple and their closely associated kin. Such exchanges may extend over a period of many generations and the alliance formed includes the obligation of members of each 'house' to perform particular ritual duties at each other's life and death based ceremonies (*lia moris* and *lia mate*).[8] At the societal level these exchanges function to reach out politically and jurally to engage with, demonstrate respect for, and create mutual support between an ever extending web of kin-based relations based on the principles of *fetosaa* and *umane* (Tetum Dili terms which I gloss in a broad sense as 'fertility-takers' and 'fertility-givers'[9]). These exchanges form the basis of local customary economies and the *barlake* process remains under negotiation and 'alive' until the exchange obligations created through particular unions are deemed to have been fully discharged. Similarly, as the ultimate giver of life, water stories and relations based on diverse origin and historical accounts continually infuse and create connections and exchange obligations between waters, 'houses' and communities. Just as *barlake* creates ongoing relations and demonstrates respect between *fetosaa* and *umane* groups, water stories and rituals are key mediums for thought, conversation, law making and exchange.

While in contrast to Bali, on island Timor the return to the source of spiritual or ancestral power is not linked to temples (but rather to springs and 'houses'), there are similarities to the account given by Lansing (2006: 195) of the role of holy water in Bali. Life in Timor revolves around the quest for positive life force or *matak malarin* (a life force of greening coolness), a state often attained through the blessing of holy water sourced at springs (Kehi and

Palmer 2012). As noted above, these springs are a threshold for exchange and reciprocity between the visible and invisible worlds. They are fundamental to life, human and non-human health and fertility and integrated with ritual practices transacted through animal sacrifices underpinned by a rich material imagination. Sacred springs can also refer to a passage between life and death (cf. Hicks forthcoming, 1996; Traube 1986: 185–186) and are often considered to be the ultimate origin source of life and death (Kehi and Palmer 2012). In the ancient kingdom of Koba Lima straddling the present-day international border between Timor Leste and Indonesia, it is clear that the broader regional 'system' of socio-cosmic dualisms or local diarchies (see Fox 1980) solidifies around the notion of mother water and father fire:

> Like many other eastern archipelagic societies, in the myth of creation of Koba Lima, it is said that in the beginning everything was water. Here, water is considered to be the mother, while fire the father. Given the original undifferentiated unity of the world, in other contexts the mother is also said to be the stars and moon (with the latter known to reflect the image of the sacred banyan and bamboo back to the earth), and the father is the sun, the eternal light and fire. It is believed, we argue, that it is through the intermingling of water and fire that the spirit of life is transformed into life itself and eventually into death.
>
> (Kehi and Palmer 2012: 445)

By tracing water's agency and presence in these foundational dualisms such as water and fire, male and female, sky and earth, wet and dry, hot and cool, light and darkness, day and night, Kehi and Palmer (2012) argue that water is an all-pervasive or holistic element which is central to both the expression of cosmological ideas and the understanding of life itself. This fact is also reflected in the way that the names of many key pre-colonial kingdoms and present-day post-colonial districts in island Timor have meanings associated with water.

While the anthropological literature of eastern Indonesia has largely focused on the ritual cycles worshipping 'rock and tree' (Traube 1986: 16), the worship of spring water, its associated vegetation (including the banyan tree, bamboo and pandanus), water spirits and ancestral ghosts is also widespread. Fox (1997: 7) notes the centrality of water in understandings of landscape in Austronesian societies, and works by Forth (1998) and Allerton (2009) on Flores; Rodemeier (2009) on Alor; Pannell (2007) in the maritime waters of the Moluccas; Grimes (1993: 174–175, 194–195, 196–197) on Buru; and Boulan Smit (1998: 110–111, 124) on Seram make it clear that the cosmological and socio-ecological understandings and roles of water are critical, if underexplored, in at least these parts of the eastern archipelago (see Map 1.3).[10] Focusing on the eastern archipelago, Hicks (forthcoming) notes the prevalence of a regional trope of water narratives which recount the ongoing exchange of life between the visible and invisible worlds, particularly deities (cf. Rodemeier 2009; Kehi and Palmer 2012). Like in other parts of the world (Langton 2006; Strang 2002; Barber and Jackson 2012;

14   *Introduction*

Brady and Prufer 2005; Lansing 2006; Reuter 1996; Boelens 2014) complex systemic socio-ecological associations are made between springs, rivers, clouds, sky, mountains, earth, underground channels and the sea (Kehi and Palmer 2012; Vischer 1992: 63–133; Boulan Smit 1998: 89; Grimes 1993: 197; Rodemeier 2009; Forth 1998; Allerton 2009).

Seen in combination these notions of sacred or holy water connected to sacred springs also suggest that the idea of water flowing from a sacred source may be as Austronesian (and indeed Australian and Andean) as it is Indic (cf. Lansing 2006). In each locality they form a key part of a sacred landscape which links associated communities into a matrix of cosmopolitical ecology with both local and extra-local significance. In Timor, while the connections at the latter level are often more materially symbolic (rather than based on actual scientifically identified and measurable water flows), they are socially and culturally foundational and will often involve an asserted connection between lowland communities and 'origin' point water sources atop mountain peaks (cf. Lansing 2007 [1991]; Rodemeier 2009). Across the region, water is the sacred oil of the earth, it is the blood and milk, a characteristic shared by the sap in the sacred banyan tree. The relationship of rain to male semen (Forth 1998: 226; Traube 1986: 173; Forman 1980), female milk (Kehi and Palmer 2012) and even to floods which are seen to arise out of earth (when the mountains and clouds merge) regulated by the mountain deity (Rodemeier 2009), suggests a powerful unity of sky, earth and below, a unity still accessible in part through springs and holy water. This bodily imagery of the land and water scape makes it clear that the watery cosmos is the flesh of the sensed world. The work of others (see Brady and Prufer 2005) suggests that ancient and contemporary indigenous use of water in karst environments is intimately connected to meteorological events controlled by the inner realms of a powerful, sacred and animate earth. As we will see, this is also arguably the case in the Baucau Viqueque region of Timor Leste where there are explicit linkages between indigenous cosmologies and the ritual use of caves for water increase and rain making rites (cf. Hicks 2004 [1976]). In this way the ethnography is further evidence of an at times 'thematic congruence in perceptions of the sacred and animate earth across linguistic and cultural boundaries' (Prufer and Brady 2005: 406; cf. Altman 2002; Sponsel 2010; Kehi and Palmer 2012; Young 2006; Langton 2006; Boelens 2014).

The intersections described above cohere socio-ecologically as complex ritual ecologies connected to agricultural cycles wherein it is *relations* not necessarily water needs (as Lansing (2006: 170, 210) also points out) which are the subjective realization of ritual network structure. Such processes can be seen in the actual material engagement between people and their agricultural or irrigation waters. Allerton, for example, has written of Flores that agricultural water is considered 'life giving oil', and its flow is ensured through blood sacrifices (2009: 276) calling 'forth long buried ancestors' (2009: 285). This she terms a type of agricultural animism, a remembering of 'all forms of ancestors' for fertility. While she notes that her case study of the modernist wet rice project in coastal southern Manggarai, Western Flores, lacks the ritual connections of swidden, in

Introduction 15

a dynamic relationship with place and process the ancestors are asked in ritual to travel down from mountains to ensure the health and wellbeing of the crop and associated communities. This example corresponds with Lansing's argument that the Balinese *subak*, long upheld as a model of egalitarian resource management, is at its heart not an entity concerned with irrigation management but rather the health and wellbeing of the fields and community (2007 [1991]: 170). Crop production is not their *raison d'être* and indeed as Reuter (1996: 23, 20–94) writes in the upland mountain communities of Bali the ritual duty of paying agricultural prestations to the *Pura Banua* (ancestral domain temples) falls not to *subaks* (which do not exist in these dryland communities) but to the *desa* (village governing authority).

As we will see in Chapter 6, in the Baucau Viqueque zone of Timor Leste, socio-ecological processes associated with agricultural water bear a striking resemblance to the 'integrated system of ritualized ecological management' described by Lansing in relation to the *subaks* of Bali (2007 [1991]: 14). For example in the town of Baucau intra-regional connections between karst springs and cave water sources creates kin relations between particular communities. These relations are honoured through interlaced ritualized practices of water management connected to spring-fed wet rice agriculture. Cooperative groupings of rice farmers and villages engage in an elaborate system of extra-local relationships which are based on historically contingent understandings of the interconnections between springs and underground flows between geographically distant communities. Yet as with the upland communities associated with the apical water temple of Pura Batur in Bali and its volcanic lake and springs, the inland community in the Baucau district (where the cave containing the 'parent' water is located) is not an irrigation community. Rather it receives annual gifts of rice from 'downstream' coastal farmers in exchange for the underground flow of fertile water. As well as tributes, there are a range of ritual ceremonies connected to water aimed at ensuring an abundant supply of water flowing between connected dryland and wetland communities. These ritual ecologies are a critical mode of communication with the spirit world which honours and renews the relationships on which all life depends.

The shared symbolism of holy water

As well as ancestral ghosts, sacred spring water can also be home to other manifestations of the water spirits: pythons, eels, shrimps, crocodiles, fish and octopus. Animal manifestations of the water spirits are also known to change into people both above and underground. Yet water itself, as well as water spirits, is also believed to have agency: it is sacred, a purveyor of life and fertility, creator of unity, source of potency; a cleanser and communicator between the visible and (usually) invisible world. Hence across the eastern archipelago we also find a shared symbolism around holy water. Along with springs, coconut water is considered holy, and rituals involving cooking with, bathing in or

16   *Introduction*

sprinkling of holy water on people, include post-natal (Graham 1991: 64; Grimes 1993: 227–234; Hicks 2004 [1976]; Therik 2004: 196; Forman 1980; Kehi and Palmer 2012), post-marriage (Neonbasu 2005: 322; Duarte 1964), health restoration and community origin rituals (Kehi and Palmer 2012; Neonbasu 2005: 322–324). The sprinkling of holy water is also carried out over animals, crops, land and at sacred house re-constructions. This may also involve the infusion of water with drops of sacrificed animal blood (see Kehi and Palmer 2012). Likewise in the context of Bali, sprinkles of holy water delivered by priests are a main part of any visit to a water temple.[11]

Along with sprinkles of holy water, ubiquitous in regional holy water practices is bamboo itself (see Kehi and Palmer 2012; Rodemeier 2009; Almeida 1976). In both Timor and Bali it is bamboo which is used to carry holy water. In Bali the *sujung* (bamboo length) is sealed and 'dressed' with sacred offerings carried back to other parts of the temple network and ultimately to *subak* fields or important family rituals or events (see Lansing 2006: 51). In Timor it may be used to carry water to found new communities, establish connections between springs or even wreak devastation on an enemy (Kehi and Palmer 2012; see also Chapter 5). In Koba Lima it is wrapped in a woven cloth (*tais*) and carried like a baby to a new location where it is thrown on the ground to create a new spring. This process is also carried out to ameliorate the effects of the forced relocation of communities as was the case in Koba Lima in colonial times when the ritual community in Portuguese Timor was forced to flee to Dutch Timor. These transformative processes allow people to better cope with movement and displacement whilst at the same time retain a tangible connection to their source, connections that continue to be honoured into the present (Kehi and Palmer 2012).

Tracing these locally specific but regionally distinctive genres of water-centred spiritual ecology throughout the chapters of this book allows deeper insights into the significance and uses of named water sources and the complicated socio-natural assemblages and processes which create interdependent networks of people, places and livelihoods. While this book makes it clear that the ongoing transformation of these localized spiritual ecologies has emerged in its 'modern' form via a messy historical trajectory of colonial and post-colonial politics (Shepherd 2013), more significantly it also shows how in historically contingent ways, local peoples have embraced this recognition space and have shown an extraordinary preparedness to risk engaging with outsiders through these processes. By gathering together these insights and linking them to a broader conceptual literature on post-humanism and vital materialism, the book is a timely contribution to the emerging critical ecologies literature. In such political engagements across plural ontologies, differently configured, if co-constitutive, socio-environmental domains have and are being continually brought into being. In contrast to much of the political ecology literature, this book will show that across these awkward zones of encounter (Tsing 2005) there is no necessary trajectory of dominance or subjugation, but spaces of opportunity variously mobilized and enacted.

Agency and the hydrosocial cycle

Within the field of political ecology a re-envisioning of a naturalistic (but equally social) hydrological cycle has seen increasing attention paid to the development of the concept of the hydrosocial cycle (Linton 2010). This concept 'envisions the circulation of water as a combined physical and social process, as a hybridized socio-natural flow that fuses together nature and society in inseparable manners' (Swyngedouw 2009: 56). A long-standing interest in the political-economy of (usually) capitalist ecologies and the need for redistributive justice has focused this political ecology literature on the 'conflict-ridden nature of the process of socio-environmental change', and on the class, gender, ethnic or other social power relations and struggles which mobilize strategies and inform discourse and arguments (Swyngedouw 2009: 57). In tracing the 'socially produced character' of hydrosocial configurations, this work is often informed by the seminal work of Wittfogel (1957) who drew the link between 'autocratic power and hydrological systems' (Swyngedouw 2009: 59). Yet despite the popularity of this thesis, even within the regions from which Wittfogel's ideas were developed, there are others who offer alternative, less autocratic, understandings of past and present hydrosocial cycles (Lansing 2007 [1991], 2006; cf. Banister 2014). As Swyngedouw himself argues, there is an urgent need for theorists to begin '[i]magining different, more inclusive, sustainable and equitable forms of hydrosocial organization', which he concludes 'implies imagining different and more effective, assumingly democratic, forms of social organization' (2009: 59). This raises the question of why we do not pay as much attention to examining already existing alternative forms of hydrosocial organization (cf. Gibson-Graham and Roelvink 2010: 342)? Is it the case that such forms are considered too marginal, non-viable or inconsequential, or is it simply because these 'arcane' and largely 'peripheral' forms eschew easily recognizable forms of democracy? Are such already existing waterworlds simply too hard to think with? These questions will be taken up in the next section and in the later discussion of the ontological frictions.

Drawing on the second generation of political ecological work which seeks to define and flesh out the analytical utility of the concept of hydrosocial cycle (see Linton and Budds 2014), I add my own extension to this reconceptualization. I advance an argument about the forms and agency of water in the hydrosocial cycle of eastern Timor and reflect on what others can learn from such alternative waterworlds. I do this by extending an understanding of the social to the concept of 'inclusive sociality'. Through this concept of 'inclusive sociality' I analyse both water's materiality (Bear and Bull 2011; Lavau 2013) and 'participation' in existence (Lévy Bruhl 1910; Sullivan 2010). I pay particular attention to the political effects of agency manifest in water and associated 'bodies' and 'things' across space and time.

First, to theorize the dynamic interplay and co-constitution of water's materiality, I examine how more recent literature on the hydrosocial cycle engages with the concept of the social. Linton and Budds define the hydrosocial cycle as 'a socio-natural process by which water and society make and remake each other

18   *Introduction*

over space and time' and seek to mobilize it both as an 'analytical tool for investigating hydrosocial relations and as a broader framework for undertaking critical political ecologies of water' (2014: 170). Developing an understanding of 'how water is not external to social relations but rather embeds and expresses them' (Linton and Budds 2014: 174), they argue we must also turn our attention to the multiple ways in which water actively shapes socio-natural worlds. Drawing on key anthropological literature on water (Strang 2004; Mosse 2003; Orlove and Caton 2010), they note that beyond material relations, people are connected to water in 'experiential, cultural and metaphorical ways' (Linton and Budds 2014: 174). They furthermore argue that the 'point is not to determine where social constructions and materialities begin but to recognize their mutual constitution' (Linton and Budds 2014: 174). While on the matter of what constitutes the social they are largely silent, they do examine the potential for the 'deep intertwining of water's material and spiritual dimensions' (Linton and Budds 2014: 174). In particular, they highlight the South American work of Boelens and his innovative development of the 'hydro-cosmological cycle' to extend the concept of hydrosocial cycle. In developing this concept, Boelens argues we need to link 'diverse water cultures, rights frames and worldviews to the socio-natural construction of hydrological flows' and 'analyze how "metaphysics" links to [water] politics and power' (2014: 245). By making a link between ancient indigenous water cultural systems and the subsequent appropriation and manipulation of these systems by the imperial powers, Boelens 'offers a tool to examine ancient and modern myths and discourses that attempt to normalize and subjugate actors to control by dominant groups in water society' (2014: 245).

The twofold task developed by Boelens (2014) creates fascinating possibilities for analysing how 'metaphysics' links to water politics and power in the Andes and elsewhere (see also Gelles 2000; Lansing 2007 [1991]). However, in a region where published ethno-historical material is minimal, rather than focusing on seeking out accounts of appropriation and the social-natural hybrids created by external 'imperial' and modernist waterscapes, I seek to examine the ontological and material dynamism of indigenous waterscapes themselves. My aim is to understand them through their own open, emergent and ever transforming notions of space and time and to analyse their proactive rather than reactive interactions with external others. As Strang writes of indigenous Australian relations with water, in such a:

> small-scale, localized, and beautifully precise cosmology, it is not difficult to see how water, and metaphors of water, move freely across ecological, social, imaginative, and corporeal domains, bringing them together in a flow of human and environmental changes over time and space. It is equally clear that water and notions of flow are ways of conceptualizing time in cyclical terms, describing how collective human and non-human actions circulate into and out of the material world and, on an individual scale, portraying the nascence, progress, dissolution, and regeneration of individual lives.
>
> (2013: 189–190)

Rather than the ways in which these indigenous water realms have or are being co-opted by external others, I am interested first in their capacities for dynamism, adaptation and invention. In this way I am also inspired by the work of Gibson-Graham who, concerned with what can be learnt from what is already there, encourages us all to pay close attention to 'the difficult process of cultivating subjects (ourselves and others) who can desire and inhabit non-capitalist economic spaces' (Gibson-Graham 2006: x). In this spirit the following challenge is posed:

> What if we were to accept that the goal of thinking is not to extend knowledge by confirming what we already know, that the world is a place of domination and oppression? What if instead we thought about openings and strategic possibilities in the cracks?
>
> (Gibson-Graham 2012: 37)

So while Budds and Linton (2014: 174) are interested in the practices which co-produce socio-natural hybrids and Boelens (2014: 246) is interested in how 'local water communities react, modify and also strategically use the ruling symbolic order', I seek to pay more attention to how local water communities react, modify and also strategically use their *own* symbolic and material orders. As Banister (2014: 205) reminds us, hydrosocial cycles do not 'translate into hierarchy or domination in any straightforward way'. In this sense, water is not, as is often presumed, merely an instrument of social control or a socio-natural hybrid but an activator of social relations within and across multidimensional complex systems. Hence while much of the literature on hydrosocial cycles has focused on 'how water is socialized' by humans, the concern in this book is to interrogate and illuminate 'water's active, agential, affective roles' (Bear and Bull 2011: 2262), its own sociality embedded *with*, not by, the sociality of humans.

Ontological frictions

To flesh out how local people modify and strategically use their *own* symbolic and material orders connected to water and trace its 'ontological politics' (Mol 1999), I make recourse to the ontologies of flux and flow that recent work on vital materialism and post-humanism has sought to activate (for an overview see Anderson and Wylie 2009; Lorimer 2012). I also draw on the work of Tsing (2005) who argues that we need to acknowledge, understand and (constructively) critique the productive (not only destructive) 'frictions' at work in the conversations between such non-deterministic natures and globalizing discourse and practices of environmental governance. The literature on non-human agency and vital materialism seeks amongst other things to remind us that all human and non-human encounters are shaped as much by the agency and friction of non-human beings and things as by that of humans (Braun and Whatmore 2010; Bennett 2010; Howitt and Suchet-Pearson 2006; Tuana 2008; Ingold 2011; Rose 2011; Tsing 2005). Such a conceptualization of agency and

20 Introduction

materiality is clearly applicable to indigenous water ontologies and to the understandings of the socio-cosmic forms at the heart of related conceptualizations of the hydrosocial cycle.

Meanwhile these relational understandings are seemingly far removed from the apolitical and ahistorical governance concepts which seek 'certainty' in comprehensively measuring, commodifying and appropriating resources such as water through encroaching processes of neoliberalism (cf. Ernstson and Sorlin 2013). However, as this book will argue, there are clear points of co-articulation, even co-production between what are in fact creatively adaptable neoliberal processes (Peck 2010) and vitalist ways of being in the world (Braun 2013). While the default position of the political ecology literature is to characterize neoliberalism as a dominant force, cajoling and appropriating the vulnerable or naïve others in its path, we can also understand non-deterministic natures as equally creative, excessive and surplus producing. In places like Timor, where the contingent assemblages of the customary realm are continually re-created through dynamic and inclusive social relations, local peoples are always attentive to opportunities which will draw capitalist resources into their worlds (whilst judicially excluding those aspects of these worlds which must remain hidden). In these vitalist ways of being in and knowing the world, one which is forever spiraling through time, refolding and unfolding in potentially novel and inventive ways, we need to ask how this process of 'lively transcendente ... can crystallize into narratives of lived practice and engagement?' (Anderson and Wylie 2009: 325). Uncovering such practices and ontological assemblages might also reveal how the frictions and co-becomings of multiple materialities are 'drawn together and held apart ... made to intermingle while sustaining ontological difference' (Lavau 2013: 416). It is through attention to such processes that we can understand social change and power.

Inclusive sociality and ecologies of spirit

Below, by fleshing out an understanding of water (and people's relations with it) as a substance, place and space of both fluid and 'congealed agency' (Barad 2003: 828), I examine how in Timor Leste water is a carrier of forms, meanings and social agency across and through space and time. Throughout the book, by tracing the relations which comprise this watery domain of ecology, sociality and religious practice, I explore the complex processes of change, interdependence, and exchange relevant to creating and transforming local livelihoods and socio-ecological modes of water governance. First, however, I need to draw out the interplay of relations between key physical objects, namely water, people, animals and plants, and advance an argument about the 'inclusive sociality' of localized land- and water-scapes (i.e. the complex and defined sets of social relations existing between humans and non-humans). As we have seen above, in this ontology where 'the space between nature and society is itself social' (Viveiros de Castro 1998: 473), water is, like other things and bodies, animated by spiritual essences. Potentially always liquid, solid or gas, water is a substance

Introduction 21

that is uniquely able to circulate life energy through time, between generations and between the visible realm of bodies and things and the invisible spiritual or 'interior' realm. As MacLeod writes:

> All matter is ultimately shared across generations. However, as the medium that carries away the dead and nurtures the unborn, water is uniquely capable of symbolizing multi-generational time. In some sense, it actually *is* multi-generational time.... Water is the ultimate medium for the conversations that continually create the world. It introduces sperm to eggs, carries nutrients to tree roots, rushes chemical messages between different parts of the body.... Smell travels in moisture ... this substance acts forever as a meeting place and medium.
>
> (2013: 49)

Exploring these unique capacities of water in this particular regional environment, and the ways that people connect with and adapt to it, expands our understanding of the productive frictions and efficacy of these spiritual ecologies and the ways in which such an inclusive human–nature sociality actually works. In order to theorize these relations I draw again from the literature on materiality and critical ecology, as well from other anthropological literature on sociality, personhood and property.

Following Ingold (1986) I define sociality as including conscious co-operation and inter-subjectivity (not just interaction). From this I define 'inclusive-sociality'[12] as consciousness manifesting in different 'bodies' and 'things' across and through space and time (cf. Pederson 2001). In expanding this definition of sociality, I open out too the definition of politics to include the notion of cosmopolitics and a more-than-human ecological or multinatural politics which is concerned about the ways in which ecologies might be 'sensed, valued and contested' (Lorimer 2012: 594; cf. Latour 2004; Latour and Weibel 2005; Sullivan 2010; Castree 2012). In short I am interested in how entities and energies sense one another through time and space and how this is manifest in particular through water or an 'aqueous ecopolitics' (Chen *et al.* 2013).

In Timor Leste, such cosmopolitical ecological constituencies find form and even voice through a storied land and waterscape of more-than-human assemblages and associated religious practices. In these multi-temporal and multidimensional ecologies, bodily forms are ever spilling over, transforming and becoming. With water as the base of all forms and the conduit for all relations, in tracing the assemblages of bodies and watery myths it is clearly the 'thoroughly materialist' (Anderson and Wylie 2009: 325) reality of the hydrosocial cycle which simultaneously forms through and breathes life into storied land- and water-scapes (cf. Ingold 2011). Yet alongside the agency of water we must also trace how localized notions of being and property congeal through complex forms of relational personhood (Strathern 1988, 1999; Ingold 2000; Strang 2009). It is these fluid agential forms which illuminate the diverse qualities of co-constituting relationships at the heart of local religious practices and

22 Introduction

property relations. Elsewhere Pederson notes that there is now a broad literature which shares a concern for 'the ontologies of complex, capricious, and emergent social forms' (2012: 35–36). He writes:

> In Melanesia, the Amazon, and northern Asia, forms are thus not mental or ideological schemata through which some fixed structure of order or symbolic meaning is imposed on an inherently disorderly world of social and material practices ... but features of the world in their own right, which must be continually recreated, recalibrated, and reapportioned for the cosmos to assume its correct proportions, and for human and nonhuman lives to unfold at a pace that is suitable to the particular dynamic configuration or continual assembling of their bodies and minds ... forms are considered to be alive, to *be* rather than to *have* force.
>
> (2011: 36–37)

Similarly Myers wrote of the need to understand how the Pintupi people in central Australia view 'an individual's internal states as extensively connected with a web of significant others or with "objects" that Western observers would describe as external to the self' (1986: 108–109; cf. Langton 2002; Stanner 1966; Tamisari 2001; Williams 1986, 1998). More recently, Sullivan, drawing on Lévy-Bruhl (1910) and Merleau-Ponty (2002), argues that within animist ecologies these complex configurations are brought about through the 'active participation of sensual perception in a collaborative bringing forth of a world of inter-subjective comprehensibility' (2010: 125). She writes that such ecologies simply affirm 'that a creative energy – and irresistible evanescence – permeates all existence'. While they share 'no interest in discerning animate or inanimate, natural or supernatural, living or dead', they are concerned with 'an immanent force conferring the possibility for a mysterious kinship and participation in phenomena, beyond the division of animate and inanimate' (Sullivan 2010: 125).

Needless to say such complex notions of personhood and relationality continue to pose a profound policy challenge to a Western liberal appreciation of individual human need, rights and desires and the interconnection between it and ecological health. This is all the more so because, as we will see in the chapters that follow, specific narrative expressions of these complex relations will 'keep pace with changing relations' (Gow 2001: 288) by simply replacing terms of old with those which have more 'popular' currency (like replacing indigenous terms for Moon-Sun deities with terms like Christ or collapsing time so as to render a founding ancestral figure synonymous with an authoritative colonial era figure or event).[13] Yet rather than a recalibration of relations, to those unfamiliar with these traditions such semantic shifts are commonly interpreted as paths or assimilative transitions to 'modernity'. In contrast, by drawing together understandings of complex personhood and emergent social forms with the transformative semantics of narrative traditions and the sensual world of perception manifest in non-deterministic ecologies, what emerges are not pathways to the certainty of 'modernist' hegemony, but a renewal of ethical structures for engaging in social relations and a world perpetually 'coming-into-being' (Ingold 2006: 10; Bourdieu 1979).

'Coming-into-being': customary renewal and transition

During the 500 years of Portuguese (and Dutch) colonialism, Timor experienced only an indirect and often tenuous foreign rule and indigenous cosmologies remained both strong and the paradigm around which daily political and economic life continued to revolve (Gunn 1999). The violence and control of the Indonesian era saw a widespread suppression of locally autonomous rule (Thu 2008, 2012). However, in the independence era there is currently a revitalization and recalibration of indigenous custom and tradition. For example, there are an increasing number of villages and sub-districts where the communal management of natural resources (fields, forests, fisheries, waters) is being enhanced by the (re)instatement of communal ritual prohibition and/or harvest ceremonies glossed as *tara bandu* (Meitzner Yoder 2005; McWilliam 2002; Palmer 2007; Palmer and Carvalho 2008; McWilliam *et al.* 2014). This and other ritual practices such as sacred house re-constructions have been variously referred to as an outcome of a resurgent diverse (Palmer 2010) or community economy (McWilliam 2011).

As Timor Leste rebuilds from its post-conflict ashes, the customary economy is frequently disruptive of attempts to put in place neoliberal logics and capitalist certainty. In recognizing the existence of a customary economy in the Baucau Viqueque zone, one is struck by the pervasive insistence of local autonomy embedded in these narratives and practices. Similarly Yang (2000) in her examinations of the resurgence of what she terms 'a ritual economy' in rapidly modernizing, post-socialist, rural south-east China, has noted an 'economic logic which is subversive of capitalist, state socialist, and developmental-state principles' (2000: 477). Calling such an economy a 'ritual-market economic hybrid' she argues that there 'the market economy and the ritual economy of expenditure emerged hand in hand' (2000: 487). A significant segment of the surplus from business enterprises and wage labour is reinvested through expenditure which is reinvigorating the ritual economy and redistributing surplus wealth. It is a case, Yang (2000: 477) argues, of an indigenous economy experiencing renewal and 'posing a challenge to capitalist principles', rather than the other way around. Similarly in his work in Mongolia on the resurgence of magic and occult practices, Pederson interrogates the unwieldy proliferation of 'fractal self-differentiation' or 'post-plural self-extension' (2012: 36). This dangerous but captivatingly powerful flourishing of liminal forms is, he argues, an outcome of the chaotic void which emerged from the post-socialist 'disintegration of stable religious, political and economic forms' (2012: 36).

In Timor the pulsing heart of the customary economy is *lulik*. Often glossed as sacred, forbidden or taboo, the term *lulik* in Tetum and its equivalents in local languages 'refer to a whole range of objects, places, topographic features,

24   *Introduction*

categories of food, types of people, forms of knowledge, behavioural practices, architectural structures and periods of time' (McWilliam *et al.* 2014: 304). In Timor I would argue that the independence era resurgence of customary relations and *lulik*, with all its attendant uncertainty and excesses, is in many ways a re-normalization of long suppressed potencies and practices. Yet the powerful potential of the always becoming (never quite settled) '*lulik* complex' (McWilliam *et al.* 2014) is undoubtedly given new form by the uncertainties, opportunities and contingencies of political and economic transition to largely neoliberal governance regimes. Meanwhile as Peck (2010) has argued in the global context, such processes of neoliberalism proliferate through increasingly honed capacities for self re-invention, processes he characterizes as 'failing forward'. In 'failing forward', concepts such as sustainability become infinitely malleable as 'rounds of neoliberal invention involve not just new models of governance, but new narratives and visions to support them' (Shaw 2013: 2160). Given the power and potential surpluses or excesses inherent then in *both lulik* and neoliberal governance, it is perhaps no surprise that their coming together creates an even heightened potential for spillage, danger and serendipity (Braun 2013; cf. Bovensiepen 2014a, 2014b on a post-independence flourishing of death rituals and 'house' ritual reinterpretation and calibration). Such thoroughly materialist and vitalist assemblages as the *lulik* complex continually rub up against and produce interpretations of equally flourishing state and international agency based forms and constructs. While these latter processes are usually determined by atomistic Western beliefs about nature, the individual and wellbeing, in the encounter between them we need to pay careful attention to what exactly these vibrant materialities in their 'multiplicities are and will become' (Lorimer 2012: 606; cf. Gibson-Graham 2006).

While it is resurgent in the independence era, it is also clear that customary governance processes centred on the 'regulation' of nature and (other) social relations are often fraught. Amongst the younger generations there is a sense that the burden of *lulik* places excessive demands on their lives. Particularly in urban and semi-urban landscapes brimming with aspirational modernity, some feel that the burden of customary obligations is overwhelming. People will often state that *lulik* is too greedy (cf. Ospina and Hohe 2001: 175). For city dwellers and wage labourers in particular, life cycle and intergenerational customary exchanges between sacred houses and the associated *fetosaa* and *umane* groups ('fertility-takers' and 'fertility-givers') in marital exchanges (of things such as buffalo, horses, goats, gold discs and swords, on the one hand, and pigs, rice, necklaces and woven cloth, on the other) are made not by drawing on family livestock and heirloom resources but via monetary payments (which are either pooled and used in the exchange directly or used to purchase the livestock and goods to be exchanged).[14] Yet while these concerns about the excessive demands of *lulik* or *lia* (customary negotiations) may lead to particular transformations in exchange practices, even in urban areas like Baucau these house-based inter-relations and rituals are on the whole reinvigorating rather than declining.[15] It is the case however, as we will see in the conclusion, that colonial era disruptions have often made ritual governance and exchange practices at the broader community level difficult to reinvigorate. The challenges of reinvigorating these broader community governance processes have led some elders to fear that the potency and wildness of *lulik*, which should be ordinarily tamed by *lisan* ('customary norms and practices'), may now re-emerge in increasingly destructive ways (cf. Pederson 2012).

What is clear is that, as a result as well of its inherent excesses, the customary economy is embedded in a lively and dynamic politics of reciprocal and deeply inclusive sociality. These beliefs and practices are not, as some might argue, invented traditions (cf. Hobsbawn and Ranger 1983), nor are they residual. Rather they are always messy, contingent convergences. This book attempts a close reading of them, in order to provoke the possibility of new environmental governance frameworks which place conceptions of multi-temporal and multi-dimensional human and non-human sociality at the centre of the new nation's governance concern. Drawing out the workings of this diverse economy, it is clear that in the customary realm's openness to and capacity for transformation (Ellen 2007), we also find the potential for creative and innovative modes of governance. Modes of governance which may assist in the task of 're-embedding social and political institutions at the local level' (Johnstone *et al.* 2012: xx). In order to do this I pay close attention to indigenous theories of this particular place and waterscape and to the fact that 'theory, particularly critical theory, is immanent in life itself' (Comaroff and Comaroff 2012: 49).

The ethnography

The fieldwork for this research was carried out using the ethnographic method, drawing on data collected from formal and informal interviews, as well as opportunistic observations and conversations with community members, bureaucrats and development workers and frequent participation in a range of household, community and ceremonial events. The research process was also facilitated by my own close and extended kinship ties with many families in the Baucau region (see Preface) enabling participation in a diverse range of social, economic and cultural activities.

To understand more about water in Baucau, a place whose history has not yet been written, it soon became apparent during the fieldwork process that I would need to immerse myself in the collection of oral histories. I began to seek out and build relationships with the locally renowned custodians of these narratives, expressing my interest in learning from them and awaiting their decisions about whether or not, or how much, they were prepared to disclose to me. What transpired has been a long, confusing, frustrating but ever fascinating journey of revelation and non-disclosure. One which has produced a tantalizing, but always imperfectly understood, story that no historiography from eastern Timor has so far been able to tell.

This account of footprints and watery trails is not a story of a village or a sub-district of Timor Leste. My research may have started out in Baucau town, but it

26   *Introduction*

became clear that as the stories traversed the landscape so too must my research. In my retelling here of the local watery histories, I investigate the width and depths of a ritual domain which spreads from the central mountains to the female (north) sea, across the sea and back again, as well as from the male (south) sea across the mountains to the female sea. In this task I needed to carry out interviews and participant observation in six local languages.

While my more formal interviews were on the whole carried out with groups of senior men, in most cases younger men, women and children would be present during these occasions.[16] Frequently women would contribute insights, a clarification or a story during these interviews and discussions but on the whole speaking publicly on water related and highly sensitive *lulik* issues is the domain of senior men (this does not preclude senior women from being centrally involved in these deliberations in private and through alternative ritual political practices). In ritual events women will often play a key role as guardians of sacred houses, dancers, musicians, singers, mourners, dispensers of betel nut and as the organizers and preparers of highly prescribed food and hospitality exchanges involving fertility-giving and fertility-taking houses. Along with child birth and care, daily cooking and household tasks, the care of guests, the infirm, the elderly and the deceased is the primary domain of women.[17] All of these roles carried out by women are considered critical to the pursuit of intergenerational wellbeing and all, including my own sustained participation in these roles, inform my understanding of the vibrant lifeworlds under discussion in this book (cf. Kehi and Palmer 2012). Women's particular relationships to water must, however, be the subject of another study.

Customary ethical processes of sharing and exchange similarly directed the research process. In many, but not all, of my more formal interviews and/or ritual participation with senior house leaders, when specific genealogical details of regional spring narratives were recounted, an animal was required to be sacrificed to *loke odamatan* and *taka odamatan* (literally to open and close the door to the ancestral realm).[18] This is the way to properly open and close a discussion of highly sensitive *lulik* matters and failure to do so could lead to sickness, death or other misfortune (see also Kehi and Palmer 2012; McWilliam *et al.* 2014; Forman 1976).

Throughout this research process, the stories I have traced and the customary activities I have engaged in have relied on the enthusiastic participation, knowledge and sustained engagement of senior ritual specialists from, in particular, the villages of Bahu, Wani Uma, Wailili, Darasula, Berecoli, Tirilolo and Ossu (see Figure 1.1). Their participation was, without exception, underpinned by a desire to have their stories told and acknowledged as important in the nation-building process. It is also pertinent to note that despite the nominally animist nature of these discussions and practices, in many instances it was Catholic religious leaders who facilitated my introduction to particular house-based leaders and communities (usually ones that they themselves were associated with). One particular ritual specialist deserves special mention. Major Ko'o Raku (Antonio da Costa Gusmao) is a respected *lia na'in* ('custodian of the words')[19] from the house of Samalari in the village of Bahu and traditional healer who has also led the renaissance in sacred house building across the Baucau sub-district (and beyond) (see da Costa *et al.* 2006). He, by his own admission, is a 'brave' (*baarani*) man (see Figure 1.2) and was able to tell me many of the *lulik* stories that figure in this book because he had already told them to his children who have written them down and in doing so have now taken them from the world of darkness into the light (see Chapter 2).[20] Richly coded and evocative, Major Ko'o Raku's stories, and those of his contemporaries in this book, are also notable because they are framed in the context of the twentieth-century social creation and transformation of Baucau town and surrounds. From them we gain critical insight into how the people of Baucau have encountered and embraced historical events and how they have recorded and framed them in the contingent realities of their own local worlds. Meanwhile it is also clear that such stories remain both immanent and becoming. Throughout the years of this research, life at many springs across the zone was punctuated by the rebuilding of sacred houses as house groups reinvigorated their spiritual ecologies and associated practices.

To begin this ethnography, the next chapter introduces the waterworld that lies deep beneath the mountains of the central dividing range. It also examines

Figure 1.1 Interview with elders at the houses of Wani Uma Chefe Sau Rai.

the ways in which these mountains are understood as the 'navel' or storage tank for all of the region's freshwater. By documenting what is a profoundly holistic, poetic and many layered understanding of being linked to water, this chapter and those that follow serve to critically explore both the complex inter-relations and future challenges for this particular socio-cosmic way of being in and understanding the world.

Figure 1.2 Major Ko'o Raku (Antonio da Costa Gusmao), Bahu *lia na'in* wearing ritual regalia.

Notes

1 These limestone reefs are 100–500 m thick (Wallace *et al.* 2012a).

2 Discharge in major springs is in a range or 1–200 litres per second (Furness 2012: 3).

3 Kawamina is a notionally Austronesian language bloc comprising the Kairui, Waima'a, Midiki and Naueti languages (Hull 1998: 4) spoken by approximately 50,000 people (15,000 of which speak Naueti) (NSD and UNFPA 2011: 204). Makasae is a notionally 'Papuan' or non-Austronesian language (Hull 2004) spoken by approximately 100,000 people (NSD and UNFPA 2011: 204). While the Makasae and the Kawamina languages are primarily spoken across the zone, Eastern Tetum is also spoken in the Viqueque district (Hicks 2004 [1976]). Meanwhile Tetum Dili, the national lingua franca, is also a vernacular language in Baucau town, an area comprised largely of Makasae and Waima'a speakers. The local cultural terms in this book are derived from all of these languages. When these concepts are being used in a general sense, unless otherwise noted, these terms are given in the national lingua franca of Tetum Dili. In places where terms from others local languages are used they are identified by the placement of an M: (Makasae), W: (Waima'a), K: (Kairui) or ET: (Eastern Tetum) prior to the English translation. An 'I' is used in the case of Indonesian language words.

4 The focus of existing studies has mostly been on Makasae marriage and mortuary exchange and dualisms (Forman 1980, 1981; Lazarowitz 1980; Guterres 1997). The exception to this is Forman (1978) who gives an insightful but brief account of political alliances and exchange in the mountainous region of Quelicai. In the 1930s, the colonial administrator of Baucau produced an account of local customs (Correia 1935). In 2006 a group of Makasae speakers (da Costa *et al.* 2006) in association with the Catholic Teacher's College in Baucau produced a short monograph on the world of the Makasae. Thu (2008, 2012) has studied post-conflict migration and rural livelihoods in the Makasae coastal villages of eastern Baucau. Hicks (1973) produced a short preliminary account of the Uaima'a [Waima'a]. Pannell and O'Connor (2005) offer some preliminary research into Waima'a cave uses. While Forman and Lazarowitz discuss wet rice agriculture neither discusses its history or associated water cosmologies and rituals.

5 Circa 200,000 individuals (CAVR 2006).

6 The country is home to an array of under-documented Austronesian and non-Austronesian influenced languages and cultures. In relation to the country's sixteen languages see Hull (1998, 2004).

7 See also Berkes (2008) on sacred ecology.

8 This may extend to assistance with agricultural tasks and also labour and gift-giving at each other's sacred house-building ceremonies.

9 While the *fetosaa* and *umane* alliances systems vary in their detail and terminology across the country, partilineal systems are usually glossed by anthropologists in English as wife-taker and wife-giver alliances (see for example Hicks 1990). In these systems the local language terms refer, in general, to the relationship formed between the marriage house of a man's sister (and her children) and the house of the man's patriline (and his children). Once the *barlake* process is completed, children belong to the house of their father (who are in effect fertility-takers from the wife's natal house). In Makasae the term for these alliance groups is *tufumata* (literally 'sister's child') *omarahe* (literally 'the perpetual house'). In Waima'a the term is *w'aa-sae lila*. While both of these systems are nominally patrilineal, men may marry into their wife's natal house in certain circumstances, in which case the children of the union belong to the mother's house (cf. Hicks 1990). For a description of a matrilineal system see Francillon (1967). In Tetum Terik the terms are *feto sawa* and *uma mane* or *feto sau mane*.

10 On Seram, Boulan Smit for example notes that the ritual centre of the region is linked to springs (1998: 110–111) and one spring is known as the 'water of origin' (1998: 124).

30 *Introduction*

11 The sprinkling of holy water also resonates with practices in the Catholic tradition where it is carried out to cool and render blessing.
12 I am indebted to Balthasar Kehi for suggesting this term.
13 Put another way the semantic repertoire of fictional possible worlds is continually refreshed by alluding to new kinds of relevance to local individual socio-cultural circumstance and materialist transformation (Boucher 2013).
14 However, in various local critiques of the excesses of the ritual economy, it is not only the replacement or phasing out of customary processes with capitalocentric approaches that are being suggested. There are also a range of precedents within the customary repertoire which draw on the power of communal ritual processes to impose a reduction on the sizes of customary payments (see Palmer 2007; Fox 1979: 32; Meitzner Yoder 2007: 47). Such cases further demonstrate the need to engage with the full range of practices embedded in the customary economy.
15 As noted above, among some educated Timorese, particularly in the capital, there is some emerging resistance to the practice of *barlake*. In addition to economic inefficiencies, concern is also expressed on the grounds of gender inequality. The latter relates to the idea that *barlake*, at least in its modern form, involves the objectification of women (Niner 2012).
16 In some water rituals carried out at particular springs the ritual power of the process is such that women are forbidden from participation. My status as an ethnographer waived this restriction in most cases.
17 As noted in Chapter 4, both women and men share the burden of agricultural work.
18 As discussed in Chapter 6, in some cases if the sacred house (complex) of the interviewees was not yet re-constructed then these ritual sacrifices were not requested as they were unable to be carried out.
19 In Makasae these people are referred to as *sobu dada* and in Waima'a as *kii-lia*.
20 His eldest son, who is nominated to succeed him as the custodian of the words, is a school teacher in Dili.

References

Allerton, C. (2009) 'Static Crosses and Working Spirits: Anti-Syncretism and Agricultural Animism in Catholic West Flores', *Anthropological Forum* 19(3): 271–287.

Almeida, de A. (1976) 'Da Origem Lendária e Mitológica dos Povos do Timor Português', *Memórias da Academia des Ciências de Lisboa* 19: 575–607.

Altman, N. (2002) *Sacred Water: The Spiritual Source of Life*, Mahwah: Paulist Press.

Anderson, B. and Wylie, J. (2009) 'On Geography and Materiality', *Environment and Planning* 41(2): 318–335.

Asian Development Bank (2004) *Integrated Water Resource Management 'Water for All – Water for Growth'*, Asian Development Bank TA:TIM 3986 Timor-Leste Integrated Water Resources Management Technical Assistance. Dili: Asian Development Bank.

Audley-Charles, M. (1968) *The Geology of Portuguese Timor*, London: Memoir of the Geological Society No. 4.

Bachelard, G. (1983) *Water and Dreams: An Essay on the Imagination of Matter*, Dallas: Pegasus Foundation.

Bakker, K. (2003) *An Uncooperative Commodity: Privatising Water in England and Wales*, Oxford: Oxford University Press.

Bakker, K. (2007) 'The "Commons" Versus the "Commodity": Alter-Globalization, Anti-Privatization, and the Human Right to Water in the Global South', *Antipode* 39(3): 430–455.

Bakker, K. (2010) 'Neoliberalizing Nature? Market Environmentalism in Water Supply in England and Wales', *Annals of the Association of American Geographers* 95: 542–565.

Banister, J. (2014) 'Are you Wittfogel or against Him? Geophilosophy, Hydro-Sociality, and the State', *Geoforum* 57: 205–214.

Barber, M. and Jackson, S. (2012) 'Aboriginal Water Values and Resource Development Pressures in the Pilbara Region of North-West Australia', *Australian Aboriginal Studies* 2: 32–49.

Barad, K. (2003) 'Posthumanist Performativity: Toward an Understanding of How Matter Comes to Matter', *Signs: Journal of Women in Culture and Society* 28(3): 801–831.

Bear, C. and Bull, J. (2011) 'Water Matters: Agency, Flows and Frictions', *Environment and Planning A* 43(10): 2261–2266.

Bennett, J. (2010) *Vibrant Matter: A Political Ecology of Things*, London: Duke University Press.

Berkes, F. (2008) *Sacred Ecology: Traditional Ecological Knowledge and Resource Management*, 2nd edn, London: Routledge.

Boelens, R. (2009) 'The Politics of Disciplining Water Rights', *Development and Change* 40(2): 307–331.

Boelens, R. (2014) 'Cultural Politics and the Hydrosocial Cycle: Water, Power and Identity in the Andean Highlands', *Geoforum* 57: 234–247.

Boelens, R. and Dávila, G. (eds) (2006) *Water and Indigenous Peoples: Knowledges of Nature 2*, Paris: United Nations Educational Scientific and Cultural Organisation (UNESCO).

Boucher, G. (2013) 'Disclosure and Critique', paper presented at Multiple Ontologies/ Ontological Relativity Workshop, Deakin University, Melbourne, December 2013.

Boulan Smit, M. (1998) 'We of the Banyan Tree: Traditions of Origin of the Alune of West Seram', unpublished PhD thesis, Australian National University.

Bourdieu, P. (1979) *Outline of a Theory of Practice*, Cambridge: Cambridge University Press.

Bovensiepen, J. (2014a) 'Installing the Insider "Outside": House Reconstruction and the Transformation of Binary Ideologies in Independent Timor-Leste', *American Ethnologist* 41(2): 209–304.

Bovensiepen, J. (2014b) 'Paying for the Dead: On the Politics of Death in Independent Timor-Leste', *The Asia Pacific Journal of Anthropology* 15(2): 103–122.

Brady, J. and Prufer, K. (eds) (2005) *In the Maw of the Earth Monster: Mesoamerican Ritual Cave Use*, Austin: University of Texas Press.

Braun, B. (2013) 'Vital Materialism and Neoliberal Natures', *RGS-IBG Antipode Lecture*, lecture delivered August 2013, London.

Braun, B. and Whatmore, S. (eds) (2010) *Political Matter: Technoscience, Democracy and Public Life*, Minnesota: University of Minnesota Press.

Burchi, S. (2005) 'The Interface Between Customary and Statutory Water Rights: A Statutory Perspective', paper presented at the International Workshop on African Water Laws, Johannesburg, January 2005.

Castree, N. (2012) *Making Sense of Nature*, London: Taylor & Francis.

Chen, C., MacLeod, J. and Neimanis, A. (eds) (2013) *Thinking with Water*, Montreal: McGill-Queen's University Press.

Comaroff, J. and Comaroff, J. (2012) *Theory from the South: Or, how Euro-America is Evolving toward Africa*, Boulder: Paradigm Publishers.

Commission for Reception, Truth and Reconciliation in East Timor (CAVR) (2006) *Chega! Final Report of the Commission for Reception, Truth and Reconciliation in East Timor*, Dili: CAVR Timor-Leste.

Conklin, H. (1980) *Ethnographic Atlas of Ifugao: A Study of Environment, Culture and Society in Northern Luzon*, New Haven: Yale University Press.

32 Introduction

Correia, A. (1935) *Gentio de Timor*, Lisbon: Agência-Geral das Colónias.

Costin, G. and Powell, B. (2006) *Situation Analysis Report Timor Leste*, Brisbane: Australian Water Research Facility, International Water Centre.

da Costa, C., da Costa Guterres, A. and Lopes, J. (eds) (2006) *Exploring Makassae Culture*, Baucau: Publicacoes Matebian-Grafica Diocesana Baucau.

De Josselin de Jong, J. (1937) *Oirata: A Timorese Settlement of Kisar, Studies in Indonesian Culture*, Amsterdam: Verhandelingen der Koninklijke Akadamie van Wetenschappen te Amsterdam.

Duarte, J. (1964) 'Barlaque', *Seara* 2 (N.S.) (3): 1–4.

Ellen, R. (ed.) (2007) *Modern Crises and Traditional Strategies: Local Ecological Knowledge in Island Southeast Asia*, New York: Berghahn.

Ernstson, H. and Sorlin, S. (2013) 'Ecosystem Services as Technology of Globalization: On Articulating Values in Urban Nature', *Ecological Economics* 86: 274–284.

Forman, S. (1976) 'Spirits of the Makassae', *Natural History* 85(9): 12–18.

Forman, S. (1978) 'East Timor: Exchange and Political Hierarchy at the Time of the European Discoveries', in K. Hutterer (ed.) *Economic Exchange and Social Interaction in Southeast Asia: Perspectives from Prehistory, History and Ethnography*, Michigan Papers on South and Southeast Asia No. 13, The University of Michigan, 97–112.

Forman, S. (1980) 'Descent, Alliance and Exchange Ideology among the Makassae of East Timor', in J. Fox (ed.) *The Flow of Life: Essays on Eastern Indonesia*, Cambridge, MA: Harvard University Press.

Forman, S. (1981) 'Life Paradigms: Makassae (East Timor) Views on Production, Reproduction, and Exchange', *Research in Economic Anthropology: A Research Annual* 4: 95–110.

Forth, G. (1998) *Beneath the Volcano: Religion, Cosmology and Spirit Classification among the Nage of Eastern Indonesia*, Leiden: KITLV Press.

Fox, J. (1979) 'A Tale of Two States: Ecology and the Political Economy of Inequality on the Island of Roti', in P. Burnham and R. Ellen (eds) *Social and Ecological Systems*, London: Academic Press, 19–42.

Fox, J. (ed.) (1980) *The Flow of Life: Essays on Eastern Indonesia*, Cambridge, MA: Harvard University Press.

Fox, J. (ed.) (1997) *The Poetic Power of Place: Comparative Perspectives on Austronesian Ideas of Locality*, Canberra: ANU Press.

Fox, J. (2001) 'Diversity and Differential Development in East Timor: Potential Problems and Future Possibilities', in H. Hill and J.M. Saldanha (eds) *East Timor: Timor: Development Challenges for the World's Newest Nation*, Basingstoke: Palgrave, 155–176.

Fox, J. and Babo Soares, D. (eds) (2000) *Out of the Ashes: Destruction and Reconstruction of East Timor*, Canberra: ANU ePress.

Francillon, G. (1967) 'Some Matriarchic Aspects of Social Structure of the Tetun of Middle Timor', unpublished PhD thesis, Australian National University.

Furness, L. (2004) *A Preliminary Assessment of the Sustainable Groundwater Yield of Timor-Leste*, Timor-Leste Integrated Water Resource Management Project, Canberra: Asia Development Bank.

Furness, L. (2011) 'Baucau Limestone Dye-Tracing Experiment', Dili: National Directorate of Water Resources, Ministry of Infrastructure.

Furness, L. (2012) 'Baucau Karst Limestone Aquifer Airborne EM Survey', Dili: National Directorate of Water Resources, Ministry of Infrastructure.

Gachenko, E. (2012) 'Water Resource User Associations in Kenya's Water Act: Real Space for Customary Governance Systems or Mere Tokenism?', *Journal of Water Law* 22(2/3): 124–138.

Gelles, P. (2000) *Water and Power in Highland Peru: The Cultural Politics of Irrigation and Development*, New Brunswick: Rutgers University Press.

Gibson-Graham, J.-K. (2006) *A Postcapitalist Politics*, Minneapolis: University of Minnesota Press.

Gibson-Graham, J.-K. (2012) 'Diverse Economies: Performative Practices for "Other Worlds"', in T.J. Barnes, J. Peck and E. Sheppard (eds) *The Wiley-Blackwell Companion to Economic Geography*, Oxford: Blackwell, 33–46.

Gibson-Graham, J. and Roelvink, G. (2010) 'An Economic Ethics for the Anthropocene', *Antipode* 41(1): 320–346.

Gow, P. (2001) *An Amazonian Myth and its History*, Oxford: Oxford University Press.

Graham, P. (1991) 'To Follow the Blood: The Path of Life in a Domain of Eastern Flores', unpublished PhD thesis, Australian National University.

Grimes, B. (1993) 'The Pursuit of Prosperity and Blessing: Social Life and Symbolic Action on Buru Island, Eastern Indonesia', unpublished PhD thesis, Australian National University.

Gunn, G. (1999) *Timor Loro Sae: 500 Years*, Macau: Livros do Oriente.

Guterres, J.M. (1997) 'The Makasae of East Timor: The Structure of an Affinal Alliance System', unpublished MPhil thesis, University of Melbourne.

Hicks, D. (1973) 'The Cairui and Uai Ma'a of Timor', *Anthropos* 68: 473–481.

Hicks, D. (1990) *Kinship and Religion in Eastern Indonesia*, Göteborg: Acta Universitatis Gothoburgensis.

Hicks, D. (1996) 'Making the King Divine: A Case Study in Ritual Regicide from Timor', *Journal of the Royal Anthropological Institute* 2: 611–624.

Hicks, D. (2004) [1976] *Tetum Ghosts & Kin: Fertility and Gender in East Timor*, Illinois: Waveland Press.

Hicks, D. (forthcoming) 'Impaling Spirit: Three Categories of Ontology in Eastern Indonesia', in K. Arhem and G. Sprenger (eds) *Animism in Southeast Asia*, Routledge.

Hill, H. and Saldanha J. (eds) (2001) *East Timor: Development Challenges For The World's Newest Nation*, Basingstoke: Palgrave.

Hobsbawn, E. and Ranger, T. (1983) *The Invention of Tradition*, Cambridge: Cambridge University Press.

Howitt, R. and Suchet-Pearson, S. (2006) 'Rethinking the Building Blocks: Ontological Pluralism and the Idea of "Management"', *Geografiska Annaler. Series B, Human Geography* 88: 323–335.

Hull, G. (1998) 'The Basic Lexical Affinities of Timor's Austronesian Languages: A Preliminary Investigation', *Studies in Languages and Cultures of East Timor* 1: 97–174.

Hull, G. (2004) 'The Papuan Languages of Timor', *Estudos de línguas e culturas de Timor Leste* 6: 23–99.

Ingold, T. (1986) *Evolution and Social Life*, Cambridge: Cambridge University Press.

Ingold, T. (2000) *Perceptions of the Environment*, London: Routledge.

Ingold, T. (2006) 'Rethinking the Animate, Re-animating Thought', *Ethnos* 71(1): 18–19.

Ingold, T. (2011) *Being Alive: Essays on Movement, Knowledge and Description*, London: Routledge.

Jackson, S. (2008) 'Recognition of Indigenous Interests in Australian Water Resource Management, with Particular Reference to Environmental Flow Assessment', *Geography Compass (Environment & Society)* 2(3): 874–898.

Jackson, S. (forthcoming) 'Indigenous Peoples and Water Justice in a Globalizing World', in K. Concu and E. Weinthal (eds) *Oxford Handbook on Water Politics and Policy*, Oxford: Oxford University Press.

34 *Introduction*

Jackson, S. and Altman, J (2009) 'Indigenous Rights and Water Policy: Perspectives from Tropical Northern Australia', *Australian Indigenous Law Review* 13(1): 27–48.

Jackson, S. and Palmer, L. (2012) 'Modernising Water: Articulating Custom in Water Governance in Australia and Timor-Leste', *International Journal of Indigenous Policy* 3(3): 1–27.

Jackson, S. and Palmer, L. (2014) 'Reconceptualising Ecosystem Services: Possibilities for Cultivating and Valuing the Ethics and Practices of Care', *Progress in Human Geography*.

Jiménez, A., Cortobius, M. and Kjellén, M. (2014) 'Water, Sanitation and Hygiene and Indigenous Peoples: A Review of the Literature', *Water International* 39(3): 277–293.

Johnstone, B.R., Barber, M., Strang, V., Klaver, I., Hiwasaki, L. and Castillo, A.R. (2012) *Water, Cultural Diversity, and Global Environmental Change: Emerging Trends, Sustainable Futures?*, Heidelberg: Springer.

Kehi, B. and Palmer, L. (2012) 'Hamatak Halirin: The Cosmological and Socio-Ecological Roles of Water in Koba Lima, Timor', *Bijdragen tot de Taal-, Land- en Volkenkunde*, 168: 445–471.

Langton, M. (2002) 'The Edge of the Sacred, the Edge of Death: Sensual Inscriptions', in B. David and M. Wilson (eds) *Inscribed Landscapes*, Honolulu: University of Hawaii Press, 427–455.

Langton, M. (2006) 'Earth, Wind, Fire and Water: The Social and Spiritual Construction of Water in Aboriginal Societies', in B. David and M. Wilson (eds) *The Social Archaeology of Australian Aboriginal Societies*, Canberra: Aboriginal Studies Press, 139–160.

Lansing, J. (2006) *Perfect Order: Recognizing Complexity in Bali*, Princeton: Princeton University Press.

Lansing, J. (2007) [1991] *Priests and Programmers: Technologies of Power in the Engineered Landscape of Bali*, Princeton: Princeton University Press.

Latour, B. (2004) *Politics of Nature: How to Bring the Sciences into Democracy*, Cambridge, MA: Harvard University Press.

Latour, B. (2009) 'Perspectivism: "Type" or "Bomb"?', *Anthropology Today* 25(2): 1–2.

Latour, B. and Weibel, P. (eds) (2005) *Making Things Public: Atmospheres of Democracy*, Cambridge, MA: MIT Press.

Lavau, S. (2013) 'Going with the Flow: Water Management as Ontological Cleaving', *Environment and Planning D: Society and Space* 31(3): 416–433.

Lazarowitz, T. (1980) 'The Makassai: Complimentary Dualism in Timur', unpublished PhD thesis, State University of New York.

Lévy-Bruhl, L. (1910) *How Natives Think*, translation by L. Clare (1985), Princeton: Princeton University Press.

Linton, J. (2010) *What is Water? The History of Modern Abstraction*, Toronto: UBC Press.

Linton, J. and Budds, J. (2014) 'The Hydrosocial Cycle: Defining and Mobilizing a Relational-Dialectical Approach to Water', *Geoforum* 57: 170–180.

Lorimer, J. (2012) 'Multinatural Geographies for the Anthropocene', *Progress in Human Geography* 36(5): 593–612.

MacLeod, J. (2013) 'Water and Material Imagination', in C. Chen, J. MacLeod and A. Neimanis (eds) *Thinking with Water*, Montreal: McGill-Queen's University Press, 55–75.

McWilliam, A. (2002) 'Timorese Seascapes: Perspectives on Customary Marine Tenures in Timor Leste', *The Asia Pacific Journal of Anthropology* 3(2): 6–32.

McWilliam, A. (2011) 'Exchange and Resilience in Timor-Leste', *Journal of the Royal Anthropological Institute* 17(4): 745–763.

McWilliam, A. and Traube, E. (eds) (2011) *Land and Life in Timor-Leste: Ethnographic Essays*, Canberra: ANU E-Press.

McWilliam, A., Palmer, L. and Shepherd, C. (2014) '*Lulik* Encounters and Cultural Frictions in East Timor: Past and Present', *The Australian Journal of Anthropology* 25: 304–320.

Madaleno, I. (2007) 'The Privatisation of Water and its Impacts on Settlement and Traditional Cultural Practices in Northern Chile', *Scottish Geographic Journal* 123(3): 193–208.

Meganck, R. (2012) 'Foreword', in B. Johnstone, I. Klaver, A. Ramos Castillo and V. Strang (eds) *Water, Cultural Diversity, and Global Environmental Change: Emerging Trends, Sustainable Futures?*, Dordrecht, Heidelberg, London and New York: UNESCO and Springer, v–x.

Meitzner-Yoder, L. (2005) 'Custom, Codification, Collaboration: Integrating the Legacies of Land and Forest Authorities in Oecusse Enclave, East Timor', unpublished PhD thesis, Yale University.

Meitzner-Yoder, L. (2007) 'Hybridising Justice: State-Customary Interactions over Forest Crime and Punishment in Oecusse, East Timor', *The Asia Pacific Journal of Anthropology* 8(1): 43–57.

Merleau-Ponty, M. (2002) *The Phenomenology of Perception*, London: Routledge.

Metzner, J. (1977) *Man and Environment in Eastern Timor: A Geoecological Analysis of the Baucua-Viqueque Area as a Possible Basis for Regional Planning*, Canberra: The Australian National University.

The Ministry of Culture and Tourism of the Republic of Indonesia and The Government of Bali Province (2010) 'Cultural Landscape of Bali Province', *Nomination for inscription on The UNESCO World Heritage List*.

Mol, A. (1999) 'Ontological Politics: A Word and Some Questions', in J. Law and J. Hassard (eds) *Actor-Network Theory and After*, Oxford: Blackwell, 74–89.

Mosse, D. (2003) *The Rule of Water: Statecraft, Ecology, and Collective Action in South India*, Oxford: Oxford University Press.

Myers, F. (1986) *Pintupi Country, Pintupi Self*, Washington, DC: Smithsonian Institution Press.

National Statistics Directorate (NSD) and United National Population Fund (UNFPA) (2011) 'Population and Housing Census of Timor-Leste: Population Distribution by Administrative Areas', Dili: NSD and UNFPA.

Neonbasu, G. (2005) 'We Seek Our Roots: Oral Tradition in Biboki, West Timor', unpublished PhD thesis, Australian National University.

Nevins, J. (2005) *A Not-So-Distant Horror: Mass Violence in East Timor*, Ithaca: Cornell University Press.

Niner, S. (2012) '*Barlake*: An Exploration of Marriage Practices and Issues of Women's Status in Timor-Leste', *Local-Global: Identity, Security, Community* 11: 138–153.

Orlove, B. and Caton, S. (2010) 'Water Sustainability: Anthropological Approaches and Prospects', *Annual Review of Anthropology* 39: 401–415.

Ospina, S. and Hohe, T. (2001) *Traditional Power Structures and the Community Empowerment and Local Governance Structures Final Report*, Dili: World Bank.

Palmer, L. (2007) 'Developing Timor Leste: Recognising the Role of Custom and Tradition', *SSEE Working Papers in Development* 1: 35–40.

Palmer, L. (2010) 'Enlivening Development: Water Management in the Post Conflict Baucau City, Timor-Leste', *Singapore Journal of Tropical Geography* 31: 357–370.

Palmer, L. and Carvalho, D.A. (2008) 'Nation Building and Resource Management: The Politics of "Nature" in Timor Leste', *Geoforum* 39(3): 1321–1332.

36   *Introduction*

Pannell, S. (2007) 'Of Gods and Monsters: Indigenous Sea Cosmologies, Promiscuous Geographies and the Depths of Local Sovereignty', in P. Boomgaard (ed.) *A World of Water: Rain, Rivers and the Sea in Southeast Asian Histories*, Leiden: KITLV Press, 71–102.

Pannell, S. and O'Connor, S. (2005) 'Towards a Cultural Topography of Cave Use in East Timor: A Preliminary Study', *Asian Perspectives* 44(1): 193–206.

Pasquale, V. (2011) 'The Poorest Countries in the World', *Global Finance*, available at: www.gfmag.com/tools/global-database/economic-data/10502-the-poorest-countries-in-the-world.html#axzz1mu5oEriP/ (accessed 3 April 2014).

Peake, G. (2013) *Beloved Land*, Melbourne: Scribe.

Peck, J. (2010) *Constructions of Neoliberal Reason*, Oxford: Oxford University Press.

Pederson, M. (2001) 'Totemism, Animism and North Asian Indigenous Ontologies', *Journal of the Royal Anthropological Institute* 7: 411–427.

Pederson, M. (2012) *Not Quite Shamans*, Ithaca: Cornell University Press.

Philpott, S. (2006) 'East Timor's Double Life: Smells like Westphalian Spirit', *Third World Quarterly* 27(1): 135–159.

Prufer, K. and Brady, J. (2005) 'Concluding Remarks', in J. Brady and K. Prufer (eds) *In The Maw of the Earth Monster: Mesoamerican Ritual Cave Use*, Austin: University of Texas Press, 403–412.

Rappaport, R. (1967) 'Ritual Regulation of Environmental Relations Among a New Guinea People', *Ethnology* 6(1): 17–30.

Reuter, T. (1996) 'Custodians of the Sacred Mountains: The Ritual Domains of Highland Bali', unpublished PhD thesis, Australian National University.

Rodemeier, S. (2009) 'Bui Hangi–The Deity's Human Wife: Analysis of a Myth from Pura, Eastern Indonesia', *Anthropos* 104: 469–482.

Rodriguez, S. (2007) *Acequia: Water Sharing, Sanctity and Place*, Sante Fe: School for Advanced Research Resident Scholar Book.

Rose, D. (2011) *Wild Dog Dreaming: Love and Extinction*, Charlottesville: University of Virginia Press.

Scheiner, C. (2014) 'The "Resource Curse" in Timor-Leste', *In Brief* 29: 1–2.

Schoffel, P. (2006) 'Timor-Leste: Community-Managed Water Supply and Sanitation: A Case Study from the 2004 Project Performance Audit Phase I and II', Asian Development Bank.

Shaw, K. (2013) 'Docklands Dreamings: Illusions of Sustainability in the Melbourne Docks Redevelopment', *Urban Studies* 50(11): 2158–2177.

Shepherd, C. (2013) *Development and Environmental Politics Unmasked: Authority, Participation and Equity in East Timor*, London and New York: Routledge.

Sherbondy, J. (1998) 'Andean Irrigation in History', in R. Boelens and G. Dávila (eds) *Searching for Equity*, Assen: Van Gorcum, 210–215.

Smith, N. (2007) 'Nature as Accumulation Strategy', *Socialist Register* 43: 19–41.

Sponsel, L. (2010) 'Religion and Environment: Exploring Spiritual Ecology', *Religion and Society: Advances in Research* 1: 131–145.

Sponsel, L. (2012) *Spiritual Ecology: A Quiet Revolution*, Santa Barbara: Praeger.

Stanner, W. (1966) 'On Aboriginal Religion', *Oceania Monograph 11*, Sydney: University of Sydney.

Strang, V. (2002) *Life Down Under: Water and Identity in an Aboriginal Cultural Landscape*, London: Goldsmiths Anthropology Research Papers.

Strang, V. (2004) *The Meaning of Water*, Oxford: Berg Publishers.

Strang, V. (2009) 'Fluid Forms: Owning Water in Australia', in V. Strang and M. Busse (eds) *Ownership and Appropriation*, Oxford: Berg Publishers.

Strang, V. (2013) 'Conceptual Relations: Water, Ideologies, and Theoretical Subversions', in C. Chen, J. MacLeod and A. Neimanis (eds) *Thinking with Water*, Montreal: McGill-Queen's University Press, 200–226.

Strathern, M. (1988) *The Gender of the Gift*, Berkeley: University of California Press.

Strathern, M. (1999) *Property, Substance and Effect: Anthropological Essays on Persons and Things*, London: Athlone Press.

Sullivan, S. (2009) 'Green Capitalism, and the Cultural Poverty of Constructing Nature as Service Provider', *Radical Anthropology* 3: 18–27.

Sullivan, S. (2010) 'Ecosystems Service Commodities: New Imperial Ecology? Implications for Animist Immanent Ecologies, with Deleuze and Guattari', *New Formations* 69(6): 111–128.

Swyngedouw, E. (2004) *Social Power and the Urbanisation of Water: Flows of Power*, Oxford: Oxford University Press.

Swyngedouw, E. (2009) The Political Economy and Political Ecology of the Hydro-Social Cycle', *Journal of Contemporary Water Research & Education*, 142(1): 56–60.

Tamisari, F. (2001) 'Names and Naming: Speaking Forms into Place', in L. Hercus, F. Hodges and J. Simpson (eds) *The Land is a Map: Placenames of Indigenous Origin in Australia*, Canberra: ANU Press, 87–102.

Tanter, R., Ball, D. and van Klinken, G. (2006) *Masters of Terror: Indonesia's Military and Violence in East Timor*, Washington, DC: Rowman & Littlefield.

Therik, T. (2004) *Wehali the Female Land: Traditions of a Timorese Ritual Centre*, Canberra: The Australian National University, Pandanus Books.

Thu, P. (2008) 'Land Forgotten: Effects of Indonesian Re-Settlement on Rural Livelihoods in East Timor', in D. Mearns (ed.) *Democratic Governance in Timor-Leste: Reconciling the Local and the National*, Darwin: CDU Press, 143–159.

Thu, P. (2012) 'Negotiating Displacement: A Study of Land and Livelihoods in Rural East Timor', unpublished PhD thesis, Australian National University.

Traube, E. (1986) *Cosmology and Social Life: Ritual Exchange among the Mambai of East Timor*, Chicago: University of Chicago Press.

Tsing, A. (2005) *Friction: An Ethnography of Global Connection*, Princeton: Princeton University Press.

Tuana, N. (2008) 'Viscous Porosity: Witnessing Katrina', in S. Alaimo and S. Hekman (eds) *Material Feminisms*, Bloomington: Indiana University Press, 188–213.

UNEP-DHI Centre for Water and Environment (2009) 'Integrated Water Resources Management in Action'.

United Nations Development Programme (UNDP) (2009) *PEI Country Fact Sheet TIMOR LESTE: Poverty and Environment Initiative*, Dili: UNDP.

Vischer, M. (1992) 'Children of the Black Patola Stone: Origin Structures in a Domain on Palu'e Island (Eastern Indonesia)', unpublished PhD thesis, Australian National University.

Viveiros de Castro, E. (1998) 'Cosmological Deixis and Amerindian Perspectivism', *Journal of the Royal Anthropological Institute* 4: 469–488.

Wallace, L., Marshall, S.K., Brodie, R.S., Dawson, S., Caruana, L., Sundaram, B.S., Jaycock, J., Stewart, G. and Furness, L. (2012b) *The Hydrogeology of Timor Leste*, Canberra: Geoscience Australia.

Wallace, L., Sundaram, B., Brodie, R.S., Marshall S., Dawson, S., Jaycock J., Stewart G. and Furness, L. (2012a) *Vulnerability Assessment of Climate Change Impacts on Groundwater Resources in Timor-Leste – Summary Report*, Record 2012/55. Canberra: Geoscience Australia.

38 Introduction

Watson, J. and Lansing, S.L. (2012) 'Using the Design of Bali's World Heritage Landscape to Empower Balinese Communities', *Subak Travelling Exhibition and Guidebook proposal, October,* available at: http://static.weadapt.org/placemarks/files/1022/52ea1a 13c508fproposal-traveling-exhibit.pdf (accessed 11 September 2014).

Williams, N. (1986) *The Yolngu and Their Land: A System of Land Tenure and the Fight for its Recognition,* Canberra: Australian Institute of Aboriginal Studies.

Williams, N. (1998) 'Intellectual Property and Aboriginal Environmental Knowledge', CINCRM Discussion Paper No. 1, Northern Territory University, Darwin.

Wittfogel, K. (1957) *Oriental Despotism: A Comparative Study of Total Power,* New Haven: Yale University Press.

Wittgenstein, L. (1979) *Remarks on Frazer's Golden Bough,* edited by R. Rhees, translated by A.C. Miles (1971), Nottinghamshire: Brynmill.

Yang, M. (2000) 'Putting Global Capitalism in its Place: Economic Hybridity, Bataille, and Ritual Expenditure', *Current Anthropology* 41(4): 477–509.

Young, D. (2006) 'Water as Country on the Pitjantjatjara Yankunytjatjara Lands South Australia', *Worldviews: Environment, Culture, Religion* 10(2): 239–258.

2 Water cosmologies

In east central Timor the rocks and soil of the Mundo Perdido[1] mountain range (also sometimes known as K: Wai Nete Watu Ba'i ('rising water, sacred rock')) are conceptualized as the skin beneath which water pools after rising up through the earth from the sea (see Map 2.1, Figure 2.1). As it rises, this salty water is transformed into fresh water. Whilst life giving, it does not yet have the necessary force to transform into life itself. Rather, life requires its activation by another element – the sun, or its associative force, fire (cf. Kehi and Palmer 2012). Emerging forth from the subterranean darkness into the light of the surface world, the life potential inherent in water is transformed into life itself by the power of fire. In this continual process of emergence and becoming a range of agencies, human and non-human, strive to balance darkness with light, night with day, 'nature' with culture.

Drawing on the work of Gaston Bachelard (1983), MacLeod (2013: 40) argues water is an important component of 'the material imagination'. If ideas are 'animated by the substance of the world' (MacLeod 2013: 48) then we might think of water as 'the ultimate medium for the conversations that continually create the world ... [a] substance [which] acts forever as a meeting place and medium' (2013: 49). Indeed, MacLeod writes that by communicating through water in myth and other 'literary' forms we invoke particular multi-generational 'relationships to time, to the past, to water and to one another' (2013: 57). In this chapter I also engage with these concepts of multi-generational and multi-time from the vantage point of a highly symbolic yet thoroughly material world of water. I am interested in the ways in which this 'world' enables me to understand the profound linkages between these thoroughly materialist ecologies and the ritual domains at the heart of eastern Timor's customary polities and cosmologies.

That the natural world, in this case water, fire and, as we shall see, particular species of animal, should be connected with deep philosophical understandings of the world, that they should bring the world into being and are connected in a variety of ways, is in the words of Wittgenstein (1979) 'obvious'. As he puts it:

> That a man's shadow, which looks like a man, or that his mirror image, or that rain, thunderstorms, the phases of the moon, the change of seasons, the likenesses and differences of animals to one another and to human

40 *Water cosmologies*

beings, the phenomena of death, of birth and of sexual life, in short everything a man perceives year in, year out around him, connected together in a variety of ways – that all this should play a part in his thinking (his philosophy) and his practices, is obvious, or in other words this is what we really know and find interesting.

(Wittgenstein 1979: 6e)

Wittgenstein then continues by arguing that:

[a]n historical explanation ... is only *one* kind of summary of the data.... We can equally well see the data in their relations to one another and make

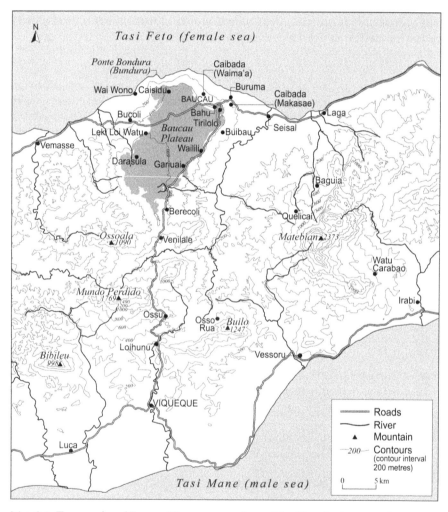

Map 2.1 Topography of Baucau Viqueque zone (copyright Chandra Jayasuriya).

Water cosmologies 41

a summary of them in a general picture without putting it in the form of a hypothesis regarding the temporal development.

(1979: 8e)

The key to this, he writes, is the 'depth of contemplation we understand through connections' where 'the depth lies in the idea ... the overwhelming probability

Figure 2.1 Mundo Perdido (Watu Nete Watu Ba'i) rocky outcrops and *tara bandu* (ritual prohibition) pole, Ossu de Cima.

42   *Water cosmologies*

of this idea … what we get from the material'. Inspired by these musings, this chapter lays out such a 'perspicuous' view (Wittgenstein 1979: 9e) and the ideas I get from this data. By characterizing the relationships between people, their ancestors and their environments through the notion of 'inclusive sociality', I describe and analyse how differently configured inter-relations co-create and order the world in the cosmologies and spiritual ecologies of north-central Timor.

People and their *dai*

To begin, I need to explore and unpack some quite opaque and esoteric beliefs about the nature of social relations between certain groups of people and certain other types of being, particularly animals. First, it is clear that sociality in the region is underpinned by more-than-human relations involving conscious co-operation and inter-subjectivity manifesting and transforming through different 'bodies' and 'things' across and through space and time. This I am calling 'inclusive sociality'. Elsewhere in Timor, Judith Bovensiepen has written that 'there is an ambiguity about the precise nature of the relationship between ancestors, *lulik* [by which I take she means spiritual energy or potency] and land [nature] spirits' (2011: 50). She concludes that 'although [these three] are conceptually separate, they are [in ritual] implicitly treated as transformations of each other and their combined presence in the land makes up its powerful potency' (Bovensiepen 2011: 50).

To say something more from this region of study about these types of relationships and what they collectively embody, I take as my starting point the cyclical movement of the world (both spatially, temporally and simultaneously) from darkness to lightness, day to night. This movement is the core principle of local cosmologies. By way of shorthand we can think of the universe as divided into two cycles: *Mu'a Gamu* in Makasae or *Namu Degu* in Waima'a refers to the dark earth period or dimension and *Mu'a Usa* (Makasae) or *Namu Rema* (Waima'a) to the bright earth period or dimension. While this blurred and often messy division is neither wholly spatial nor temporal, it does in some contexts become historicized and may even at times refer to the era of 'nature' or *natureza* (where the dark earth is referred to in combination with terms for 'sacred earth', W: *ria luli* or M: *mu'a falun*) on the one hand, and on the other, the incremental arrival of Portuguese Catholicism some 500 years ago. It is also, however, always comparable to the Earth spinning on it axis, with its halves forever switching between night and day and its whole pervaded by both.

From a historicized point of view, the era of *darkness* is understood as the transformative period when the world was created and shaped into being. At the beginning of this period people did not yet know fire or water nor did they know the differences between animals and themselves. Throughout the period, form or 'skin changing' between humans, animals and physical objects was commonplace. As the world evolved, this period of continual transformation solidified around cultivated relations between certain groups of human beings

Water cosmologies   43

and certain other species of animal (most commonly we find special or totemic relationships between named groups of people and crocodiles, snakes, eels and other water-based species, civet cats, rats, bees, bats, monkeys, birds and termites). These ancestral animal spirits are 'fed' in special ceremonies usually revolving around agricultural rites. Some origin groups have these same special relationships with ancestral fire and water. Eventually the earth moved into the period of lightness, 'culture' (customary norms and practices referred to as *lisan* in Makasae and Waima'a) emerged and the transformations between people, animals and physical objects became less common. As other power objects, such as gold discs, swords and books, emerged these were also considered to give power to the particular clan houses they became associated with.

Over time, then, as people came to know about fire and water, they learnt the differences between people and animals and began to eat cooked foods. Eventually as the darkness truly receded into light people also learnt to write and from this they could live and rule in the manner required by the foreigners who had by then long been in the land. This period of lightness, or perhaps even enlightenment, really began when now immutable human bodies sought out objects and processes of cultural change, processes that are still in this era of lightness being perfected.

We can see then that it was with the emergence of 'culture' that respectful relations were instigated and solidified between clans and particular ancestral animal species or *dai* as they are referred to in the Makasae and Waima'a languages (or *malae* in the national language of Tetum).[2] These *dai*, and their living animal counterparts, inhabit sacred waters, mountains, rocks and trees. Unlike people it is said they have no shame and no secrets to hide. While even in the era of lightness all of nature is considered to have agency, ancestral *dai* which are connected to particular peoples have particular significance as their powers have been 'tamed' and channelled via an ongoing relation to the 'culture' (*lisan*) or laws of a particular group.

What elucidated best for me this complicated relationship between people and their *dai* was the practices of house-based traditional healers who are routinely consulted when illness afflicts a household member[3] (see Figure 2.2). As is common in animism, these healers' perspectives on the spirit world embrace both the inter-human and the extra human. But what is most important in their healing practice is the appeal to the relationship between them and their non-human and human ancestors through time (something more akin to totemism). Particular non-human as well as human ancestors share a genealogy to particular named groups of people. Within clan groups, these ancestral animal spirits or *dai* are believed to actively seek out human host bodies. These hosts are known as *kuda* (horses) and the *dai* sit down on their shoulders. It is these *dai*, or more specifically in Waima'a *bo'o dai* (ancestral *dai*), in their various forms, who give magical healing powers to house-based traditional healers (known as *dai kuda*). All *dai* have a propensity to 'wildness', they are unpredictable and easy to anger. While in some cases *bo'o dai* may also be named human ancestral spirits, the origins of these human *dai* will be traceable to an animal ancestor. Meanwhile

44 Water cosmologies

truly wild *dai*, those not or no longer in a reciprocal relationship with humans, are believed to wander the landscape randomly at night. Referred to as wild animal spirits (Makasae: *itibi*, Waima'a: *kele ba'i*) they may sometimes appear in human form and they attach themselves to a person's soul causing sickness often resulting in death.[4] Some other types of traditional healers actively seek out and make sacred compacts with the healing powers of these *dai*.

Figure 2.2 Major Ko'o Raku carrying out a healing divination, Ono Seri, Buruma.

In their healing practice, house-based traditional healers will draw on the power of their own 'tamed' *dai* and use this power to carry out particular diagnostic processes, usually auguries of particular substances. Once the assistance of these *dai* has been garnered and the illness addressed, animal sacrifices are then carried out to 'feed' and placate them. If you do not reciprocate this sacred exchange your *dai* may leave you, take away your power, kill you or make you sick. It will then go to someone else, usually a close or even distant family member. Other more 'modern' Timorese healers with affinities to the Catholic faith may channel assistance and read the wishes of the spirit world through prayer and candle flame. Yet from within the 'traditional' sphere it is said that the origin or trunk of all these spirit manifestations can ultimately be traced to an original ancestral animal *dai*.

Alongside and interwoven with these complicated communicative and avoidance relationships between people and *dai* it is clear that at the cosmological level all beings (living humans, living animals and *dai*) comprise an organic unity which we might think of as conscious nature or a spirit collectivity. In this unity the categories of animal, human and spirit are 'continuous rather than discrete' (Brightman 1993: 3). To explain how this tension between a greater unity and the discontinuity of named groups connected to particular ancestral spirits is reconciled I take my lead from Ingold (2011) and make recourse to the deployment of storied knowledge. What Ingold (2011) proposes is that it is through attention to the inter-related stories through which beings and things are 'alive' we are able to transcend notions of unity and disunity or language preoccupations with networks and classification. For example in the secreted ancestral names and bodies invoked by healers and other ritual specialists the relations between people, animals, physical objects and spirits simply 'happen, they carry on, they *are* their stories and their names … they are not nouns, but verbs' (Ingold 2011: 175). Narrating the movements and speaking these names, they are forever 'alive', continuously woven *together* into the fabric of the world: 'As [these beings] meet up with one another and go their various ways, their paths converge and diverge, to form an ever extending reticulate meshwork … the meshwork of storied knowledge' (Ingold 2011: 168). It is then by focusing on the fabric which is woven and rewoven through these inter-related stories that we can understand 'inclusive sociality'. It is to these stories, specifically about water, that I will now turn.

The hydrosocial cycle

To link the segregation of the world through homologous identification with the simultaneous process of analogous identification which connects all beings, I now need to introduce local conceptualizations of the hydrosocial cycle and pathways. Below I draw on one ritual narrative which weaves together the relations between people, animals, physical objects and the spirit world. It is a sacred or *lulik* story and revolves around the boundary crossing capabilities and spiritual energy of water where social agency is also ascribed to the non-human.

46 Water cosmologies

It is commonly recited at major sacred house-building ceremonies or at major spring rituals in Baucau.

Detailed knowledge of these ancestral connections and powers are closely held clan secrets, to which only certain ritual leaders and healers will be privy. To reveal these secrets is to risk angering the *dai* and to invite misfortune or death. It is said that the arrival of Portuguese into the region triggered a process whereby the ritual leaders of many clans or house societies forfeited aspects of their leadership role, entrusting political leadership to other houses whose leadership was not versed in the detail of these clan secrets. These new 'political houses' were asked to stand up alongside and speak to the foreigners, while the true knowledge-holders retreated back into the darkness to keep their ancestral secrets and the powers of their *dai* safe and hidden.

Interestingly, outsiders, whether they are Portuguese or others, are also known as *dai*. They are referred to as *dai* for two reasons. First, many (but as we will see not all) are considered wild like animals. Yet while they are thought to have no laws or cultural connection, they are powerful (as are nature spirits or *natureza* in general). Second, some are considered to have heightened powers by virtue of a specific cultural connection to their homeland but this source of power is hidden. They too can change their 'skins' and they are known to periodically return to their homelands to do so (the portals to these homelands are often natural locations within Timor itself). For example the most important site atop Mundo Perdido is a place, once a spring, called Wai Taka ('closed water'), a powerful portal to the 'other world'. It was through this transitional space that Timorese lieutenants of the colonial Portuguese army were said to have been sent by their superiors to train in Macau. Entering this 'door' to the other world, some would later return to roam the peaks as men in animal costume, causing havoc for the gardens of the local population. Yet at some point the Portuguese closed 'the door', placing on the site a cemented mountain cairn.[5]

As we will see below in a narrative which records the creation of life and the cycle of life and death, the generative space of *dai* is premised on the interaction of three foundational cosmological elements – water, earth and the sun.[6] Together they create the hydrosocial cycle. At a general level, water is believed to be the blood or energy of the earth, the underground place from where spirits emerge as they are drawn up out of the ground and given life by the power of the sun. These beings ultimately return in death to the ocean before rising up through the underground to begin again the cycle of life. The narrative I relay here begins in the ocean and traces the emergence, movements and names of successive generations of non-human *dai* which are connected to the agency and rule of the eastern Timorese ritual and political centre of Luca on the south coast. The ancestors of this dark world moved and indeed still move across the landscape until they reach the end, the ocean (and emerge once more into the light).

This hydrosocial cycle has been narrated to me in Makasae on several occasions by Major Ko'o Raku, the leading ritual specialist (M: *sobu dada*) and a well known healer in the Makasae and Waima'a speaking village of Bahu. He is by his own admission both extremely knowledgeable and brave and it is for this reason that in this telling he elaborates somewhat on the story's meaning (the square brackets are my own interpretations):

In the beginning all is ocean
[There arises]
Luka Bui, [*Bui* = a type of (civet) cat known to shape change with the eel]
Duka Woi Wa
Dai Duka Wai [*Dai* = ancestral animal spirit]
Duka Dai
Loi Ela [*Ela* = wild animal of the night]
Baru Ela
Ela Loi
Turns into
Loi Ofo [*Ofo* = python] the last ancestral name
Turns into
Ofo Bere [large python]
Turns into
Bani Bere dae fitu [large seven-headed bee]
This seven-headed bee brings culture [knowledge of water, fire, clan houses, ritual objects and boundaries]
This is why today when we carry out rituals we always place seven of things
Bani Bere [large bee] caught hold of *Bere Watu* [large sun]
Bere Watu
Mau Watu
Solu Watu
Dara Watu
Lela Watu
Leki Watu
Watu [sun]
Ira [water]
Dara Ira [forest water]
Ira Ba [water goes to]
Meti [the sea]

While this period of darkness and transformation ends in death in the sea, the earth which has now been wholly made in consort with the sun also transforms from darkness into light and following the pathway of water, life again emerges from the sea. Yet in this narrative of creation, after seven generations or cycles, subsequent ancestral pathways and subsequent ancestral names are no longer called, the paths have been made and life in this hydrosocial cycle must simply renew and transform itself again.

48 *Water cosmologies*

While, as we have seen above, Wai Taka is or was a major doorway or portal for movements between worlds, these doorways are also said to be connected to other spring complexes across the region. In Makasae these portals are known as *gituba ginana*, the 'places where the water pools and flows forth'.[7] *Gituba ginana* is associated with the beginning of life, the place from where the ancestors emerged (in Waima'a the term is *wai haba wai mata*). These springs are the doors through which the living are able to communicate with the ancestors (see Figure 2.3). As will be discussed below, central to ancestral movements to and from these *gituba ginana* is the agency of eels and other aquatic species, including pythons, which enable the underground water pathways between origin and 'child' springs to be forged.

This hydrosocial cycle is the foundational story of all life. At *oma lakasoru* [M: major origin house] re-construction ceremonies in the Baucau region, Major Ko'o Raku will be present to narrate the cycle, to open up the power of the relevant *gituba ginana* (portal) and activate its particular pathways through the bodies of lineage members. Before returning to a discussion of the ritual political dimensions of this cycle, I first explain in more detail the spiritual ecologies connected to spring water in Baucau.

Figure 2.3 Wai Kinari spring, Caibada Makasae.

The spiritual ecology of spring water in Baucau

With the exception of some Makasae words (mainly adjectives like big/small), the names for most springs in the Baucau district are rendered in one or other of the dialects of the 'Kawamina' language group and begin with the word *Wai*. The name for a spring in Waima'a is *wai mata*, with *wai* = water and *mata* = eye (having in addition associations with 'navel', 'womb' and 'source', cf. Hicks 1978). The animal being custodians of important spring or cave water portals may live in these water sources or be stationed at cave doors. A range of animals, but particularly snakes and eels (known collectively as *tal-ibere*), are said to be embodiments of the ancestral rulers of the area.[8] These beings are also referred to as *wai buu* (W: custodians of the water or *ira gauhaa* in Makasae). Other manifestations of the *wai buu* are shrimps, crocodiles and fish, and, in at least one fresh water spring, octopus.[9] Eel manifestations of the *wai buu* are also said to change into the civet cat when they venture out of the springs at night, often in search of fresh palm wine (W: *tuo*). In some accounts, particular named eels and civet cats are the founding ancestors of particular sacred houses. Similarly, as we will see below both these eels and spring water are believed to have been able, at least in the distant past, to completely shift location by emerging from the ground and changing into human form. These newly transformed family groupings would then travel across the landscape to relocate to a new site before morphing back into the land as eels and spring water. Likewise, even in the present period, spring water may be ritually moved by people and physically carried in bamboo containers from one location to another to create a new spring source (cf. Kehi and Palmer 2012; see also Chapter 4).

Hicks (2004 [1976]: 33) who worked with the Eastern Tetum in Viqueque places the *wai buu* (ET: *bee na'in*) in the same category as *ria buu* (ET: *rai na'in* = owners of the land, land spirits, custodians) and refers to them as (at times malevolent) free nature spirits and agents of mother earth. As we will see below the custodianship of both land and waters is clearly interrelated. Meanwhile Traube, working with the Mambai in central Timor, also writes of a category of ancestor spirits which she calls 'shades': unnamed ancestors who are called to the threshold of the spring from the sea. She writes that:

> the dead who depart overseas are transformed into various forms of marine life ... the sacred eels who guard the entries of the springs are the leaders of this marine host. As mediators between the land and the sea and between below and above, their role is to negotiate cosmic exchange.
>
> (1986: 194)

In Baucau's water sources all renderings of these beings are present and such beings may be called forth as (land or water) nature spirits or as named and unnamed ancestors. At water increase ceremonies carried out at Wai Lia Bere, a cave water source on the Baucau plateau, the (Makasae speaking) Ledatame

50   Water cosmologies

ritual custodians of the water communicate with the guardians of the cave door, in this case manifest as pythons, in the following way:

Nawa asi dada asi nanu Wai Lia Wai Lobi	Please receive this offering our ancestors from Wai Lia Wai Lobi
I ini mua gi gauhaa,	You are the owner/custodian of the land
I ini kuba ere gi gauhaa	You are the owner/custodian of this savanna
I mau do inai gunirai	We will hide your name
inai nama rai, inai guni bare	We will honour your name, we will hide your name
I ini kuba ere gi gauhaa	You are the owner/custodian of this savanna
iha i ini rata	and the ruler of this land
I ni ge'e naga ma rau gini	Come and we will give force to all that is ours (yours)
I ni ge'e naga ma rau gini	Come and give force what is yours (ours)
I noto nelu	We will not forget
Ini I noto ma isa nelu gini	We will never forget you
Naga isi I loki[10] *gene lolo*	We will always call your name
Naga isi ma I fa'ana	We will always 'feed you' (make offerings to you).

As is the case across much, if not all, of the Timor region, springs custodians have a further aspect to their identity as they are also living humans incorporating the spiritual essence of water custodianship concurrently in differentiated forms (human and non-human bodies) (Hicks 2004 [1976]; Kehi and Palmer 2012; McWilliam 2011; Carvalho 2011). These living custodians of the water are in most cases also synonymous with the living *ria buu* (ET: *rai na'in* = 'custodians of the land') of the adjacent land. While spring water for example is usually shared collectively amongst a particular community there are particular people and 'houses' who are themselves known as the *wai buu* (or *ira gauhaa* in Makasae) who have particular custodianship rights and responsibilities for this water. Connected to ancestral *dai*, these living human water custodians obtain this designation through descent or as a sacred gift which is subsequently handed down through the lineage. As with knowledge of all ancestral *dai*, the details of their esoteric knowledge and ancestral corpus connected to springs are a closely guarded secret. These human water custodians are linked into broader land and social relations through their own sacred houses and affinal kin, they are also, like healers, in communication with their *dai*.[11] As the embodiment of the ancestors, traditionally around most springs, eels and snakes cannot be eaten. Meanwhile the human manifestations of the water custodians are the critical link to the 'dark' world and their 'bodies' ability to communicate with the various non-human manifestations of the *wai buu* or *dai* in the spring system is essential to the wellbeing of themselves, their clan and others dependent on those waters.

In the Baucau region, eels have another very important role in many spring related myths. In many tellings it is the eels (W: *thuno*, M: *wasu* also known in this context as *talibere*) who are responsible for channelling water underground, moving it across the landscape from spring to spring. Surface channels or openings may be said to be the domain of pythons (also known as *talibere*), terrestrial beings whose scales more obviously refract and capture the power of the sun. Meanwhile in the version of the hydrosocial cycle above it is Banibere, the seven-headed bee, who is credited with bringing 'culture' to Timor and with it knowledge of water, fire, clan houses, ritual objects and boundaries.[12] At some time prior to this, however, this version of the cycle begins with Luka Bui, an ancestral being from the great eastern ritual domain of Luca. This ritual domain, as we will see below, is prevalent in the stories of springs from across the region.

According to Major Ko'o Raku, at some undefined point after the emergence of mountain peaks and dry land from a world of water, the first people of what is now Baucau descended from the central peaks of the Mundo Perdido range (according to this account they descended at the same time as four other parties who founded settlements elsewhere in the north-east region). The two people who arrived in Baucau were a husband and a wife and they found themselves in a stony dry land bereft of water. So that they might eek out a living in this place, the husband set off for seven days and seven nights and returned to his wife with a bamboo cylinder (W: *ae*) full of sacred water from the southern kingdom of Luca. He threw down the water between the gap in his wife's legs and a spring spewed forth out of the ground. This man took on the name of Wai Lewa[13] and he became the founding father of Baucau, which was known then by the name of its spring Wai Lewa (W: *lewa* = garden). Similarly the Waima'a-speaking custodians of the related spring complex of Wai Husu in nearby Teulale (see Chapter 4) also record that their ancestors arrived from Luca, but in this case in the form of an eel which emerged from the spring and transformed into a woman. Ritual verse from the village of Wani Uma records the arrival of Luca in the spring grove of Teulale:

Viqueque Luca mai Luca Tirilolo	Viqueque Luca comes to Luca Tirilolo
Teulale Lumu Lumu	Teulale is all green
Koi Kota Daru	And the stone walls are made.

The hydrosocial cycle and the ritual centre of Luca

The people of Luca, the once great kingdom of the east, also record their relations to eels, water and the sea in narrative verse. The verse below recounts in Eastern Tetum the words of a long ago ruler of Luca who says:

52 *Water cosmologies*

Hau naran Lu Leki meti oan hau	I am Lu Leki, the son of the tides
Hau naran Lu Leki tasi oan hau	I am Lu Leki, the son of the sea
Hau katak ba tasi, tasi sei nakduka nuu lor ba	I command the sea to recede, it obeys me
Katak fali ba meti, meti sei nakduka nuu lor ba.	I command the tide to recede, it obeys me.

Luca's rule of the sea is then juxtaposed with that of We Hali, the once great kingdom of western Timor, whose ruler is said to be both the son of and the commander of the sun and the moon. Meanwhile the eastern kingdom of Luca is divided according to the parts of a buffalo:

Isin lolon Rai Luka	The main body is in the land of Luca
Dere too Wai Bobo	Its head extends to Wai Bobo[14]
Dikur balu We Masi, balu We Soru.	Its one horn is to We Masi, another is to We Soru.[15]

While historians and anthropologists have long written on the subject of the great western kingdom We Hali (Therik 2004; Francillon 1967; Schulte Nordholt 1971; Hägerdal 2012; Gunn 1999; Soares 2003) and its relation to other major ritual centres, here I want to give an account of Luca and explain its pre-eminent status in the hydrosocial cycle of eastern Timor. This account focuses on the nature of Luca as a pre-colonial centre of ritual power and cosmological force, its changing role and fate during the colonial era will be developed in subsequent chapters.

Across the eastern part of Timor Leste, Luca's central political and ritual power is continually encoded in myth and narrative, many of which are connected to springs. Yet as with its paired ritual counterpart We Biku We Hali, it is important to stress the fact that this domain is as much a ritual-political concept or symbol as it is an actual political realm (Francillon 1967: 113). Schulte Nordholt (1971) for instance argues in relation to We Hali's regional power that this relatively dynamic and open system of politico-ritual power was in fact held together by mythic accounts of the power of the centre (an immobile core of ritual power and skill (*matenek*)). It was the ensuing ritual connections of the immobile centre to surrounding emissary sub-kingdoms which held the domain together. While, as with We Hali (ET: 'banyan tree water'), the political importance of Luca has long since declined,[16] its symbolic meanings and its encoding in ritual form remain central to many mythic narratives across the region. In many of these narratives it is Luca's power to communicate with the sea (and through this its capacity to access the wealth of the underworld) which remains a recurring theme.[17] As well as a once expansionary and pre-eminent political presence in the region (see Chapter 5), by virtue of its power to tame the sea, Luca is the pre-eminent communicator with '*rai seluk*' (the other world).[18]

While there is much in the oral history record which links Luca to the expansion of the kingdom of We Biku We Hali (see for example Spillett 1999), David Amaral the *lia na'in* ('custodian of the words') of the apical house of Uma Kan Lor in Luca relayed to me a narrative concerning seven siblings who emerged from the earth (see Figure 2.4).[19] These seven siblings commenced tilling the land (ET: *fila rai*) around Luca which had until then neither fields nor water. As a consequence the youngest of the siblings was continually beaten and sent to fetch water from the far west and the far east of the island. One day as the youngest sibling sat exhausted under a banyan tree he sobbed out loud that it would be best if he took his own life. Yet as he spoke these words, water started to gush out from beneath his feet. Later after a dog ran off to find the older brothers, they arrived to see that their youngest brother had morphed into water from the chest down. The boy, whose name was Nai Leki, told his older siblings that he had now transformed into the sacred spring of We Lolo. His head then transformed into a water bowl (*we lolo*) and lodged in the banyan tree now called Nai Leki. The spring water then flowed from We Lolo to sea passing through the sacred tidal lagoon of Luca called We Liurai (ET: 'ruler's water') at the coast. Luca became a kingdom of seven villages and a centre of power. Meanwhile these sacred origin waters of Luca are known metaphorically as *we ai balun* ('wooden safe water'[20]) as it is from these waters that the wealth of Luca has been distributed across the land.

Figure 2.4 David Amaral, Luca *lia na'in* (right) and apprentice.

54   *Water cosmologies*

In mythic narratives found across the region it is to Luca that people have long travelled to receive, or emerged from to decree, the power to rule. Following a ritual ceremony at the springs of Luca, emissaries would leave as the kingdom's 'arms and legs' (*ain liman*) and execute the authority of the ritual centre across the east. As a part of this process, as we have seen above, Luca's sacred waters would be carried across the region to create child or subsidiary springs.

Yet not all peoples are so concerned with the metaphor of Luca's ritual power. The people of Wai Riu (who we will encounter in Chapter 3) to some extent challenge the politico-ritual accounts of the pre-eminent rule of either Luca or We Biku We Hali across the east. In contrast to other houses in their region who did receive sacred objects such as the sceptre (*rota*), drum (*tamboor*) and dances (*tebe no bidu*) from Luca, the Wai Riu people of Mundo Perdido (Wai Nete Watu Ba'i) assert their sacra emerged from the waters under the earth, the very place from where they emerged. We Biku We Hali they say arrived by way of Luca some thirteen generations ago. It was they who brought with them a monarchical system, intermarried and ruled over the kingdoms of Luca and Viqueque. Others, like Timorese historian Antonio Vicente Marques Soares (who is also an elder from Lacluta in Viqueque), maintain that the ritual political centre of Luca emerged as the Tetum Terik speakers of We Biku We Hali arrived into a Waima'a speaking region which was then loyal to the inland domain of Ai Sahe (see also Spillett 1999: 348). As we will see in the conclusion, in other versions of the hydrosocial cycle which I have been told by Major Ko'o Raku, it is ancestral beings coming from across the sea (or alternatively from the 'other world') which travel across and populate the land (via but not beginning in Luca).

At whatever point it was that Luca's power expanded across the region it is also clear that the new houses and spring water sources its emissaries 'created' would become sites for rich agricultural groves, including irrigated rice production (see Chapter 4). Yet in these narratives it is not only the agency of humans which is stressed. Rather it is the agency and subjectivity of the spring water itself and its own alliance with the kingdom of Luca which is the recurring theme. Water is said to have its own needs and desires which includes the need for its interactions with humans to be grounded in respectful and mutually supporting relations. For example on the high southern slopes of Mundo Perdido at a place called Seu Baru (M: 'the cooked meat'), the Kairui and Makasae peoples of the area recount their story of a spring called Mau Lau (M: 'the place of the civet cat') which in distant times simply disappeared (see Figure 2.5). The custodian of Mau Lau, an eel from Luca, was tired of being abused by the local residents (who were capturing and eating eels from the spring) so one day the spring water morphed into a family, led by a man called Wai Leki (who had transformed from the eel). This group of old men, women, children and their animals gathered up their magic basket and other belongings and walked off across mountains to the north. When they reached the north-eastern edge of the Baucau escarpment in a village known today as Wailili they met an old man and asked him for a place to rest. The old man kindly pointed them to a shady tree and they set down their belongings and made camp. When the old man returned the next day the entire family and their belongings had disappeared. Meanwhile a spring had now appeared in the ground beneath the tree where they had made camp. Mau Lau and his people never returned to Seu Baru and to this day the people of the Seu Baru region are fearful of the repercussions of bathing in the potentially hostile springs of Wailili.

In yet another often repeated story from the southern high slopes of Mundo Perdido, we find a spring Wai Lesu whose waters once drained back to its origins in Luca.[21] The spring takes its name from a *lesu* (K: a wooden rice husking implement). In its origin story the waters emerged from the ground following the fall of the *lesu* which was being pounded beneath the pillars of a sacred house located on a high precipice. Recovering the *lesu* from a newly emerged spring at the bottom of the precipice, the house of Wai Lesu began making ritual offerings to feed the custodians of the spring. But at some point in time these rituals ceased and as a result the spring water simply drained back down the mountain to its rightful home in Luca (indicating that the rice husking implement was also connected to the ritual power of Luca). By the time the water arrived back in Luca it had metamorphosed into human form and had told the ruler of Luca that the people of Wai Lesu no longer respected the spring. Meanwhile the house of Wai Lesu, bereft at losing their water, sent out a

Figure 2.5 Water blessing for new arrivals (Gari Modo, water custodian for Mau Pula spring, Seu Baru, Mundo Perdido).

56 *Water cosmologies*

messenger to Luca to negotiate the return of the spring water. The ruler of Luca gave this messenger sacralized betel leaves and told him to return to Wai Lesu and prepare sacrifices for a ritual at the spring. There when all the necessary sacrificial objects and animals had been readied, the messenger of the house 'called' the ruler of Luca using betel leaves which he placed to his ear. 'Are you [the water] coming yet or not he asks?' 'We are coming', was the reply. As the messenger recited a prayer the sacrificial buffalo fell to the ground dead (a sure indication of the power and correctness of the prayer). Suddenly the spring water re-emerged, gushing from the ground to swallow up all the things prepared as an offering.

Discussion

Most Timorese remain attentive to the diverse needs and wishes of the ancestral spirit world and much of this is believed to be communicated through signs in the behaviour of living animals or physical elements. These people lay their belief and trust in the agency and power of their ritual specialists and traditional healers to carefully cultivate relationships, rapport and reciprocal exchange relations between the living (animals and humans) and the dead (objects, animals and humans). In common with other complex spiritual ecologies, in the interface of religion and ecology, nature and spirit are both multiple and inseparable (Sponsel 2012: 170–171). What unites them is their inclusive sociality, a process 'that weaves together persons of all sorts, be they humans, animals, or spirit entities' (Pederson 2001: 416). This inclusive sociality configures and patterns the cosmos and is synonymous with a sense of the cosmos as a living being, as an 'aliveness' which is forever becoming, holding together in disparate ways and breathing life into storied land- and water-scapes (cf. Ingold 2011).

What is also clear from this material is the firm conviction that the prerequisite to harnessing the power of life and taming the wildness within *all* beings is careful attention to a meshwork of cultivated and proscribed relations. 'Culture' or *'lisan'* in the local idioms correlates not so much to 'the tending of something' (Williams 1983: 87) as to the tending of affective socio-ecological relationships.

While Luca is a kingdom of great politico-ritual pre-eminence in many of the mythic narratives found across the east, it is also clear that in the existential realm, the realm of ultimate origin, the ritual relationships encoded through the narratives of the hydrosocial cycle link people, the spirit world and water in socio-ecological relationships which are both hierarchically horizontal and vertically circular (Hicks 1990; cf. Reuter 1996: 271). Hence while, as Mullin argues, we need in our analysis of human–non-human relations to pay attention to 'social change, power, agency and the negotiation and instability of categories and meanings' (Mullin 1999: 219), we also need to pay attention to how some things, however inflected through time, always stay the same. This chapter has recounted stories of water, the sea, eels, snakes and other animals with which many Timorese houses have an ancestral connection and which feature in accounts of the hydrosocial cycle, more recently it seems those connected to

Luca. In such invocatory speech the flow of words or blessing has been likened to the flow of water (Waterson 2012; Schefold 2001) and indeed an argument could be made from this material that the link between the flow of words and the flow of water is not only poetic but instrumental, that it is the inextricable link between invocatory names and words, water and mobility which in fact enables all relations.

It is for this reason that we can also understand the relationship between Luca (ruler of the sea/water) and We Hali (ruler of the sun/fire) as symbolic of the mystical occult state or as politico-religious centres of the Timorese cosmos (Francillon 1967: 113; cf. Hicks 1990: 102). What is highlighted in the mythic narratives of Luca across the eastern part of Timor is its pre-eminent communicative relationship with the power of the sea. Elsewhere, Jones writes that tides[22] and other extra-terrestrial forces animate water into agency which are then 'folded into a range of ecosocial systems' (2011: 2287) all of which are characterized by an ecological temporality that 'has a great richness' tracing 'through assemblages and bodies and affective life (human and non-human)' (2011: 2289). Recognizing the power of such temporal ecologies (their change and rhythms) on ecosocial assemblages in eastern Timor, Luca's connection to the power of sea is indeed traced through to cosmological power. In this context it is the symbol of the ritual centre of Luca which enables nature's 'activity, unpredictability and unruliness' (Jones 2011: 2290) to be recognized, engaged and tamed. It is to this necessary relationship that '*lisan*' (customary norms and practices) focuses people's material arrangements.

Notes

1 Referred to as Mundo Perdido (literally 'lost world' in Portuguese) by the Portuguese in the early twentieth century, this mountain range is known by many local language names depending on your origin house, your language, and what part of the mountainous landscape you are referring to and why. In everyday conversation Timorese now also refer to this mountain as Mundo Perdido. Its other names are generally reserved for ritual use when many names referring to particular rocky peaks, features and springs are called out in succession.

2 *Dai* may also be translated as the 'custodian of power'.

3 Alternatively the other broad category of traditional healers in the region draw their power not from ancestral spirits but 'nature spirits' or '*natureza*' more broadly.

4 They may be coloured white, red or black.

5 Traube (2007) recounts a similar story told by Mambai speakers about the peaks of Timor's highest mountain Ramelau. Here a sacred spring is also understood to be a portal, a place where during the Indonesian occupation an American counter-invasion was predicted to emerge. It was also believed by the Mambai that it was through this 'door' that their ancestors had once departed to Portugal before later returning to rule Timor (Traube 2007).

6 As we will see in the conclusion, in other tellings, a fourth element wind is also central.

7 *Gituba ginana* may also be translated as the 'entry/exit' point. *Ginana* means umbilical cord.

8 Detailed stories of eels, their characteristics and journeys, appear in many spring myths. The life cycle of freshwater eels was long a mystery to Western science. It is

58   *Water cosmologies*

now understood that they are catadromous, living in freshwater but spawning in the deep sea (after which time they die). Land barriers in their long journey to and from their chosen freshwater habitats and the sea are negotiated by wriggling across land at night. Their bodies also change colour from initially clear when spawned in the sea to a pigmented yellow or brown colour after migrating to freshwater. Sexual maturity is indicated by a silver underbelly and even darker head and back at which time they return to spawn in the sea (which is always tropical). Adults settle to live in their freshwater habitats from between 5–20 years. It is believed their common ancestor probably appeared in Indo-Pacific close to present Indonesia between 30–50 million years ago (Lecomte-Finiger 2003).

9 In their biology all of these beings share two qualities: they refract colour in sunlight and metamorphize from eggs laid outside of the body. With the capacity to abruptly change in bodily form, metamorphosing eels, pythons and other reptiles, fish, aquatic insects, and molluscs are *lulik* species for many clans across the region.

10 M: *Loki* = basket and may be used to contain sacred items in sacred houses.

11 The *dai* or ancestral beings connected to springs were usually discoverers or creators of these water sources and the founders of spring connected communities.

12 A migratory species, worker bees produce honey in their tree hives by feeding raw nectar and pollen to the queen bee. Like the mixture of water with fire, these (social) exchanges transform the raw materials of life, into the golden sweetness of honey, the substance of life itself.

13 On account of his posthumous baptism he is also known as Fransisco Wai Lewa.

14 A neighbouring kingdom to Ossu and east of Mundo Perdido.

15 The buffalo is being used here to explain, amongst other things, the territorial power of Luca as the main kingdom, whose head reaches (*dere*) Wai Bobo (symbolizing the East here), whose two horns symbolize the North and South. We Soru [ET: 'woven water'] is Vessoru and We Masi [ET: 'salty water'] is Vemasse.

16 'Between 1642 and 1645, Luca was evangelized by Father António de S. Domingos, OP, who baptized the queen of Luca, as well as her son, the nobles of the kingdom and innumerable commoners' (Belo 2011: 336). Luca also paid tribute to the Portuguese in Lifao (Belo 2011: 336). Hägerdal (2012) refers to a number of historical sources which briefly mention the colonial significance and expansion of the kingdom of Luca suggesting it remained a significant kingdom into the nineteenth century. As a result of its alliance with the Portuguese monarchy, Luca's regional power peaked in the 1700s (Soares pers. comm. 2010) but began to decline after its first anti-Portuguese rebellions in the 1781 (Belo 2011: 336). See also Chapter 5.

17 Luca's wealth (usually expressed as buffalo and gold) and power over the sea is also evident in the ethnography of the Viqueque region carried out by Hicks (2004 [1976]) in the 1960s. Hicks notes that Luu Leki, the ruler of Luca, was said to own much gold (2004 [1976]: 66). He also writes of one particular king from Luca who was sent by the Portuguese to jail on Atauro and in a show of pre-eminent power opened the sea and walked straight across from Dili to the island (Hicks 2004 [1976]: 66–67). A large land south of the eastern archipelago and a kingdom, 'Lukak', rich in gold was reported in the fourteenth-century accounts of Marco Polo (Francillon 1967: 474).

18 See also Conclusion.

19 Hicks (1990: 107) recounts that the eel (ET: *tuna*) clan from Caraubalu (near to Viqueque town where he carried out his ethnography) were originally from Luca, a place where they still had rights to farm. Their clan origin history, which he recorded in the 1960s, correlates in many respects with the spring narrative told to me by the *lia na'in* of Uma Kan Lor.

20 *Ai-balun* can also refer to a coffin.

21 While in some tellings this is said to be a modern era story, others refer to it as a story of ancient times.
22 There are seven-day intervals between spring (maximum) and neap (minimum) tides. The wild 'male' south coast of Timor has on average double the tidal range of the calmer 'female' north coast.

References

Bachelard, G. (1983) *Water and Dreams: An Essay on the Imagination of Matter*, Dallas: Pegasus Foundation.

Belo, D. (2011) *Os Antigos Reinos de Timor-Leste*, Baucau: Edição Tipografia Diocesana Baucau.

Bovensiepen, J (2011) 'Opening and Closing the Land: Land and Power in the Idate Highlands', in A.R. McWilliam and E.G. Traube (eds) *Land and Life in Timor-Leste: Ethnographic Essays*, Canberra: ANU E-Press, 47–60.

Brightman, R. (1993) *Grateful Prey: Rock Cree Human-Animal Relationships*, Berkeley: University of California Press.

Carvalho, D.A. (2011) 'Ritual Sira Kona ba Jestaun Bee Nudar Aplikasaun Matenek Local iha Timor Leste', in D.A. Carvalho (ed.) *Matenek Lokal Timor Nian*, Jakarta: UNESCO, 70–83.

Francillon, G. (1967) 'Some Matriarchic Aspects of Social Structure of the Tetun of Middle Timor', unpublished PhD thesis, Australian National University.

Gunn, G. (1999) *Timor Loro Sae: 500 Years*, Macau: Livros do Oriente.

Hägerdal, H. (2012) *Lords of the Land, Lords of the Sea: Conflict and Adaption in Early Colonial Timor, 1600–1800*, Leiden: KITLV Press.

Hicks, D. (1978) '"Mata" in Tetum', *Oceania* 48(4): 299.

Hicks, D. (1990) *Kinship and Religion in Eastern Indonesia*, Göteborg: Acta Universitatis Gothoburgensis.

Hicks, D. (2004) [1976] *Tetum Ghosts & Kin: Fertility and Gender in East Timor*, Illinois: Waveland Press.

Ingold, T. (2011) *Being Alive: Essays on Movement, Knowledge and Description*, London: Routledge.

Jones, O. (2011) 'Lunar-solar Rhythmpatterns: Towards the Material Cultures of Tides', *Environment and Planning A* 43(10): 2285–2303.

Kehi, B. and Palmer, L. (2012) 'Hamatak Halirin: The Cosmological and Socio-Ecological Roles of Water in Koba Lima, Timor', *Bijdragen tot de Taal-, Land- en Volkenkunde* 168: 445–471.

Lecomte-Finiger, R. (2003) 'The Genus Anguilla Schrank, 1798: Current State of Knowledge and Questions', *Reviews in Fish Biology and Fisheries* 13: 265–279.

MacLeod, J. (2013) 'Water and Material Imagination', in C. Chen, J. MacLeod and A. Neimanis (eds) *Thinking with Water*, Montreal: McGill-Queen's University Press, 55–75.

McWilliam, A. (2011) 'Fataluku Living Landscapes', in A. McWilliam and E. Traube (eds) *Land and Life in Timor-Leste: Ethnographic Essays*, Canberra: ANU E-Press.

Mullin, M. (1999) 'Mirrors and Windows: Sociocultural Studies of Human-Animal Relationships', *Annual Review of Anthropology* 28: 201–224.

Pederson, M. (2001) 'Totemism, Animism and North Asian Indigenous Ontologies', *Journal of the Royal Anthropological Institute* 7: 411–427.

Reuter, T. (1996) 'Custodians of the Sacred Mountains: The Ritual Domains of Highland Bali', unpublished PhD thesis, Australian National University.

60 *Water cosmologies*

Schefold, R. (2001) 'Three Sources of Ritual Blessings in Traditional Indonesian Societies', *Bijdragen tot de Taal-, Land- en Volkenkunde* 157: 359–381.

Schulte Nordholt, H. (1971) *The Political System of the Atoni of Timor*, The Hague: Martinus Nijhoff.

Soares, A.V.M. (2003) *Pulau Timor: Sebuah Sumbangan Untuk Sejarahnya*, Baucau: Edicao Tipografia Diocesana Baucau.

Spillett, P. (1999) 'The Pre-colonial History of the Island of Timor Together with Some Notes on the Makassan Influence in the Island', unpublished manuscript, Museum and Art Gallery of the Northern Territory, Darwin.

Sponsel, L. (2012) *Spiritual Ecology: A Quiet Revolution*, Santa Barbara: Praeger.

Therik, T. (2004) *Wehali The Female Land: Traditions of a Timorese Ritual Centre*, Canberra: Pandanus Books.

Traube, E. (1986) *Cosmology and Social Life: Ritual Exchange among the Mambai of East Timor*, Chicago: University of Chicago Press.

Traube, E. (2007) 'Unpaid Wages: Local Narratives and the Imagination of the Nation', *The Asia Pacific Journal of Anthropology* 8(1): 9–25.

Waterson, R. (2012) 'Flows of Words and Flows of Blessing: The Poetics of Invocatory Speech among the Sa'dan Toraja', *Bijdragen tot de Taal-, Land- en Volkenkunde*. 168: 391–419.

Williams, R. (1983) *Keywords: A Vocabulary of Culture and Society*, London: Fontana Paperbacks.

Wittgenstein, L. (1979) *Remarks on Frazer's Golden Bough*, edited by R. Rhees, translated by A.C. Miles (1971), Nottinghamshire: Brynmill.

3 Watery histories

During his years spent incarcerated in an Indonesian prison in the 1990s, the Timorese independence leader Xanana Gusmão wrote a poem entitled 'Oh! Freedom!' in which he expressed his longing for his country, 'drinking from springs which would murmur in the air legends of Timor' (1998: 31). Meanwhile many historical accounts have been written about Timor and Hägerdal (2012) laments that the history of the island is destined to be written through recourse to the colonial record. Indeed it is the case that while he and others have produced intriguing accounts of the colonial encounter and its attendant history making on the island, largely absent from these accounts are the stories that are told and retold in particular contexts by local communities across Timor. Apart from the fact that these accounts are transmitted in oral form (and are extremely time-consuming to collect and analyse), another reason for their absence from the historical record is their frequent preference for cyclical time and a preoccupation with identity, relationship and hierarchy (Schulte Nordholt 1971; cf. Hägerdal 2012: 10–13). Yet it is clear that within the recurring motifs of local narrative genres, vibrant oral accounts of place and place-making contain highly localized and nuanced interpretations of events recorded as well in Western historiography. While these ethno-histories are always partial and open to interpretation, so too are those emanating from their Western archival counterparts.

Taking my lead from Gow's 2001 book *An Amazonian Myth and its History*, this chapter and those that follow begin the task of retelling and engaging with indigenous accounts of the region's history. A task which in the words of Levi-Strauss is like 'gathering the scattered threads [of] the actors of a play for which we do not have the script [but which] have left their footprints' (Levi-Strauss 1982: 228). In this account it is springs and the mythology connected to specific springs which I am treating simultaneously as the objects and, as we saw in the last chapter, subjects of history. The historical method for this retelling begins in my own ethnographic data and it is my own interpretations of mythic modalities and accompanying historical vignettes and conundrums that have been woven together to produce a 'general account' (Gow 2001: 23). 'Only then', writes Gow, 'can the archive start to speak to us of what we hope to find there' (2001: 23).

62 *Watery histories*

Yet this chapter and those that follow also make clear that while general accounts of localized histories are possible, historical specificity in a Western sense is not. The narratives on which I rely are both contingent on history and on their specific retellings, which as Levi-Strauss reminds us have an inherently transformative potential. The local retellings of these narratives (whether to me or others) occur in an ever shifting context which accords with what interests people, their own interpretation of the importance of changes they experience and the specificities of the audience at that moment (cf. Gow 2001: 312; Bovensiepen 2012; Fox 1980; Traube 1989). Representing the past through 'a mix of history, memory and myth' these accounts are generative of place and relations over linear time (Attwood 2011: 177). In contrast to history's conception of a 'clean break' (Certeau 1986: 4) between the past and the present, memory entangles the past with the present, it has presence (Attwood 2011: 178; cf. Chakrabaty 2011). So too, as we shall see, does myth. As Gow writes:

> myths are casually related to history but, when threatened with historical events which would render them meaningless, they simply transform, in order to preserve themselves from such meaningless.... In this reaction to a changing world, myths obliterate time [and] act to reset the temporal scale of the lived world [creating with it] new sets of meaningful connections to be explored and lived.
>
> (2001: 285)

In this way, these myths are forever semantically reinterpreted to form the basis of dynamic relational actual worlds (Boucher 2013). Worlds which, as we saw in Chapter 2, are co-produced by and interwoven with complex understandings of personhood, transgenerational immanence and spirit ecologies.

James Fox argues that all historiography 'must be concerned with relating certain structured events within some framework of time and place' (1980: 10). He writes that '[t]o be history, a narrative must establish a chronology and a location' (1980: 10). Drawing from narrative histories on Roti, an island to the west of Timor, he argues that local 'true tales' are those which are rooted in particular domains and which account 'for some feature of that domain's organization' (1980: 17). These 'true tales', he writes, are also related to other similar sorts of tales (1980: 17). However, he also contrasts these 'true tales', dynamic and contingent as they are, with tales divorced of specificity 'told for the telling itself', something he aligns with folk literature not folk history (1980: 25). In a similar way, Gow (2001) asserts that there is a difference in his Amazonian material between stories of the ancestors told outside of historical context and stories told by the ancestors set within a chronology and location. He writes that while the former eschew time and place, in the latter 'agent, event and narrative complexity are suddenly and dramatically restored' (Gow 2001: 289).

Both of these types of tales, the folk literary and the historical, are present in much of what follows. Many for instance revolve around accounts of knowledge of water and fire. While in their historical specificity these tales relate to actual

Watery histories 63

named springs (*bee matan*) and actual ancestral hearths (*ahi matan*) or sacred houses (*uma lulik*), in their folk literary context they also tell us stories of how the world came into being, of how people's lives developed in relation to others and the hold that these lives have over people across particular spans of generations. Hence alongside their historiography, these tales simultaneously express an ontology through which spring water is the autochthonous giver of life and the ultimate arbitrator of truth. Meanwhile, fire is both the transformer of life and, through its connection to the hearth of sacred houses, the harbinger of jural status (Kehi and Palmer 2012; cf. Hicks 2004 [1976]). As such the search for narrative cohesion and a general account of local histories through these stories of waterscapes is always interceded by the agency of both water and fire, of life giving liquidity and transformative radiance which in combination are forever recasting life and responding to historical contingency.

In my analysis of people's relations with water through the spring mythscape of north-central Timor, my search was both 'to understand "the hold that life has", and to understand the way in which *this* life comes to have *this* hold' (Gow 2001: 26). Through a series of localized accounts of the inter-relations between time, water and fire this chapter is a thoroughly materialist reading of regional history (and oral history), a reading in which nothing is 'spirited away onto a higher plane or exorcised into a nether world' (Doel 2004: 151 cited in Anderson and Wylie 2009: 319).

The emergence of the world

To begin this task I will relay a summary of the origin story told to me in Makasae by Major Ko'o Raku, a *lia na'in* of the Bahu village in Baucau which is comprised of both Makasae and Waima'a speakers. While Makasae originates from a Papuan or non-Austronesian language family, Waima'a is thought to be derived from a notionally Austronesian bloc termed by linguists Kawamina, which comprises the Kairui, Waima'a, Midiki and Naueti languages. Both language groups, the Makasae and the Kawamina, are spoken across the region of this study.[1] This origin story, however, is of a time before languages, a time when everything in the world was water and the first lands of Timor emerged:

> In the beginning Timor was created by a foot sparring pair of brother and sister birds (M: *ketu*). Their sparring kicked back the sea and so created the first dry land in the form of three mountains: Ramelau, Cabalaki and Matebian [see Map 5.1]. Sometime later *Christu* [a term (along with *Maromak* or God) which is now used interchangeably with the term for the preeminent indigenous Moon-Sun deity (M: *Uru-Watu*; W: *L'ara Wulo*)] descends and creates from the mud a human figurine.[2] *Christu* then [like the wind] breathes life into the figure and fashions another figure from its rib. He then announces he will return in seven days and orders the two people not to eat the forbidden fruit. Yet these two people listened instead to the python (M: *talibere*) and disobeyed the order. From this act they knew shame and hide

64 *Watery histories*

their bodies under bark clothing. Later other people came from across the sea (Makasar) and showed them how to make *tais* (woven cloth). As their penance for eating the forbidden fruit, in order that they could have food to eat, they and their descendants were now destined to labor in fields growing rice and other crops. In order that he could help his older brother carry rice back from the fields, the younger brother of the first people secretly began transforming back and forth from person to horse. This act is known as *kuda resa* [M: 'rice horse'] and it is from such [transformative] acts by the first ancestors that we came to know 'culture'. Today as descendants of these first people we continue to make offerings at large springs [the portals to the other world of deities and ancestors] in order to feed the spirits of the ancestors, imploring them to make the springs flow freely so that the people can live and grow their rice and other crops.

Despite its distinct Catholic inflection, what over time became evident to me from this story (told to me early in my fieldwork period) were clues to the connections between people, localities and spiritual ecologies stretching from the mountains to the sea. It was not until many years later that I was able to piece together the story's meanings and understand the transformative roles of its key protagonists, to see the connections and lay them out in the sort of 'perspicuous' view inspired by Wittgenstein's simultaneous critique of certainty and search for clarity:

The perspicuous presentation makes possible that understanding which consists just in the fact that we 'see the connections'. Hence the importance of finding *intermediate* links ... [to] draw attention to the similarity, the connection, between the *facts*.

(1979: 9e)

While this myth was told by a ritual leader from the north coastal zone, its central themes reverberate through the creation oriented myths of other communities who also tell stories of how they came to be, of why they continue to toil hard in their fields, to make their offerings to their ancestors and to continually confront treachery and trickery at the same time as they strive for a way of life that is respectful and prosperous. What is uncanny about all of these tellings, however, is how much of their content correlates with what we know, or think we know, from the archaeological and historical linguistic record. These scientific interpretations paint for us imperfect pictures of how it was that people and their languages migrated through the islands of the archipelago and of how they collided, transformed and internally spread across the islands which they settled. Likewise in local narrative traditions we find accounts of people transforming from a solely hunter gatherer to a mixed hunting, gathering and sedentary agricultural existence, of the coming of 'culture' and laws, and of the ways in which outsiders have been installed and thus transformed the fabric of these worlds. The ways in which people negotiate and memorialize these

Watery histories   65

momentous changes to their worlds and interactions with each other is there in these stories. Whilst, as ever, narrative unity and linear cohesion remains elusive, pieced together as 'intermediate connections', these stories can also offer a tantalizing glimpse of an ever transforming world, one impossible to construe from history and science alone. Perspicuity, then, is a way of identifying the patterning of phenomena, of seeking out connections whilst maintaining openness to other possibilities and intellectual humility in the face of the unknown.

Moving beyond our fabulous narrative of the whole island being brought into being, I now need to explore more localized accounts of this history. In these stories, found both at the mountains and the coast, we are often told about a first peoples, the progenitors of an origin clan of a particular locality, who emerged either out of the ground or moved into this 'uninhabited' locale through journey. Whether their 'emergence' is from a vertical or horizontal journey, we then learn much about how they subsequently negotiated their place in the world. Movement in most of these stories is facilitated through or by spring water, a substance which connects the world of the living with that of the dead.

Water, fire and Mundo Perdido

Major Ko'o Raku also told me the story recounted in Chapter 2 of how a group of first ancestors in the Baucau region descended from the central mountain range of Mundo Perdido – the lost world as the Portuguese presciently named it. In this chapter I recount a perhaps related story told by the Makasae-speaking people of Wai Riu on the Mundo Perdido (Wai Nete Watu Ba'i) range, wherein we encounter Wai Riu the first man to emerge from the earth. It is important to note here that across the Mundo Perdido range the languages of Makasae and Kairui are most commonly spoken.[3]

In this story of the first ancestors of the house of Wai Riu all of the central characters are named (although I do not reproduce them all here). The original custodian of Mundo Perdido was an old man named Wai Riu (K: *riu* = bathe) who spoke Makasae. When the old man first emerged out of the ground through a cave he did so via an upward flow of water which later disappeared. He also had with him a book, which he subsequently lost after his offspring took it with them on their journeys to other locations closer to the coast. For the people of Wai Riu, a smooth rocky outcrop called Wai Taka atop Mundo Perdido acts underground like a door periodically opening to send the mountain's stores of karst water both to the male south sea and the female north sea.

When Wai Riu emerged from the ground he came with his wife Kasa Loi or Wai Badu [K: *badu* = firestick]. These first ancestors of the world had many children and grandchildren. To this day the people of Wai Riu worship animals rather than cultural objects like swords or gold discs. In the beginning it is said that the people of Wai Riu ate only raw foods. This was until

66 Watery histories

Wai Riu's grandchildren (two brothers and two sisters) were out hunting and met up with people from the house of Wai Lia to the south-east who were out doing the same at a place called Seu Baru (M: roasting meat) to the south of Mundo Perdido's peaks. The two hunting parties were successful in the hunt and killed the captured animals. The grandchildren of Wai Riu began to eat it straight away but the people from the house of Wai Lia had brought with them flints (K: *watu kili* and M: *afa kili*) which they struck together with palm fibres (M and K: *baru*) creating fire. They proceeded to roast the meat over fire inside bamboo lengths (M and K: *tukir*). The grandchildren of Wai Riu asked if they could also have fire-making implements. They were given them after which they placed them in the house of Kasa Loi/Wai Badu where they are worshipped to this day.

The grandchildren of Wai Riu were naked, while the grandchildren of Wai Lia wore loin cloths (M: *baa gutu*, K: *tahi waa*). As well as fire, they gave the people of Wai Riu clothes, loin cloths to the men and woven cloth (M: *rabi*, K: *noro lolo*) to the women. This event occurred at a place called Watu Laku (K: civet cat rock). However, almost immediately the people of Wai Riu forgot how to light fire. Later 'nature' or *natureza* reminded them in the form of an insect which flew over and started to repeatedly hit a piece of bamboo with its wings, causing smoke to appear and finally fire.

After Wai Riu received this knowledge of fire, the women of the lineage bore children and fire was said to have spread across the world. The men set out from Mundo Perdido following the path created by the spreading fire and teaching others how to make and control it. In each new locality they put in place the boundaries (ritual rocks and poles) to stop its spread. With fire clearly a metaphor for clan formation (symbolized as it is by the sacred hearth of each house), it is said that soon the whole world understood about fire, how to make it and how to create its boundaries. Henceforth, the world to the south as far as Natarbora and to the north as far as Laleia and Vemasse are said to have become orderly.

When these men returned from their journeys across the island, they said to the women that they now needed to stop living like animals and build houses. They went to cut house posts in locations referenced by bodily co-ordinates and returned to make their house at Kasa Loi. These men then began to level out rice paddies at a place named Kai Tui on the mountain's lower slopes. However, one man, an elder brother, remained living on the mountain top. Meanwhile, on the mountain slopes his younger brother successfully grew rice paddy and set aside these first grains (one per person) for his wife to cook. Yet when he had grown rice enough to fill one basket of rice, his older brother suddenly descended from the mountain top and ruined the crop, declaring angrily: 'if you are going to grow paddy you need to fetch a small bamboo length for water (M: *noka*), a sword, rope, a hen and a dog and I will first make the offerings for you to the spirits of the land.' They did this and the younger brother was able to recover his basket of rice and carry it to the house. Yet, the family still did not know how to thresh and prepare the rice. Eventually the man's son married a woman from elsewhere (from where is not specified) who knew how to pound rice in a coconut shell and she taught this process to the family. Then they too cooked the rice and began to traverse the lands teaching people how to grow and prepare rice for eating.

In a classic Timorese tale of a split between the world of darkness and the world of light, the protagonists in this next happening are four brothers from the houses of Kasa Loi and Wai Riu. In this story, two of these brothers decided to stay on Mundo Perdido, while two descend towards the north to live in Kai Oli Lale (W: 'inside the great forest', near Venilale in the upper reaches of the Seisal River valley). It was at this time that the book that had emerged from the ground originally with Wai Riu was taken by the descendants of Wai Badu/Kasa Loi to Kai Oli Lale and the book (symbolic of the era of lightness) was henceforth lost to the people of Wai Riu. This is why it is said that to this day those that stayed atop Mundo Perdido in the houses of Wai Riu and Kasa Loi do not know how to write. Those that went to Kai Oli Lale also took with them the knowledge of paddy making and spread it from there across the land, creating and naming springs and creating a network of spring groves and rice paddies. As Wai Riu (and Mundo Perdido) is the source of all water, wherever they spread, even to a dry mountain top, all they needed to do was dig for water and a spring would emerge.

These stories of Wai Riu suggest more than a few things to us about local interpretations of the early history of the region. The first people originated (by way of water) out of the earth, their hunter-gatherer existence was transformed by the acquisition of fire, clothing, houses, rice and rice culture all of which were enabled through various journeys and marriages and ultimately by the expansion outwards across the land. The coming of clothing correlates with what we have seen in our opening creation story where, according to Major Ko'o Raku, it is people from Makasar (Celebes/Sulawesi) who are said to have brought the knowledge of how to grow cotton seed (*kabas fuan*), spin the cotton and dye the thread with mud before weaving it into *tais*. Prior to this, he asserts, people wore only clothing made from the bark of trees.

Central to the story of Wai Riu is the original connection between these mountain peoples and the waters of Mundo Perdido, waters that make all life possible. Loss and recovery is also a recurring motif. The ancestors emerged from the ground with water which they lost but ultimately through movement regained access to. They also gained the knowledge of fire which they lost but through the assistance of an animal recovered. It was thus their connection to and knowledge of water and fire which enabled them to spread out across the world. But in one area, recovery has not been possible. Those who remained on Mundo Perdido remain in a world of darkness, their book of light was taken from them and the 'good life' moved elsewhere.

We will return to the story of Wai Riu and the coming and going of light. But first it is salutary to turn to the historical record and examine what this can tell us about the settlement of the central mountainous zone and the Baucau–Viqueque corridor.

68 *Watery histories*

The speculations of historical linguistics

Linguist Geoffrey Hull (1998), writing about the history of Austronesian languages in Timor, proposes that the Celebes (Sulawesi) is the likely source of the Austronesianization of Timoric languages. Hull notes that the famous Timorese origin myth (from the central kingdom of Belu) of a crocodile sailing east from *rai-Makasar* and turning itself into island Timor, correlates with the way the term *Makasar* is often used by Timorese to refer to Celebes in general (1998: 150).[4] Celebes is, he says, 'thought to have been Austronesianised from north by 2000 BC' (Hull 1998: 150).

Analysing the etymology of the vocabulary used in the present-day Kawamina language and aligning it with languages of Western-Malayu origin, Hull (1998: 150–152) goes on to speculate that the origins of the Kawaimina language may be linked to the history of a movement out of the eastern Tukung Besi islands of Celebes during the Fabronian (blacksmith) expansion (sometime prior to the eleventh century). This expansion, he argues, came from the Celebes through the eastern archipelago to the island of Wetar. From Wetar around the eleventh century, he hypothesizes that these peoples crossed the seas to the eastern central Timor (see Map 3.1). Some, he says, made incursions into the Makasae lands centred on Matebian to the east while the majority headed across the south coast and in a westerly direction. Hull's thesis correlates with the work of Portuguese anthropologist Almeida (1976) who writes that some Naueti speakers claim to have come by sea from the north settling in the mountains of Matebian (see Map 2.1) and then heading south to the coastal lands (where they now dominate). Yet other Naueti speakers on the south-eastern coastal strip are said by Almeida (1976) to have descended from the mountains of Matebian after another wave of 'foreigners' had arrived on the south coast and asked for the mountain people to join them. Meanwhile of the Waima'a, Almeida says that '[t]hey don't know their origin, although, anthropologically and linguistically, they are akin to the Macassáes, to whom, as a matter of fact, they recognise that they are related, receiving from them the designation of *Ãsu Wai Mu'a*' (1976: 363). This connection will be explored further below.

Concurrent with the Austronesianization of Timor from the west, Hull (1998) argues that there were important influences occurring at a smaller scale as a result of trade contacts between people on island Timor and Ambonese language speakers from the central-Malayu region. This influence was enhanced in the twelfth and thirteenth centuries through the expansionary journeys of Ambonese aristocrats (see Map 3.1). During this period, Hull (1998) argues that Kawamina and Tetum (from which the national lingua franca is derived) became heavily influenced by Ambonese languages. He notes that Ambonese toponyms correlate with Timorese ethnonyms including Waimaha even possibly the island name of Leitimor (Hull 1998: 162).

In a 2004 paper Hull argues that the Makasae and Fataluku speakers of the far east of island Timor were part of a separate and much earlier neo-Bomberaian expansion from the eastern tip of the island of Papua. Based on linguistic and

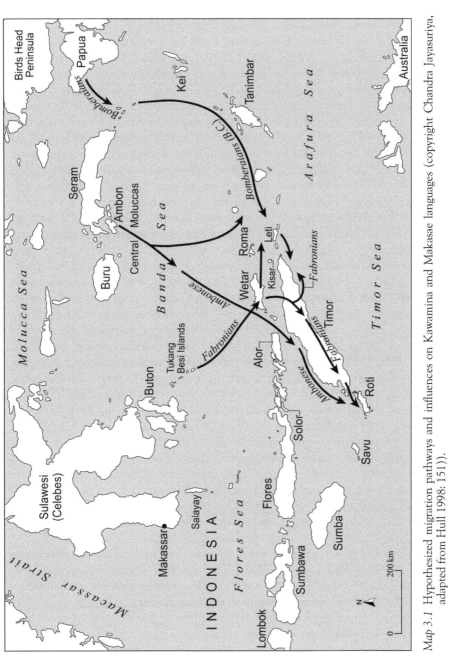

Map 3.1 Hypothesized migration pathways and influences on Kawamina and Makasae languages (copyright Chandra Jayasuriya, adapted from Hull 1998: 151)).

70 Watery histories

archaeological evidence, he argues that in Papua these people were already in contact with Austronesian settlers some 3,500 years ago (cf. Wurm 1975, 1982). This type of 'Austronesian cosmopolitanism' (McWilliam 2007a: 371) was followed by a Trans New Guinea expansion involving south-west journeys down through the islands of Kei, Ceram, Roma and Kisar ultimately to Timor (Hull 2004: 65; see Map 3.1). While Hull (2004) notes that the Fataluku arrivals in the far east of island Timor have largely retained their cultural distinctiveness and myths of marine voyage origin (cf. McWilliam 2007a), he states that the Makasae of the central eastern zone came eventually to assimilate Kawamina myths of origin from the Celebes. Yet the source for Hull's speculations that these later myths come from the Celebes is again the work of Almeida based on an oral history he collected from the Laga/Quelicai region (1976: 343). Yet my own ethnography collected as well from elsewhere in the Kawamina region (Baucau and Mundo Perdidio for instance) suggests that while Makasae and indeed Waima'a, Midiki and Kairui myths of origin may mention journeys and intermarriages from across the sea in almost each case (apart from stories from Laga/Quelicai) these are said to be the journeys of returning ancestors who originally emerged out of the ground on island Timor. According to Hull, such myths of naturalized origins are usually equated with non-Austronesian speakers.[5] Hence if, as Hull concludes, the Makasae language and mythic structure is now fashioned on Kawamina then one might also conclude (as Hull himself speculates for different reasons) that the Kawamina language itself might be fashioned from some early non-Austronesian language, perhaps an alloglot language not 'unlike that of Alor prior to the waves of Austronesian expansion' (Hull 1998: 146).[6] Such speculation can similarly be gleaned from a Waima'a myth of Catholic inflection told to me at the spring and village of Aubaca just west of Baucau town. In this story the protagonist is an old man called Rubi Lai who lived alone high on a mountain peak of Matebian. At this time the world was once again emerging from flood, and as the waters began to descend two women from the west travelled across the island from their abode on the Illi Manu ranges (an area of Manatuto still characterized by many Timorese as home to hunter-gatherer peoples). They followed the smoke signals from Rubi Lai's fire to reach him atop Matebian. From their union emerged twelve children who subsequently received from God (who may be known by the names of *Maromak*, *Amadeus* or *Lara Wulo* [sun-moon deity]) the gift of language. From there these children spread out to populate the world.

In these language puzzles it is useful again to draw on Levi-Strauss who writes of the way in which in a world of multiple languages and cultures, people have explained the world and represented and elaborated the universe to themselves and each other 'in an unceasing and vigorous dialogue' (Levi-Strauss 1982: 145). Water, particularly spring water, is central to both assertions of autochthony and settlement legitimacy, and is frequently a key 'topic' (Latour 2009) of conversation between founders and settlers. In this region, the historically contingent worlds of the Makasae, Kawamina and as we shall see in the next chapter the Eastern Tetum were and *are* filled with people living 'elbow to

Watery histories 71

elbow' (Levi-Strauss 1982: 145). As Gow writes and 'Levi Strauss insists', the challenge is to 'search for how this immediate local context is being made in space and time as part of a much wider system' (2001: 298).

The returnees

In some stories from north-central Timor, as we have seen, people emerge together with water out of caves on mountain peaks, in other stories which will be discussed below they emerge out of springs closer to the coast (cf. O'Connor *et al.* 2013). What is also interesting is that in many of these stories, like that of Wai Riu, those that emerged from the mountain peaks are said to have spread out from there to populate the world beyond, some even travelling across the seas, returning later with the heightened knowledge of fire and metals, water and wet rice production. While some of these 'explorers' returned to their original mountain and dry land rocky abodes, others are said to have returned to settle by the springs which are scattered across Baucau's coastal marine terrace zone.[7] From this point the stories tell us they began producing wet rice. Meanwhile another group is said to have arrived into the region from Luang (Leti) by way of Laga and travelled up to (re)settle in the mountains of Matebian. Major Ko'o Raku refers to these people as the Butu generation (other named groups with a similar migration pattern are called Luang, Dala Hitu (see below) and Makasar). Over time these Butu people began to descend from the high rocky outcrops of mountains and settled in the savanna plain to the south of Baucau. As they were largely dry land farmers, these Butu people are counterposed with the wet rice farming people from the coast.[8] They are also characterized as 'hairy people' with extremely long facial and armpit hair, even hairy mouths. While the Butu people eventually established relations with the coastal zone growers of irrigated rice, the division between largely dry land peoples and those living around the rice paddies and lush spring groves of the marine terrace zone was for a long time a jealously guarded boundary (see Figure 3.1). A Makasae ritual poem (*masa*) recounts:

Butu usa, nasa nasa loi casa	I Loilau Katilau [ancestors of a founding house of Boile Komu in Baucau]
Gel bobo, bobo casa gel	make my rice fields and swidden here
Loi Lau Kati Lau mu'a gasi	I ban you from descending
Rim liu gas rini	You live in your place in the rocks up above.

Overtime Butu men, some of whom descended through underground water sources, married into the families of these coastal irrigated rice growers and the cultures intermingled, resulting in complicated ritual governance relations (see Chapters 4 and 6). According to Major Ko'o Raku, Butu people have a sacred or *lulik* connection to *futu*, a Makasae word meaning subterranean termites.[9]

At the edge of the savanna on the Baucau plateau at a spring called Au Baka (Aubaca) and its associated origin house Kai Leki (W: 'Leki's forest') comes a

72 *Watery histories*

Figure 3.1 View of Mount Matebian from Berecoli ricefields.

story of people emerging through water out of the ground. It is said that at a time in the distant past, three brothers emerged from the earth clinging to the back of a buffalo. The oldest brother was sitting closest to the head of the buffalo, but his younger siblings then scrambled to grab onto the buffalos horns and hence they emerged first. The old brother conceded defeat, allowing his brothers to clamber into the light, he returned back underground into the darkness with his buffalo charge. Before doing so, however, he relayed to his younger siblings a range of strict prohibitions (*lisan*) with which they must abide to be able to live in the light earth. Lastly he told them to be sure to return to this same location the next morning. When they did so the next day, they found a spring had emerged from out of the ground and floating on the water asleep inside the leaves of a rootless lily (*bili*) was a baby girl who came to be known as Bui Bili. When this girl grew up, she married the older of the two brothers, whose name was Baka [Au Baka]. Meanwhile the youngest brother descended from the savanna to the marine terrace zone and married the daughter of the (rice growing) house of Weu Ho'o in the village of Boile, which today forms a part of central Baucau.[10]

The returning 'rice growing people' of Baucau's marine terrace zone are significant for other reasons as well. They also brought with them the knowledge of metalwork. Oral histories recount stories of these peoples heating and beating metal in the fire, before combining it with mud and heating it again to beat into shape ornamental discs and swords. These prized objects, as we will see below, were then exchanged with other local groups (including the Butu), eventually forming the basis of the local marriage exchange economy. This metalwork industry is said to have been first established at the beach called Mau Ba'i, below the Baucau village of Buruma. As the industry emerged Butu people were increasingly drawn down from the mountains eager to engage in trade and participate in this emerging culture.

Baucau and the origins of irrigated rice production

Both the Waima'a and Makasae settlement histories of coastal Baucau area record the arrival of people, usually brothers, from the Peaks of Matebian and Mundo Perdido. In the myth recounted by the people of the Waima'a village of Wani Uma [W: 'house of the bees'] to the north-west of central Baucau, three named brothers descended from the mountains 'in darkness' down the river valleys towards the coast. When they reached the coast the youngest brother had an injured leg and could no longer continue. It is recounted that as it 'was getting light', he had neither the necessary strength nor speed to continue this journey. At a place called Buruma [W: 'house of monkeys'] he heard the winged serpent crow, signalling to him this was the place he should settle. He did so and sent his elder brothers on their way.

Waima'a ritual verse (*loli*) from the village of Wani Uma records this event, although unusually it does so in Makasae:

Asa bui bere du'u	We male birds have come from the mountains
Kokoroe dana kokoroe	But the earth is already light
Nadani la'a do	You two go on to the rocks beyond
Afasika na Wasika na isi la'a	I am going to stay here.

Eventually the descendants of this man, in some accounts comprising a party of another three brothers, headed across the sea to settle on the island of Roma. Importantly, however, at unspecified intervals two of these brothers later made their way back to island Timor. One brother settled to the east of Wani Uma inland on the Laga coast beneath the Matebian range. This brother, who arrived at the house of Boleha, brought with him a particular breadfruit tree (*kulu kai*: 'the seedless Kai breadfruit'). The other settled to the west of Wani Uma in a coastal zone near Bundura called Wai Wono. This man brought with him another kind of breadfruit tree (known as *kulu roma*: 'the seeded Roma breadfruit'). Hence while both brothers symbolically shared the same trunk, the fruit of their respective branches was distinct. Oral histories recount that the branch which first settled with the Boleha house headed south up into the mountains of Matebian to a place called Baguia where they intermarried with the local clans (the nearby Afalokai is said to be the origin settlement from where first peoples

74 *Watery histories*

of Wani Uma descended to the coast). In a story reminiscent of the Butu, the descendants of these *kulu kai* people (who are also said by the people of Wani Uma to have been hairy) then descended from Matebian in waves. Meanwhile the other group of returnees who arrived to settle at Wai Wono continued to move slowly east along the coast to Baucau. They first settled on the spring fed plain by a hillock called Wai Mata Me below Wani Uma (see Figure 3.2). Later these people moved to the beach of Mau Ba'i below Buruma (see Figure 3.3). At this beach there is a natural rock pillar of the same name which is sacred (*lulik*) and said to be the metamorphosed body of the crocodile ancestor on whose back the returning people of Wai Mata Me arrived from Roma (later arrivals are said to have come on the back of a whale (M: *afibere*) and octopus (M: *tala dau*)).

A Waima'a ritual poem (*loli*) records the arrival of these two waves of migration, referred to as the brothers of Kulu Roma and Kulu Kai:

Kokoroe Koe e	The male bird crows
Kokoroe koe la	The male bird crows
Ro mai-e – la dopa mai-e	The boats are coming
Kokoroe koe e	The male bird crows
Kokoroe koe la	The male bird crows
Roma mai-e la	The boat is coming from Roma
Ro mai e	The boat is coming
La ro mai la teu Rai Malaku	Another boat comes from Malaku
Tasi tuku tasi tena	These sons have been brought up across the sea
Iti ana watu rai tena	They come to plant breadfruit and level the land (make paddy)
Kaiwetu kei aku resa kei.	In separate hamlets and houses.

These first people to settle at Wai Mata Me were a brother and a sister and they commenced their settlement below Wani Uma by creating two rice paddies which were named Bui Laku Bui Liri. They also brought with them bamboo lengths filled with water and when they moved to their final settlement site at Mau Ba'i on the coast below Buruma they created (M: *saun* = planted) there two springs known as Wai Mata Oli (W: large spring) and Wai Mata Me (W: small spring).

Meanwhile Major Ko'o Raku recounts that it was two ancestors whose names were Leki Roma and Loi Roma who brought with them to the spring of Wai Mata Me buffalo of the same name. The buffalo wallowed in the mud and broke up the earth below with their horns. From this act the springs were created and the water began to emerge. By the spring of Wai Mata Me a sacred house was built. From the spring at Wai Mata Oli the water was channelled to feed the rice fields below in the coastal area of Mau Ba'i (where the practice of metalwork or *tuku besi* was first introduced). These fields were

Figure 3.2 Wai Mata Me hillock and coastal irrigation channels, Baucau.

named Da Holo, Ra Buti, Ria Siaka, Aha Isi, Manu Waru, Ra Gia and Wai Sara. Once the water had been canalized all the way to Mau Ba'i, the owners of the buffalo sacrificed the buffalo by the springs.

Other ancestors (also a brother and sister) are also remembered by Major Ko'o Raku as Kulu Kai. They arrived to the join the house of Boleha near Laga, later moving the incoming male house known as Sa'a Dahu (six posts) in

76 *Watery histories*

Figure 3.3 Mau Ba'i beach and coastal features, Baucau.

Makasae up to the mountainous region of Matebian in Baguia. When they too moved down to coastal area they joined with the house complex of Wani Uma (see Chapter 4) where this male house is known in Waima'a as Rikainena (six posts). In contradistinction to the longer 'Makassan' swords prized in marital exchanges by the other houses of Wani Uma, the house of Rikainena is identified with the tradition of the short sword.

Kisar and respectful relations

The wet rice production and metalwork that is recounted in these stories as co-emergent with at least one of these groups of north sea returnees brings with it a radical transformation of life. These cultural transformations are recorded in other stories as the result of local marriage relations and exchanges with island Kisar (an island located between Timor and Roma). These stories, emanating from confusingly unspecified time periods, centre on a woman called Ono Loko (a daughter alternatively of Wai Lewa the founding ancestor of Baucau (see Chapter 2), or of the infamous nineteenth-century ruler of Baucau Dom Joao Vicente Paulo from Boile (see Chapter 5)). Ono Loko married with a ruler from Kisar known as Coronel Dala Hitu (Dala Hitu or 'seven times' was also the principal kingdom of the Ambonese in the twelfth century).[11] Ono Loko travelled

Watery histories 77

to Kisar with a local midwife from Baucau. The pair possessed knowledge which was until then unknown on Kisar, the knowledge of birth. Prior to this time, it is said that every birth on Kisar was a result of the cutting open of the mother's stomach (a procedure leading inevitably to the death of the woman). Yet with the assistance of her midwife, Ono Loko is able to give birth to eight healthy children, although each time this happens in secret. The nobility of Kisar were astounded and wondered how this could be possible. They checked Ono Loko's ears, nose and mouth looking for clues as to where the baby had emerged. Finally after the birth of her eighth child, the secret of birth was shared by Ono Loko and her midwife and the gift of life was given to the people of Kisar. In return, the Baucau region received back its eight sons and daughters who returned to found their own sacred houses. These children brought with them various objects which are, even today, central to marriage exchange relations in the region.

In these stories of the return, the sons and daughters of Coronel Dala Hitu and Ono Loko arrive at a beach called Hare Lai Duro below the village of Boile in Baucau. They bring with them gold discs and weapons. After this they form relations through marriage with other groups and eventually these objects brought with them from Kisar become objects of marriage exchange, creating and cementing respectful exchange relations between fertility-giver and fertility-taker groups across the region. Later, more boats arrive from Kisar and they bring with them the much coveted Makassan swords which also become central to respectful fertility-giver and fertility-taker exchanges and relationships.[12] These boats landed first to the west in Laleia and near Vemasse at Ren'bo and Wai Wono. Following this further arrivals from Kisar brought coral necklaces (M: *gaba*) and these were given by fertility-givers to fertility-takers in exchange for Macassan swords. It can be seen that the original marriage of Ono Loko with Coronel Dala Hitu formed a pattern of marriage exchange whereby men and women moved across the water in both directions until the early twentieth century (see Correia 1935; see also Chapter 5).[13] From this original exchange of goods (sourced from Kisar, Makassar and Ambon) subsequent generations in Timor have developed their own etiquette of marriage exchanges and respectful relations. Macassan swords, buffalo and horses given in exchange for coral necklaces (*gaba*), woven cloth (*tais*), rice and pigs remain central to marriage exchange practices in this area of Baucau.

Yet further along the coast, the arrival of a different 'branch' of people, the Kulu Kai ('seedless breadfruit'), to the region near Laga created a different expectation of exchange through marriage. These people brought with them other types of sword, one short (known as *gurnisa*) and one longer (known as *biragaba*). These swords were subsequently traded as these people moved up into the mountains of Matebian. While around Baucau town Makassan swords are still demanded by the fertility-giving houses in their marriage exchanges with others, the fertility-giving houses around Laga and Matebian demand the *gurnisa* and *biragaba*.

78 *Watery histories*

Discussion

In his powerful critique of the lack of serious engagement with indigenous histories in Peru, Gow has written that:

> Because we assume their ideas to be so fragile, we do not bother to enquire into their historical trajectories, or even to ask seriously about their real world meanings. We therefore miss out on how such ideas might actually inform the ways in which indigenous Amazonian people live the lives they do, and on the potentially profound continuities hidden within their mercurial transformations.
>
> (2001: 310)

From this chapter we can see that in Baucau, as elsewhere in the indigenous world, the arrival of Europeans was not a 'privileged moment of rupture' but in many ways merely 'another form of others' who entered a 'lived world richly provided with the means for exploring their potential' (Gow 2001: 309). The next and subsequent chapters will continue excavating the historical nuances and lifeworld meanings of these mythic narratives of journeys, oceans and spring water and how, over time, they incorporated a European presence.

Informed as well by historical linguistics, my materialist analysis in this chapter of a largely symbolic mythscape has raised a number of questions for further investigation. Who exactly are these 'hairy people' found in stories across the region and who it appears provide us with both naturalized creation stories as well as links to a migrating (or returning) people from the north. Archaeological investigations have identified an ancient rock art record which suggests that during some period in the distant past they were one cultural bloc of peoples stretching from the mountainous zone of Matebian to the coast of Baucau and Ponte Bondura (O'Connor and Oliveira 2007).[14] As we shall see in Chapter 4, the place names and autochthonous clan names of the Baucau region are predominantly Waima'a in origin rather than Makasae. If Hull's speculations on Kawamina as an alloglot language are correct then perhaps it is possible that the stories recounted in this chapter give us insight into a chain of migrations stretching from 'original' peoples to later migrations of both neo-Bomberaians and Austronesian language speakers.

Whatever their historical resonance, what is clear is that these myths and mythic genres are themselves continually unfolding, transforming and remaining meaningful to people's lives in ever changing contexts (cf. Gow 2001). Indeed this chapter's opening (Catholic inflected) myth of creation and other stories of subsequent journeys down from the mountains resonate closely with a myth collected by Almeida (1976) in Laleia to the immediate west of Baucau over half a century earlier. In what Almeida characterizes as a central myth of the eastern region, a snake ancestor from Mount Cabalaki travels east to Mount Matebian where another snake also emerges out of the ground (see Map 5.1). The two snakes transform into a man and woman and they produce seven sons. While the man and the woman then once again transform back into snakes, the snake-father is finally transformed into jewels (coral necklaces and gold) and the snake-mother becomes a woman. This woman and her sons carry with them their sacred jewels as they descend from the mountains to Laga (see Figure 3.4). There on the coast two of the sons settle, one heads further east and four migrate west towards Baucau and Manatuto. Almeida writes that '[t]his reptile was the distant ancestor of the Macassáes, Uái Má'as, Ná Ines, Nái Damos and other peoples of the far east of the island of Timor' (Almeida 1976: 346).

Reptilian ancestry (and given its link to the python, in this I include the eel) is a recurring theme for many houses across the region (see also Appendix 3, and while I do not discuss them here, crocodiles are also a powerful ancestor across Timor[15]). As we have seen in some stories when snakes emerge from the waters below the earth, through their encounter with the sun (fire) they gain the capacity to reproduce and transform their radiant hue into human form as well as gold and other sacra (see Dos Santos (1967) on Vemasse and Chapter 4). While in the period of light, shape changing between people and animals is rare, as night follows day in this intensely cosmic and localized hydrosocial cycle water remains a key portal (M: *gituba ginana*) of communication between these worlds of dark and light. It is the material substance which carries the essence of shared origins and inclusive sociality through all bodies and things. Even in 'modern' creation narratives (like the one recounted on p. 63), the underlying theme is still one of the sun (fire) blowing (like the wind) into a mixture of earth and water (mud) to create life enabled by the agency of a snake. At every encounter, the radiance and excesses of fire continues to transform life (water) into life itself, connecting and enlivening mythic origins and settlement patterns across the region.

Figure 3.4 Laga coast and ricefields.

80 *Watery histories*

Notes

1 In this and other Timorese multilingual settings the local preference is to highlight cultural inclusiveness and synergies, not linguistic differentiation (cf. Schapper 2011). Local myth narratives often centre on two brothers, one who spoke Makasae and one who spoke one of the 'Kawamina' dialects. Differentiation between groups, when asserted, is made on the basis of divisions between 'houses' and their customs (T: '*lisan*'), not language. As we will see in Chapter 4, although the Makasae language now dominates in the Baucau district, the names and origin histories of many Baucau sacred houses, along with place names themselves, suggest that some time in the past the Baucau region was dominated by the Kawamina language group (cf. McWilliam 2007a).

2 Correia (1935: 68) writes that '[i]f one insists that the indígenas translate for us the notion of God (Deus), it is clear that they designate "Him" with Uru-Uato, a composite word that as much in Makassae as in Uaimaa, the most common languages in the circumscription, means Lua-Sol' [Moon-Sun].

3 Waima'a speakers often refer to the Kairui dialect spoken on Mundo Perdido as Waima'a. The Kairui spoken further to the west, where the village of Kairui is located, is inflected to a greater degree by Galoli and far less familiar to them.

4 This priority given to Makasar could also be a result of the histories of connection established between the two regions as a result of trade between seafaring 'Makassans' and locals from the sixteenth century or earlier (cf. Spillett 1999; McWilliam 2007b). See also 'The Legend of We-Hali We-Bico' which recounts how the south-west coastal region was 'invaded' by peoples from the Malay Peninsula by way of Makasar (Correia 1935 cited in Belo 2011: 459–461; cf. Spillett 1999: 155–205).

5 The Mambai belief that their ancestors came from mountains and are progenitors of other tribes on Timor is not dissimilar to the stories we have so far heard of origins from the peaks of Matebian, Mundo Perdido and Cabalaki. Hull (1998) asserts that Mambai is linked to an earlier Aboriginal language.

6 Hull (1998: 165) asserts (in contrast to earlier studies) that Kawamina does not exhibit significant Papuan traits and suggests that (at the time of his writing) the study of Timoric languages has revealed negligible pre-Butonic Austronesian stratum (1998: 152). While he says that Kawamina has no significant Papuan exotic element he qualifies this by adding no 'Bomberaian' exotic element (Hull 1998: 165). He notes that the intractable elements in the Butonic languages of Timor without Austronesian connection do not concord with Bunak, Makasae or Fataluku and suggests words 'from a pre-Austronesian sub-strata quite distinct from (and possibly older than) the surviving Papuan languages on the island' (Hull 1998: 146).

7 Karst fed springs of the marine terrace zone combined with a pattern of denser vegetation and cave overhangs or 'wave cut notches' are also believed to be early inhabitation sites (Metzner 1977: 25; cf. Glover 1986). Glover has dated habitation sites in this area to 15,000 years BCE (Glover 1986).

8 *Butu* in this context can also mean growers of dry land cereals.

9 Which are perhaps not incidentally connected to underground water sources.

10 In myth from this house recorded by Antonio Vicente Marques Soares in the early 1970s, there is a subterranean connection between the spring of Au Baka and Wai Lia in Baucau. I have so far been unable to locate the published version of this myth and its original teller is now deceased.

11 Ono Loko at others times is asserted by Major Ko'o Raku to be the daughter of the founding ruler of Baucau, Wai Lewa. Wai Lewa's other daughters are said to have married into houses in Berecoli and Bucoli. Wai Lewa's sons married women from Seisal, Caibada and Tirilolo. The title of Coronel ('Colonel') emerged in the early eighteenth century when the Portuguese title system came into use for indigenous rulers (Belo 2011).

12 The 'Makassans' of Sulawesi were famous for producing knives and swords from the early sixteenth century and their recorded presence in Timor is from the early seventeenth century (Spillett 1999; McWilliam 2007b, Hägerdal 2012).
13 See Correia (1944: 299–301) for a summary of Kisar–Baucau relations.
14 See also Gomes (2014).
15 Along with the famous Belunese origin myth of island Timor originating from the body of a crocodile (see above), connections of particular houses to crocodiles are common across the coastal zones of Timor (including low-lying regions of the Baucau district. Near Seisal at the spring of Bui Leme, crocodiles are a critical messenger between peoples and the underworld of the sea). The crocodile is commonly referred to in Tetum as 'avo-sira' or grandparents. In Tetum Terik they are referred to as 'Nai Bei', the great ancestor, and in the ancient kingdom of Koba Lima they are connected to the maintenance of the division between the land and the sea (Kehi and Palmer 2012). On the south coast of Viqueque in the sub-district of Watu Carabao, representatives of particular houses are responsible for guarding the coast and maintaining lulik relationships with crocodiles. These people are known as 'friends of the crocodiles'. In Luca this crucial role is referred to as 'marrying with crocodiles'.

References

Almeida, de A. (1976) 'Da Origem Lendária e Mitológica dos Povos do Timor Português', *Memórias da Academia des Ciências de Lisboa* 19: 575–607.

Anderson, B. and Wylie, J. (2009) 'On Geography and Materiality', *Environment and Planning* 41(2): 318–335.

Attwood, B. (2011) 'Aboriginal History, Minority Histories and Historical Wounds: The Postcolonial Condition, Historical Knowledge and the Public Life of History in Australia', *Postcolonial Studies* 14(2): 171–186.

Belo, D. (2011) *Os Antigos Reinos de Timor-Leste*, Baucau: Edição Tipografia Diocesana Baucau.

Boucher, G. (2013) 'Disclosure and Critique', paper presented at Multiple Ontologies/ Ontological Relativity Workshop, Deakin University, Melbourne, December 2013.

Bovensiepen, J. (2012) 'Words of the Ancestors: Disembodied Knowledge and Secrecy in East Timor', *Journal of the Royal Anthropological Institute* 20: 56–77.

Certeau, M. de (1986) *Heterologies: Discourse on the Other*, translated by Brian Massumi, Manchester: Manchester University Press.

Chakrabaty, D. (2011) 'The Politics and Possibility of Historical Knowledge: Continuing the Conversation', *Postcolonial Studies* 14(2): 243–250.

Correia, A. (1935) *Gentio de Timor*, Lisbon: Agência-Geral das Colónias.

Correia, A. (1944) *Timor de Lés a Lés*, Lisbon: Agência Geral das Colónias.

Doel, M. (2004) 'Poststructuralist Geographies: The Essential Selection', in P. Cloke, P. Crang and M. Goodwin (eds) *Envisioning Human Geographies*, London: Arnold, 146–171.

Dos Santos, E. (1967) *Kanoik: Mitos e Lendas de Timor*, Lisboa: Ultramar.

Fox, J. (1980) Retelling the Past: The Communicative Structure of a Rotinese Historical Narrative', *Anthropology* 3(1): 56–66.

Glover, I. (1986) *Archaeology in Eastern Timor, 1966–67*, Canberra: The Australian National University Press.

Gomes, J. (2014) 'Waima'a Culture Glimpsed', *Tempo Semanal*.

Gow, P. (2001) *An Amazonian Myth and its History*, Oxford: Oxford University Press.

Gusmão, X. (1998) *My Sea of Timor: Poems and Paintings*, Porto: Granito.

82 *Watery histories*

Hägerdal, H. (2012) *Lords of the Land, Lords of the Sea: Conflict and Adaption in Early Colonial Timor, 1600–1800*, Leiden: KITLV Press.

Hicks, D. (2004) [1976] *Tetum Ghosts & Kin: Fertility and Gender in East Timor*, Illinois: Waveland Press.

Hull, G. (1998) 'The Basic Lexical Affinities of Timor's Austronesian Languages: A Preliminary Investigation', *Studies in Languages and Cultures of East Timor* 1: 97–174.

Hull, G. (2004) 'The Papuan Languages of Timor', *Estudos de línguas e culturas de Timor Leste* 6: 23–99.

Kehi, B. and Palmer, L. (2012) 'Hamatak Halirin: The Cosmological and Socio-Ecological Roles of Water in Koba Lima, Timor', *Bijdragen tot de Taal-, Land- en Volkenkunde* 168: 445–471.

Latour, B. (2009) 'Perspectivism: "Type" or "Bomb"?', *Anthropology Today* 25(2): 1–2.

Levi-Strauss, C. (1982) *The Way of Masks*, Seattle: University of Washington Press.

McWilliam, A. (2007a) 'Austronesians in Linguistic Disguise: Fataluku Cultural Fusion in East Timor', *Journal of Southeast Asian Studies* 38(2): 355–375.

McWilliam, A. (2007b) 'Looking for Ade: A Contribution to Timorese Historiography', *Bijdragen tot de Taal-, Land- en Volkenkunde* 163(2/3): 221–238.

Metzner, J. (1977) *Man and Environment in Eastern Timor: A Geoecological Analysis of the Baucua-Viqueque Area as a Possible Basis for Regional Planning*, Canberra: The Australian National University.

O'Connor, S. and Oliveira, N. (2007) 'Inter- and Intra-Regional Variation in the Austronesian Painting Tradition: A View from East Timor', *Asian Perspectives* 46(2): 389–403.

O'Connor, S., Pannell, S. and Brockwell, S. (2013) 'The Dynamics of Culture and Nature in a "Protected" Fataluku Landscape', in S. Brockwell, S. O'Connor and D. Byrne (eds) *Transcending the Culture–Nature Divide in Cultural Heritage: Views from the Asia-Pacific Region*, Canberra: ANU Press, 203–234.

Schapper, A. (2011) 'Finding Bunaq: The Homeland and Expansion of the Bunaq in Central Timor', in A. McWilliam and E. Traube (eds) *Land and Life in Timor-Leste: Ethnographic Essays*, Canberra: ANU E-Press, 163–187.

Schulte Nordholt, H. (1971) *The Political System of the Atoni of Timor*, The Hague: Martinus Nijhoff.

Spillett, P. (1999) 'The Pre-Colonial History of the Island of Timor Together with Some Notes on the Makassan Influence in the Island', unpublished manuscript, Museum and Art Gallery of the Northern Territory, Darwin.

Traube, E. (1989) 'Obligation to the Source: Complementarity and Hierarchy in an Eastern Indonesian Society', in D. Maybury-Lewis and U. Almagor (eds) *The Attraction of Opposites: Thought and Society in the Dualistic Mode*, Ann Arbor: University of Michigan Press, 321–344.

Wittgenstein, L. (1979) *Remarks on Frazer's Golden Bough*, edited by R. Rhees, translated by A.C. Miles (1971), Nottinghamshire: Brynmill.

Wurm, S. (1975) 'Papuan Languages and the New Guinea Linguistic Scene', *New Guinea Languages and Language Study Vol. 1*, Canberra: Research School of Pacific Studies, Australian National University.

Wurm, S. (1982) *Papuan Languages of Oceania*, Tubingen: Gunter Narr.

4 Water pathways

To understand the ongoing import of localized social relations enabled through and with water, I now turn to a consideration of specific subterranean pathways which configure relations between groups in or across particular zones in this region. These pathways also give us insights into both regional settlement and subsequent localized dispersal patterns. They are pertinent to processes of social and political identity formation and integration and enable some understanding of power and local governance configurations across time and space. It is, I will argue, these relational, dynamic and opaque watery pathways which create a thoroughly material basis for engagements between people, ancestral spirits and place. This actual and metaphorical fluidity of movement highlights the multiple life-giving qualities of springs and the dependencies of people on them.

As we saw in the previous chapter, the mythic narratives which recount the movements and settlement stories of people across the landscape prioritize relationships – their making, severance or continuance – over linear time. As these relationships change they may also recalibrate the mythscape making space for new connections and eliding others in their reconfigurations of socio-political power. In these dynamic relational narratives aspects of ancestral names will usually be retained (if secreted and added to) through time, while the particular origins, characteristics and actions of these same ancestral protagonists may change. For example, many of the stories relating to the origins of Baucau town revolve around the area's springs and the actions of three brothers named Tai Loi, Leki Loi and Wono Loi (see also Correia 1935; Spillett 1999). In these tellings, which were first recorded in the early twentieth century, the cultural origins and historical trajectory of the three brothers changes according to the time period of the telling as well as the socio-political locatedness of the teller(s).

Along with three brothers, another constant trope is that of people travelling through underground waters to emerge and make connections with other communities. These stories, which are found across the region, will usually have as their narrative base a protagonist male who is led to a previously unknown water source by an animal (usually a dog) and a trail of ash. Upon entering the subterranean waters the protagonist will have encounters with trickster eels and pythons which guard the world below. After these misadventures the protagonist

84 *Water pathways*

will emerge in the new locality where he will be found by a local woman who he later marries. This underground journey often connects the two communities in ongoing ritual exchange relations. In contrast to the three brothers' stories, I have no written sources with which to compare the present-day tellings of these subterranean narratives. However, research carried out by Fox on the island of Roti shows that similar local 'histories' about the discovery of springs (and people's subsequent rights to that water) are subject to the vagaries of time and social situatedness. Demonstrating that such 'true tales' or historical narratives are 'intended to communicate the present as well as the past', Fox concludes that ironically this category of tales are more unstable than plain (ahistorical) tales (Fox 1980: 65). Hence while various tropes and motifs in these historical narratives remain constant through time (male ancestors, dogs, ash, tricksters), the sequencing of events or particular relationships between protagonists shifts through time to reflect dynamic socio-political relations.

It is both this ongoing flow of water and the flow of words between people that gives these narratives their currency and their magic. Recounting these mytho-historical narratives in written form risks flattening them out and decontextualizing them from their unique specificities of time, place, teller and audience (Gow 2001). To avoid this, I carefully draw out both the entangled historical contexts and the socio-ecologically located 'streams of talk' (Gow 2001: 36) that characterize these multiple tellings and retellings and their present-day meaning and significance.

The descent: the story of Wani Uma and their water

While, as we saw in Chapter 2, the founder of the central Wai Lewa spring in Baucau town descended from Mundo Perdido (referred to occasionally on the coast as Wai Ba'i), we are not told in this story if this ancestor arrived to an empty or already occupied land. Such details are provided in the stories told by the Waima'a-speaking elders of Wani Uma, a sacred house complex (see Figure 4.1) and sub-village in the present-day village of Caibada (Waima'a), a few kilometres to the north-west of central Baucau (see Map 4.1). When their ancestors arrived in this coastal region the land, they say, was bereft of people. It was also, as in the Wai Lewa narrative, an area largely bereft of surface water.[1] The Wani Uma elders recount that when the earth was still dark, clan groups moved down into the region from the mountains of Matebian. These people came in three main waves over an unspecified time period (to specify this is forbidden (*lulik*)). The first two waves came down via rivers and travelled along the coast west to Baucau. The third wave came down by travelling via the central zone (Mau Koi Mako Leki) via the Mundo Perdido range (see Map 2.1). In each of these waves particular clan groups carried with them water in bamboo lengths drawn from their origin springs in the mountains. Upon arrival at their chosen settlement site, this water was ritually poured into the ground (usually in places with an extant, if very meagre, water source) and a powerful spring would then emerge from the ground.

Water pathways 85

The story told to me by Joao Ximenes (Ossu Watu), the Wani Uma 'historian of the light', is summarized below:

> Wani Uma came from the peaks of Matebian. This land here was wild. We were the first to arrive, there were no people living here. The clan of Watu Naru came first, together with Boile Mauduku. These houses have three

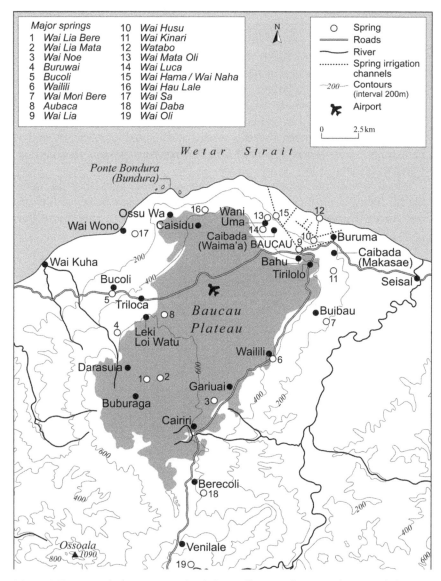

Map 4.1 Baucau sub-district map (with key villages and springs from text) (copyright Chandra Jayasuriya).

parts – the older house, the middle house and the youngest house. It is always like this.

These first clans of Wani Uma left their origin houses at Afalokai [near to Baguia below the eastern peaks of Matebian]. They came together with Wai Luo and Wai Hau [the first peoples of Caisidu. In other accounts Wai Luo are said to have arrived from Alor].

Wani Uma came in three main stages. Each major house group travelled together with their own. Originally we followed the rivers to the coast but in the third stage people came through the central corridor. Wani Uma's path has branched over time from Afalokai, south to Watu Carabau, west to Watu Lari and then north to Waukau [Baucau]. Later a branch went from Waukau to the island of Atauru.

Our spring water was brought with us from Matebian. We carried it here and established springs here. Wai Hau brought the source water for many of our springs. They put it in bamboo and carried it down where they threw it on the ground. Then they dug the ground and recited sacred words and a permanent water source appeared. There were three groups that carried water with them.

Much later another group came from the south from Luca, they also went via Illi Manu [a mountain range to the west] and brought water with them from there. This spring is called Wai Naha. There is also a spring called Wai Luca [nestled beside the original Wani Uma sacred house complex].

Figure 4.1 Wani Uma sacred house complex, Baucau.

Water pathways 87

In the stories of Wani Uma (as well as those of other clans across the region), sub-sequent dispersals from those living together in the new settlements were triggered by intra-group or clan conflict (usually between older and younger brothers). These disputes resulted in new settlements being founded elsewhere and in many cases those that moved out took with them specific clan sacra and/or water sources:

> There is a spring on Atauru [the island opposite Dili] called We Krang. There was a dispute between two brothers from Wani Uma. The younger was coming to participate in a ceremony, but then he and his group saw the smoke rising from the sacred fire at the sacred house complex and they knew their kin had decided to carry out the ritual without them. They decided they must leave. They fashioned a canoe and set off with a bamboo length full of water and settled on Atauru. This water became a spring on Atauru called We Krang.
>
> Wai Luo and Wai Hau settled at Bundura [near the present-day settle-ment of Caisidu]. That is their place. They share the custodianship of area's *luli* (W: sacred, forbidden) complex with Watu Naru. Boile Mauduku was originally together with them, but after a dispute over buffalo they set off on their own and made their own *luli*. Together these groups created their sacred 'rock and tree' (ancestral offering places) and called the names of the land and the waters and made them sacred. They built their sacred houses by the springs to make the water sacred (*luli*) and ensure the continuation of a permanent water supply.

While their ancestors augmented these water sources with their own ancestral waters from the peaks of Matebian, it is also said that subterranean waters flow like rivers through the area and originate from Mundo Perdido. Each of these flows have with their own particular paths:

> Baucau's water comes from Wai Lia Wai Lobi [the Wai Lia Bere complex on the Baucau plateau]. Its source is Mundo Perdido. Wani Uma's water also comes from Mundo Perdido. Through this path we receive a little water here, but most of it is lost to the sea. The water from Matebian goes to the south coast. Both mountains give water. But it was the water that was brought from Matebian that we 'planted and grew' (W: *diku*) here.

It is clear then that there are multiple material-symbolic associations at work in these accounts, each layered with the meaning derived from specific histor-ical contexts. While water is said to circulate underground between the moun-tains of Matebian and Mundo Perdido and the sea, where this water emerges to form springs is dependent on the connections between in-migrating groups of people and their origin spring or *hun* (trunk). Water from ancestral origin springs is known as the 'mother water' (*bee inan* or main source of water), and it is this water that is carried with migrating groups to new places. When it is subsequently thrown onto the ground, it is the ancestral essence of this 'mother water' which connects with the subterranean sea or 'other world'. Accessing its

88 *Water pathways*

origins in this 'other world', the 'mother water' draws forth a 'child' spring to the new location. The spirit agents of this 'other world' are typically eels and great snakes and together it is they who forge the subterranean pathways between mother and child springs.

The expansionary presence of Luca

As we have seen in Chapter 2, in spring narratives across the region the ritual-politico kingdom of Luca is repeatedly reported as the 'mother' or power source for many springs. However, in these watery narrative journeys, Luca's influence over or creation of specific springs is usually subsequent to earlier ancestral movements of both people and water. During this earlier time, house-specific ancestral sacra also emerged. As people (and water) spread out across the region settling in new places and intermarrying, the sacra connected to particular centres of ritual power also spread through the region. As we have seen above, all these waters are understood as being connected to the 'other world', a world often identified with the sea. Yet it was because of Luca's pre-eminent relationship with this other world of the sea that it emerged as the ritual centre of the eastern region of the island (see Chapter 2). During this period it was sacra (such as betel leaves and golden objects) and *lulik* waters drawn from the springs of Luca which gave its emissaries the right to (re)create new centres of power. Dominion was frequently established in localities now associated with lush spring groves and irrigated rice production (see Figure 4.2).

Figure 4.2 Wailili spring, irrigation channel and spring grove.

Water pathways 89

This sequence of events is also suggested in changes in the 'origin' and 'conquest narratives' told about present-day Baucau, a rich spring grove with hundreds of irrigated rice terraces. In the early twentieth century Armando Pinto Correia (1935: 126–128), the famous Portuguese administrator of Baucau district, recorded an origin story for Baucau linked to three sons of the local patriarch. In this narrative, the patriarch divides the area between his three sons named Wono Loi, Tai Loi and Leki Loi and the sons found the town's present-day villages of Bahu (Wabubo), Caibada and Tirilolo respectively (see Map 4.1). Yet by the 1980s when the historian Peter Spillett visited Baucau, in the accounts he heard these same three brothers had transformed into invaders from the south (Spillett 1999: 275).[2] Meanwhile in the nearby village of Buruma, these three brothers were characterized as founding ancestors of the coastal region who had subsequently set out across the north sea to the island of Roma. One of them, Loi Leki, later returned to Buruma on the back of a crocodile (Spillett 1999: 275; see also Chapter 3). In the course of my own research, I have been told versions of all of these stories. While confusing for an ethnographer in search of historical insight, what became clear to me over time was that the trope of these three named brothers, the one constant in all of these stories, enabled all tellers to connect people, differentiate groups and shift hierarchical relations across great distances and time periods. What was being prioritized was the forging of dynamic relationships.

Like Peter Spillett, Correia (1935: 129–133) was also told a story of the conquest of Baucau. However, his story features three un-named brothers from Makadiki in Viqueque on the southern side of the central ranges. These brothers, who lived by a spring, came into dispute and two of them migrated away in search of a new home and spring. As they travelled north across the landscape others joined their party. They arrived in the north and found Baucau's (now) six villages at war with each other (two against four). These southern newcomers were fierce warriors and because of this they were asked to join one of the warring parties. The southern warriors joined the battle as requested and the war was won. While the southerners' ferocious battle tactics shocked their new allies, the locals were pleased with the victory and asked the newcomers what they sought in return. Their reply was that they only sought the rights to drink the waters of the region. The right was granted and a victory party was held. However, during these festivities the local (presumably Waima'a-speaking) inhabitants were tricked by the southerners into participating in a ritual during which iron spikes (brought from the south) were plunged into their heads. With the local leadership now dead, the southern newcomers settled in to rule the region.

The similarities and differences between the stories told first to Correia (1935) and later to Spillett (1999) are perhaps best explained by the fact that by the 1980s much had changed in Baucau. The in-migration of many Makasae speakers (discussed below) meant that many of the original Waima'a-speaking houses of the area had either left the region or had, by then, long intermarried with Makasae speakers. In one of these origin narratives relayed to Spillett

90   *Water pathways*

(1999: 270), the first king of Baucau was said to be a Makasae man named We Lewa who had three sons, Tirilolo, Bahu and Caibada (although a fourth brother, Buruma, is also mentioned). This king was killed by a warrior from Viqueque whose own sons then divided up the area between themselves. In another conquest narrative told to Spillett, a party of 600 invaders attacked the area led by three brothers from Luca whose names were Tai Loi, Leki Loi and Wono Loi (Spillet 1999: 270–272). To try to repel these attacks the local (presumably in this version Makasae) inhabitants of Baucau sought the assistance of a group of eighty neighbouring newcomers who hailed from the Waima'a-speaking area of Vemasse (and whose leader's names were Bahu, Caibada and Tirilolo). These southern invaders defeat the Waima'a newcomers, killing their leaders and driving them out. After this the brothers from Luca took control of the water supply (from the extant Makasae rulers), married with local women and acquired livestock.

While all these transgenerational accounts of origin and conquest have a stable core of three brothers, they vary according to the situatedness of the teller and the time period of the telling. In 2010, the people of Wani Uma also relayed to me their own story of the arrival in Baucau of three brothers named Wono Loi, Tai Loi and Leki Loi. These arrivals occurred in a period referred to as '*tempu monarchia*' ('the time of the monarchy', which I take as referring to the rise of Luca's expansionary power linked to the Portuguese crown). Following the arrival of these brothers, changes in locally configured rights to land and water meant that they were forced to 'buy' (*sosa*) their own water through ritual and land exchange. While this period will be explored in detail in Chapter 6, the people of Wani Uma characterize their ancestors at this time as 'stupid people' with no comprehension of politics. As a result they simply gave away a significant amount of their rice fields and rights to water to the newcomers. It is said the invaders came and settled by the main water source of Wai Lewa in Baucau, eventually expanding irrigation canals and taking control of the water.

Meanwhile, in Baucau the people descended from the ancient village of Boile (now a part of the village of Bahu) trace their lineage back to the ancestor buried in the spring of Wai Lewa. While Boile is said to have descended from the central ranges, the first group of arrivals sojourned westwards to Wai Cuha near Vemasse before later returning to settle at the Wai Lewa spring (see Map 4.1). The name Boile is derived from the Waima'a and Makasae verb '*boi*', the practice of gathering together in a circle to dance and sing and 'make place' (*le* is said to derive from the Waima'a *le'he* meaning 'a place in the spring groves').

According to Boile elders, the pre-eminent origin house of Baucau's central spring complex is the house of Boile Komu (W: *komu* = to gather together) (see Figure 4.3). One of the elders of Boile Komu explained to me that in the beginning their ancestors came from the central ranges:

> They came down in groups, everyone around the same time. Some descended to Laga, some went to the female sea, some to the male sea, some went to the west. Today we call one of these mountains Matebian,

'the mountain of spirits', because our ancestors are buried there. It is also called Umu Rafa in Makasae. Across Timor some of us say we are descended from eels, others say they are from crocodiles. It is like this. The ancestors of Boile Komu gave to us the sacred identity of eels and civet cats. These we can not eat. All of Ana Ulu (the eldest brother houses of the village of Bahu) are descended from Loilau Katilau [civet cat and eel respectively]. This is what belongs to Liurai and Resirai[3] [the ancestors who descended from the peaks of Matebian].

Emergence and division: the house of Loi Leki

As noted above, over time many of the original Waima'a-speaking houses of Baucau either departed the area or intermarried with Makasae speakers. This historical shift is also evident in the narratives associated with the house of Loi Leki, a once prominent Waima'a-speaking house in the spring grove and village of Wailili (ten kilometres south of Baucau) (see Figure 4.2). Taken as a whole these stories recount how in ancestral times people emerged out of springs ruling themselves, until later coming under the rule of Luca and finally intermarrying with incoming Makasae speakers.[4] Yet even when these 'houses' now predominantly speak Makasae, in the realm of *lulik* an earlier cultural and linguistic footprint is acknowledged as remaining in their ritual language and practices.

Figure 4.3 Boile Komu sacred house renovation, Bahu (January 2012).

92 Water pathways

This suite of stories, which were told to me by the elders of houses descended from the origin house of Loi Leki, are glossed below.

In a 'plain tale' of their ancestors, a tale largely devoid of the specificities of place or time (Fox 1980), one elder recounts how in the beginning a woman ancestor of the house of Loi Leki emerged from the earth below and turned herself into a beautiful deer. Later, a man descended from the sky and married this deer which then transformed back into a woman. As a result of such connections the descendants of the house of Loi Leki continue to worship wild animals. An elder from another branch house tells how, in the dark earth period, each night eels would emerge from a spring called Wai Lakulo and turn themselves into civet cats feasting on the fruits of the land. By morning they would return to the spring as eels. Eventually when the first people of the house of Loi Leki also emerged from the waters of Wai Lakulo, their pre-eminent ancestral spirit or *dai* was both the eel and the great snake, another manifestation of the eel. In past times, it is said these eels would emerge from the spring and change into people, with ears like civet cats, or else they might change into snakes.

Other stories told by the descendants of the origin house of Loi Leki tell about the coming of Luca. In the beginning the various origin houses of Wailili[5] (which would later come together with others under the rule of Uma Medai from Luca) comprised only one house, Loi Leki. These descendent houses are still considered the mother-father clans of the area (M: *ina-bobo*) and have ritual preeminence as custodians of Wailili's spring groves, land and waters. However, their political pre-eminence was overthrown at some point by the arrival of a man from the kingdom of Luca. Denied marriage with a local woman, this man returned to Luca to collect a bamboo length of water. On his arrival back to Wailili he threw this water on the ground by the woman's family home. This triggered an eruption of subterranean waters which swallowed the hamlet in its entirety, drowning the people and creating a new spring known as Ira Luca.[6] This man, Dukai from Luca, is characterized in ritual verse as seeking to control everything from the mountains to the sea.

The making of relationships: the story of Wai Lia

Meanwhile, in present-day Baucau, the spring complex surrounding the founding Wai Lewa spring is now known as Wai Lia (W: 'cave water') (see Map 4.1). The story of this spring complex is both connected to the story of Wai Lewa and a more 'recent' story. As we shall see, over time the narratives and ritual practices connected to this spring complex have also undergone significant change. At their core, however, these stories function to connect through sacred relationship disparate and changing agricultural communities from across the Baucau plateau and marine terrace zone. One of these communities is Wailili.

The more 'recent' story of the Wai Lia spring, the so named headspring in the complex now also known as Wai Lia,[7] gave the original impetus to my research on water in Baucau (see Preface). While it continues to be a poignant story demonstrating the connectedness of sacred houses and whole communities through spring complexes and subterranean water pathways, it has also turned out to be a far less straightforward tale than I originally thought (see Palmer 2010). But this is to jump ahead of myself. First I need to tell the story of the Wai Lia spring as told by senior ritual leaders (*lia na'in*) of the spring connected communities.

While I have been told a number of versions of this narrative, taken as a whole what they highlight is the way in which the management of this water source is intimately embedded in the most important organizing principle of Timorese social life: the marriage exchange between fertility-takers and fertility-givers (*fetosaa omane*) and older sibling–younger sibling (*maun–alin*, *bin-alin*) traditions. A man from the parent water source on the drylands of the Baucau plateau marries a woman from the Wai Lia spring grove in Baucau, creating an ongoing asymmetrical ritual and exchange relationship between the peoples from the two areas and linking together their water resources. This actual and symbolic marriage ensures a generative intergenerational exchange of gifts and counter-gifts throughout the (agricultural) ritual cycle of both communities, who in this case are linked not so much by specific houses but by specific waters. Hence in order to ensure the ongoing gift of fertility and life giving (a plentiful supply of water, crops, animals and children), ceremonies must be carried out at both water sources. The people of the four Baucau villages must provide these sacrifices (and as we will see in Chapter 6, annual tribute) to their water's *hun* (trunk, origin, source) and the custodians of the water from the plateau must also carry out their own ceremonies. Each of the versions I have heard of this story varies in relation to the genealogies and marriage arrangements of the protagonists as well as the time scale involved (this is discussed to some extent below and in Chapter 6). What follows is a summary of one account told to me early in my research by Major Ko'o Raku, the *lia na'in* of Bahu village:

> Wai Lia spring has its *fuu* [M: trunk, origin, source] on the Baucau plateau near a place called Darasula [see Map 4.1]. In the beginning there were two brothers there tending buffalo. One day they were hungry so they decided to dig, cook and eat some yams. But then they were very thirsty. While they were sitting down wondering where they could get water they remembered the day when their dogs went missing and came back all wet. They wanted to know where the dogs got this water. So they made a plan. They cooked some more yams to give to the dogs, but before they gave them to the dogs they made a bamboo collar – tied with string – for one of the dogs' necks. Inside the hollow piece of bamboo they placed ash from the fire and made a small hole in the bamboo. Then they gave the yams to the dogs to eat. The dogs were thirsty and headed off. In about one hour they returned all wet. Now the brothers had a way to find the water. They followed the ash that had trickled from the bamboo collar until they came to a big cave with water inside. They both went down into the cave and drew water, which they carried back out of the cave to drink.

94   *Water pathways*

After this they were still thirsty so the younger brother then went down again to fetch water. Inside the cave there were two places to draw water. On one side was a big cave; on the other side was a small cave. From the large opening the younger brother could hear the water flowing very loudly. He went in to have a look at what was making such a loud noise and suddenly he fell down into the water. He was under water a long time [in other versions this is specified to be a period of seven days and seven nights during which time he encountered two eels, one white and one black/yellow. Both offered to help him find his way out. He chose to go with the white eel] and eventually he emerged in the still water of another cave – Wai Lia in Baucau [if he had chosen the black eel he would have followed the waters underground path to the sea (the 'other world') and never re-emerged in this world again].[8] During his long journey he had eaten his clothes [the white eel had warned him that if he had eaten the fruits of the gardens he encountered under the water he would never have emerged from that world]. Arriving in the spring waters of Wai Lia he was now naked, and so he decided to stay there beneath the surface and wait.

Then to the spring came two women, the daughters of a woman from Bahu. The older sister entered the cave and drew water from a very clean source. The man from Darasula was crouching beneath the surface and saw this woman drawing water but decided not to do anything. Then the younger sister came in to draw water, but when she exited the spring she saw that in contrast to her older sister the water she had drawn was dirty. She drew water two more times and each time it was dirty. 'What is making my water dirty?', she thought with frustration. She looked down into the water and beneath it she made out a naked man. The naked man explained: 'I am from the savanna; I was tending buffalo there when I was thirsty and went down into a cave to draw water. Then I somehow ended up here.' 'But what do you want?' asked the women. 'Could you go and ask your brothers to bring me some clothes to wear?' asked the man. So the women went to ask their older brothers to take the man a *tais* [woven cloth] to wear. They did this and he got dressed in the water.

When he came out of the water the two sisters and their older brother who had brought the *tais* were still there. It was decided that the younger sister would now marry this man. So they got married and lived together at the woman's home and they had a child together. And then the woman said, 'Now it is time for us to go to try to find your place so I can see where you come from. Do you still have family there, I wonder?' So they set off to look for this place, telling his story along the way and asking people if they knew of his brother and if he was still alive. Eventually they found some of his possessions hanging in a tree: his carry basket, cotton spinning stick, spear and digging stick. 'This is the place where I was tending buffalo the day I became lost', he said. He got down his possessions and they kept walking.

They kept asking people they met about his brother and finally one man responded: 'Yes, it is me, I am your older brother. I thought you were lost forever.' The two hugged each other and cried together. The older brother explained that now as the younger brother had returned to his *fuu* [M: trunk/origin], they would now make a sacred house here at this place by the cave with water. The house was needed so that offerings could be made to the water and the story would not be forgotten. 'When the time comes for us to make offerings to give thanks to the water which we both found together, the people from Bahu, Caibada, Buruma, Tirilolo [the four villages in Baucau that receive water from Wai Lia] must also come together to kill goats, buffalo, pigs and chickens and then also bring some of them here for us to make our offerings at Darasula.' 'You must also make a sacred house at Wai Lia', said the older brother. This was so the four villages could also make the same collective offerings at Wai Lia spring in Baucau.

After this they made their sacred houses in both places so they could remember this story and give thanks to the water. Each year the local population would carry out ceremonies so that the two springs would never be dry. This meant that they could make fields and plant rice and have plenty to eat.

However, eventually the people from the four villages sharing the water from Wai Lia forgot to make their sacrifices. The water stopped flowing and many animals, crops and trees began to die. The people from Baucau went to the custodians of the water on the plateau and asked, 'Why is our water dry?' The custodians of the water explained the reason: 'You have not been making the sacrifices and you need to start doing this again.' So the people in Baucau started to make the required sacrifices again and after this their rice could grow again.[9]

This story is emblematic of the ways in which place and place-making in the region is both 'aquatically conceived' (cf. Jennaway 2008: 26) and aquatically enabled. It also shows how caves, springs and their water flows constitute a domain of ritual and spiritual ecology which continue to make and connect water-sharing communities. The broader Wai Lia complex in Baucau town is in fact made up of seven inter-related springs which includes the origin spring of Wai Lewa. The water from this complex feeds the irrigation channels running east and west to rice fields of the villages of Bahu, Caibada, Tirilolo and Buruma. The basis for the sharing of this irrigation water is the fact that these villages are in a sibling relationship, as established in the (wildly divergent) stories of the three brothers Wono Loi, Tai Loi and Leki Loi. As such the specific custodians of the water and the ritual leaders of these villages (particularly Bahu, Caibada and Tirilolo) are expected to carry out the ceremonies required to properly manage the springs in the complex. These sacrificial processes – known in Tetum as '*fo han*' (feeding) – involve small-scale annual sacrifices to ensure that the irrigation waters travel down the man-made water channels to the fields below. They also involve the larger collective seven-yearly ceremonies ('*tinan hitu dala ida*') which involve all the water-sharing communities over a period of seven days. In both ceremonies, ritual experts will call forth and commune with the sacred eels that inhabited the springs. While the seven-yearly ceremonies have been highly irregular in recent times (this is discussed in Chapters 6 and 7), they are considered critical community events involving much communal singing and dancing (*tebe*).

The cave on the plateau which is said to feed the flow of water to Wai Lia in Baucau is known in Makasae as Wai Lia Bere ('the great Wai Lia') and similarly in Waima'a as Wai Lia Oli ('the great Wai Lia'). This cave is also understood to be a gateway or 'door' for water flowing to other springs in the region, and as such is considered a critical source for springs across the marine terrace zone (see Map 4.2 for a cartographic representation of this knowledge). Underwater springs in the ocean are believed to be the final exit points for much of this subterranean water.

Custodians of the savanna: Wai Lia Bere and Wai Lia Mata

The ritual custodians of the Wai Lia Bere spring on the Baucau plateau are the Makasae-speaking house of Ledatame Ikun (see Figure 4.4). They are a plains people, also characterized by Major Ko'o Raku as being intermarried with Butu migrations from the peaks of Matebian (see Chapter 3). During water increase rituals carried out at Wai Lia Bere the sacrifices of larger animals (buffalo, goats) will take place outside the entrance to Wai Lia Bere, while the sacrifice of additional smaller animals takes place at Wai Lia Bere's *wii*, or wife, a cave

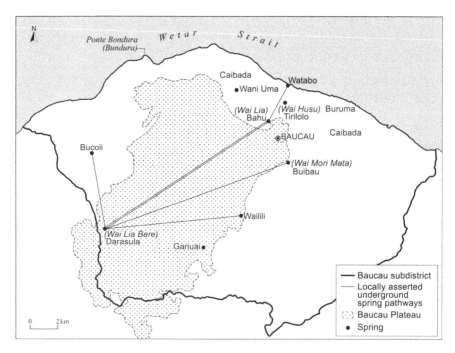

Map 4.2 Locally asserted underground flows from Wai Lia Bere (copyright Chandra Jayasuriya).

Water pathways 97

Figure 4.4 Water custodian of Wai Lia Bere (Wono Loi, left) at Ledatame Ikun sacred house, Darasula with Major Ko'o Raku (right).

water source known as Wai Lia Mata (M: *mata* = small) which is located two kilometres away. While the main ceremony and sacrifice is carried out above ground (see Figure 4.5), a portion of the cooked meat and rice will be placed on plates fashioned out of bamboo lengths and carried by ritual leaders down into the water cave where it is left on a ledge as an offering to the *ira gauhaa* ('custodians of the water') who are manifest as pythons (as discussed in Chapter 2).

98 *Water pathways*

Figure 4.5 'Closing the door' (*taka odamatan*) ceremony at Wai Lia Bere.

As a past and present focal point for the coastal region water increase ceremonies, the Wai Lia Bere and Wai Lia Mata cave springs are critical to the organization of a regional water ritual ecology. Yet the sub-village of Darasula (M: 'the edge of the savanna') in general and Darasula's Ledatame Ikun sacred house have only a few hectares of wet rice cultivation themselves. Irrigated by a small seasonal spring called Wai Lobi these rice fields are known as the 'plate' (M: *ra'u*) which feeds the ancestors of the Ledatame sacred house. With their water predominantly subterranean, the Waima'a and Makasae speaking peoples of Darasula are largely dryland agriculturalists of rice, peanuts and other vegetables. In addition to tending candlenut plantations they also graze many livestock across their unfenced lands. According to the Ledatame ritual custodians of the water, one of the conditions of the sacred oath between the Ledatame ancestors and those from other communities connected through 'downstream' subterranean water flows, is that these latter communities can only farm the very edges of escarpment zone and the marine terraces below it. As the underground water from the plateau descends to feed and make fertile the lush spring groves of the marine terrace zone, this sacred agreement ensures that the coastal populations refrain from grazing their livestock on the savanna proper (see Figure 4.6). The savanna is the domain of dryland agriculturalists of Darasula and surrounds.

Figure 4.6 Buffalo and herder, Baucau plateau (with central ranges in background).

Complicating things: Wai Lili-Wai Wa and Wai Husu-Wai Lewa

Yet the story of this ritual ecological relationship forged through water gets more complicated the further one probes into these regional narratives. While I was used to hearing what I imagined were disparate or contested accounts of people's relations to particular springs, it later became clear to me that what they also reflected were changes through time and socio-historical circumstance. Hence a story which is widely asserted to precede the current narrative of Wai Lia, is based on the relationship between two rice-growing communities and also contains similar assertions of an underground journey. These communities in this story are those connected to the spring groves of Wai Husu-Wai Lewa (present-day Baucau) and Wai Lili-Wai Wa (present-day Wailili) (see Map 4.1).

Prior to the version of the Wai Lia narrative relayed above, the ritual centres of Baucau and Wailili had also been linked together in a ritually binding fertility-giver and fertility-taker relationship. The catalyst for this relationship was the accidental fall of a son of Wailili (from the house of Loi Leki) into a cave containing water. Following this he travelled through the underground waters, emerging, as we have seen above, at Wai Lia spring. In this account the connections forged by this event extended into networks much denser than

100 Water pathways

simply the Ledatame Ikun sacred house in Darasula. Ledatame is in fact a branch house of Loi Leki and this earlier story relates to a time when the origin house of Loi Leki was still at the peak of its ritual and political power in the village of Wailili.

In this story, after the marriage of a son of Wailili to a daughter of Bahu, other daughters of Bahu also began marrying into the houses of Wailili. The two spring complexes and ritual centres known respectively as Wai Lili-Wai Wa and Wai Husu-Wai Lewa became focal points for collective post-harvest rice rituals with each centre expected to actively participate in the rituals of the other. Over time, as these relations entrenched themselves, the two ritual centres held a ceremony in which they exchanged the respective ancestral names of their spring complexes.[10] This exchange gave each spring community the right to invoke each other's ancestral names to harness their power and protective blessing in community rituals. This relationship then transformed into a shared approach to the regional ritual regulation of land and resources and the two centres began gathering at each other's spring complexes for major seven-yearly ceremonies. At these ceremonies it was the Baucau villages' responsibility as fertility-givers to contribute rice and pigs. Buffalo and goats were expected as the contribution from the fertility-takers of Wailili. The purpose of these ceremonies was to cement the ties between the centres, maintain peaceful relations, and respect each other's boundaries, fields, produce and livestock. Today this type of ritual relationship is glossed as *tara bandu* (see Chapter 7).

Yet it was not long after their ancestor had travelled through the water to Wai Lia, that a now unknown (or undisclosed) dispute divided the house of Loi Leki, a division that continues to this day. While subsequently the political power of the various houses of Loi Leki became subservient to the dominion of Luca, in later periods these houses divided again between northern and southern zones known as Fatumaka Leten and Fatumaka Kraik (this was also to become the key colonial administrative division of the former Wailili kingdom in the nineteenth century). By this period, the houses of Wailili had also become places for the in-migration of Makasae speaking houses from the Matebian foothills. Bringing with them 'knowledge of fire' and stores of gold, from these early beginnings the Makasae language spread throughout the region of Fatumaka.[11] By the twentieth century, as Portuguese colonial control increased and the Catholic Church installed a grotto by the spring of Wai Lakulo, Wailili had diminished as a centre of ritual power. By the end of the Second World War Japanese occupation, the ritual relationship between the rice-growing villages of Baucau and Wailili was in disrepair.

Yet throughout this time the number of branch houses derivative of Loi Leki had grown and they had spread throughout the region to establish sacred houses elsewhere, including on the savanna of the Baucau plateau. Sometime during this migration from the spring groves of Wailili to the drylands of the plateau, the most recent version of the connection between Wai Husu-Wai Lewa and Wai Lili-Wai Wa emerged: this time configured through the connection between Wai Lia and Wai Lia Bere (see Chapter 6 for more).[12]

While the stories associated with the Wai Lia spring in Baucau differ slightly, all feature underground water channels which carry with them men from the plateau who are received by and marry women from the coastal zone. The purpose of all these stories is to make connections and shared governance relations between people. In yet another story relating to this period, Augosto do Rosario Xavier (Anu Watu), an elder from the Loi Leki branch house of Neligia in Wailili, tells the story of the near demise of the house of Loi Leki. At an unspecified time when all that remained of the house was one childless couple,[13] a man suddenly descended (from where is not specified) to live with them and later the elderly woman produced a child. When this child reached adulthood it was he who discovered, fell into and travelled through the underground water to Wai Lia. One of his names was Belu Mau ('my friend Mau', *mau* can also refer to brother) meaning to makes friends with people. This man, asserts Major Ko'o Raku, was a descendant of the (in-marrying) Butu generation.

In this connection between Wai Lili-Wai Wa and Wai Husu-Wai Lewa, the latter are represented by the settlements of Bahu, Tirilolo, Caibada, Buruma, and by some accounts Bucoli (see Map 4.1). In these stories of the relation between the two regions, the house of Boile Komu is said by Major Ko'o Raku to be one of the parent houses of Wai Lewa.[14] The other, as we will see below, was a house connected to the ancestors of the people of Tirilolo, a group who now live largely in Caisidu.

The exodus: the movement to Caisidu

As Makasae-speaking clans became increasingly widespread in the eastern part of the marine terrace zone, around central Baucau a new wave of population shifts began to occur. In Bahu there is a story of a snake entering the village in the guise of a pale-skinned man (we can assume that this is a son of Luca). He impregnates a woman who produces two sons. When these human offspring find out that their father is a snake they are incensed and the father offers his own reptilian body to them. In death his body turns to gold.[15] This gold then gives the sons the powerful basis from which to marry and extend their local rule. However, later the people from the powerful Makasae-speaking houses of Afagua near Wailili steal this golden sacra from the people of Bahu. These incursions lead to a war at the frontier of the two ritual centres, during which time both Boile Komu and Luca are defeated.

Around five generations ago, it is said that many of the original Waima'a-speaking peoples of Teulale in Tirilolo were compelled to move out of the area as a result of the increasing presence of Makasae newcomers. While these Waima'a houses moved westward as far as Vemasse, they finally returned to settle in the barren plateau of Caisidu near Bundura [Ponte Bondura] (see Map 4.1). In Caisidu they were welcomed by the origin clans of Wai Hau and Wai Luo (the mother-father clans of the area or *woi-ba'a* in Waima'a). As the ritual custodians of the land and resources, these mother-father clans carried out rituals and initiated the newcomers into the

102 *Water pathways*

traditions of the area. Even in the independence era, the people of Caisidu assert that they defer to Wai Hau and Wai Luo in all rituals or dispute mediation that concerns the land, water or other natural resources in the area (but see also conclusion). Meanwhile the exiled population of Teulale continue five generations on to return each year from Caisidu to Baucau to carry out ancestral rituals at the spring of Wai Lewa. They also descend to another spring, Wai Husu, to carry out other rituals to feed the spirits of that spring in Teulale (see Map 4.1). The story of this exodus and their ongoing connection to Wai Husu was told to me by one of the area's *lia na'in* Joao Graciano Simoes (Tetu Noko):

> The house of Caime went from Teulale to live at Caisidu. The younger brother house of Loime in Tirilolo stayed in Baucau [and intermarried with the Makasae]. First they travelled west to Vemasse, Lenau, Wai Wono and then back to Ossu-Wa [near Caisidu]. The owners of the land (Wai Luo and Wai Hau) received them and said you can not return to Teulale you must stay here. They had a ceremony and killed many animals. They were told that they must respect the sacred water, rocks, forest, potatoes, yams and trees. We respect their custodial jurisdiction over these things until this day. They are the mother-father clans. Our main house is Kotalale.
>
> Water is scarce here. We must travel to the springs of Wai Haulale, Tuo Ho'o Oli, Aubaca, Caibada and Wani Uma. When we fetch water we use bamboo and measure its use carefully. This is a dry land.
>
> Where we came from in Teulale there is a spring called Wai Husu [whose spirit guardian originates from Luca]. This does not belong to the Makasae, although they live in that area now. At this spring we always offer pigs to the water spirit from Luca. The people from Kotalale, Caisidu return each year to carry out these ritual offerings at Wai Husu. The Makasae people living there now can not carry out these rituals. We carry out the ritual feeding. When it is time for the ceremonies we will always take pigs for the sacrifices.

Meanwhile atop the barren drylands of Caisidu there was once a spring. Known today as Wai Taka (W: closed water) a decision was made (presumably by Wai Hau and Wai Luo) at some point to close it over and ensure that outsiders would not be tempted to settle there.

Discussion

Similar to the story of the ongoing ritual relations at Wai Husu, movements of Waima'a speakers to the west of Baucau mean that the original ritual custodians of many springs across the marine terrace zone are now absent from the area.[16] As we have seen in Wailili the disruptions to its land and waters through the twentieth century has meant that ritual activity at this once prominent centre of power has now retreated back into the darkness and the guiding fertility-giver,

Water pathways 103

fertility-taker relationship between Wai Lili-Wai Wa and Wai Husu-Wai Lewa is now something of the past. Yet it is also clear that in its place other manifestations of these intra-community relationships have emerged (this is discussed further in Chapters 6 and 7). History in this sense is valued primarily for what it can tell us about 'the making, living out, and unmaking of kinship' (Gow 2001: 290).

As incoming migration patterns resulted in origin communities spreading out from lush coastal spring groves to the dry savanna, the changing divisions of labour and resources resulted in the need to regulate a new suite of socio-ecological relationships. New ancestral connections emerged to regulate the waters teaming under the dry lands of the Baucau plateau (see Map 1.2). This resulting ritual ecology of water characterized in the most recent Wai Lia story encouraged both socio-ecological co-operation and co-reliance between what were emerging as otherwise separate 'agricultural' communities (cf. Peterson 1978). They signified a new era of ritual exchange relationship between dryland agricultural communities and escarpment edge and coastal wet rice cultivators (cf. Traube 1986; this is further discussed in Chapter 6). These emerging relations (and conflicts) between dry and wet land communities across the ecotone – a transitional or threshold socio-ecological zone – are encoded in these dynamic watery pathways of connection. As Chen argues, '[m]apping watery place is best practised by taking multiple perspectives into account' (Chen 2013: 293) and realizing that 'we practise and imagine the past and future only through continuing iterations' (Chen 2013: 287).

In the past it is claimed that the whole of the region from Matebian to the Baucau coast was the domain of the Waima'a, who received waves of newcomers over time and continue to do so. As we will see in the next chapter, when these newcomers integrated themselves into and respected the local moral economy of fertility-givers and fertility-takers they were generally embraced by the extant community. Those who did not show this respect or who lapsed in their commitment to these sacred arrangements were eventually repelled. In the accounts of these processes, springs are central agents of change and enablement. Even the power of warriors was sourced from these sacred springs, creating debts which must be repaid across the generations.

Notes

1 Wai Ma'a means empty of water.
2 In Correia (1935) Baucau stories are told by Belmiro Belo from Tirilolo. Spillett (1999) was also told his story by a Belo from Tirilolo.
3 Which can be translated in Eastern Tetum as 'bigger than the land' and 'cannot fit into the land'.
4 As discussed in Chapter 3, Waima'a is a part of the Kawamina language group said by Hull (1998) to be both potentially alloglot and substantially influenced by the eleventh-century Fabronic wave which emerged from the Celebes/Sulawesi. See Map 3.1.

104   Water pathways

5 Neligia, Ledatame, Baduno, Duruwa.
6 I know of at least four other similar stories from localities in the central eastern region (in Venilale, Cairiri, Wailili and Lacluta). The protagonist in such stories is always a son of Luca or connected to it through one of its sub-kingdoms, Vemasse and Vessoru (characterized as the buffalo horns of the Kingdom of Luca). In connection to Vemasse see the story of We Tasi in Lacluta (Soares 1971).
7 Once known as Wai Husu-Wai Lewa (see below).
8 White is synonymous across Timor with the sun (and all it represents), yellow and black with its opposite. Eels, or glass eels, are translucent when they first migrate inland from the sea to inhabit freshwater. In freshwater they pigment turning yellow or brown before sexually maturing (signified by a silver belly and darker head and body) and returning to spawn (and die) in the sea (Lecomte-Finiger 2003).
9 This is an amended version of a narrative that was previously published in Palmer (2011).
10 The ancestral names of the eels and civet cats connected to both spring complexes were called out in ritual verse at these ceremonies, one of these names, that relating to the civet cat ancestor, is the same for both springs.
11 In some accounts the Makasae-speaking clans of the northern Matebian foothills were invited into the region by Waima'a speakers to drive back the expansionary power of Luca and force their retreat from the north coastal zone.
12 However, the descendants of the Waima'a-speaking area of the Wai Daba spring in Berecoli assert that these first underground travels from the plateau to Wai Lia involved a man from the hamlet of Cairiri on the edge of the savanna just south of Gariuai (which was also once a part of Wai Lili) (see Map 4.1). This hamlet (which in some accounts is a branch house of Loi Leki) had a long association with Luca (its *rota* (sceptre) and water were received from there). The man who entered the cave system and emerged in Wai Lia is said to have been a son of a marriage exchange relationship between Wai Daba and Cairiri. According to this version of events, Wai Lia has a direct connection to Wai Daba and these ancestral travels created marriage exchange relationships between them and the Baucau villages.
13 While it is not specified by the teller, this near demise of the Loi Leki house may have occurred in the wake of the arrival of rulers from elsewhere, possibly Luca.
14 The house of Lakudarabaha is another parent house of the Wai Husu-Wai Lewa complex. In the accounts from the spring of Wai Mori Bere in Buibau, the various Makasae custodian houses of the spring recognize that these waters as the domain of Lakudarabaha (see Map 4.1). In the account of the house of Alawa'a they, and their sibling house Lalabu, were requested by Lakudarabaha to settle at the spring many generations ago and establish a '*guarda*' or staging post for Makasae speakers visiting Baucau from Matebian. In the account of the neighbouring Makasae-speaking Leb-alaku Fofa house their ancestors came to the area from Utabailema and married with a woman from the house of Lakudarabaha establishing an ongoing fertility-giver and fertility-taker relationship. While the houses of this spring community now have their own ritual relationship with Wai Lia Bere (and the house of Ledatame Ikun) the pathway to this relationship was through Lakudarabaha, the true 'owners' of the spring. In 2010 a large collective ceremony was held at the Wai Mori Bere spring to re-establish the relationship with Wai Lia Bere and ensure that the post-independence flow of water would be strong.
15 As noted in Chapter 3 a similar golden reptilian patrimony is found in the origin story from Cabalaki and Matebian recounted by Almeida (1976: 346–347) and in a story about the founding of the kingdom of Vemasse (see dos Santos 1967).
16 Wai Kinari in Caibada (Makasae) is another spring where a Makasae-speaking house is the present-day custodian (see Map 4.1, Figure 2.3). At certain ritual events the original Waima'a custodians of the spring who now live in Caisidu will be asked to return and carry out the ritual prayers.

References

Almeida, de A. (1976) 'Da Origem Lendária e Mitológica dos Povos do Timor Português', *Memórias da Academia des Ciências de Lisboa* 19: 575–607.

Chen, C. (2013) 'Mapping Waters: Thinking with Watery Places', in C. Chen, J. MacLeod and A. Neimanis (eds) *Thinking with Water*, Montreal: McGill-Queen's University Press, 274–290.

Correia, A. (1935) *Gentio de Timor*, Lisbon: Agência-Geral das Colónias.

dos Santos, E. (1967) *Kanoik: Mitos e Lendas de Timor*, Lisboa: Ultramar.

Fox, J. (1980) 'Retelling the Past: The Communicative Structure of a Rotinese Historical Narrative', *Anthropology* 3(1): 56–66.

Gow, P. (2001) *An Amazonian Myth and its History*, Oxford: Oxford University Press.

Hull, G. (1998) 'The Basic Lexical Affinities of Timor's Austronesian Languages: A Preliminary Investigation', *Studies in Languages and Cultures of East Timor* 1: 97–174.

Jennaway, M. (2008) 'Aquatic Identities, Fluid Economies: Water Affinities and Authenticating Narratives of Belonging in East Timorese Myth and Ritual', *Oceania* 78: 17–29.

Lecomte-Finiger, R. (2003) 'The Genus Anguilla Schrank, 1798: Current State of Knowledge and Questions', *Reviews in Fish Biology and Fisheries* 13: 265–279.

Palmer, L. (2010) 'Enlivening Development: Water Management in the Post Conflict Baucau City, Timor-Leste', *Singapore Journal of Tropical Geography* 31: 357–370.

Palmer, L. (2011) 'Water Relations', in A. McWilliam and E. Traube (eds) *Land and Life in Timor-Leste: Ethnographic Essays*, Canberra: ANU E-Press, 141–162.

Peterson, J. (1978) 'Ecotones and Exchange in Northern Luzon', in K. Hutterer (ed.) *Economic Exchange and Social Interaction in Southeast Asia: Perspectives from Prehistory, History and Ethnography*, Michigan Papers on South and Southeast Asia No. 13, The University of Michigan, 55–72.

Soares, A.V.M. (1971) 'Lenda do água do mar em Lacluta', A *Provincia de Timor: Boletime de Noticias*, 18.

Spillett, P. (1999) 'The Pre-Colonial History of the Island of Timor Together with Some Notes on the Makassan Influence in the Island', unpublished manuscript, Museum and Art Gallery of the Northern Territory, Darwin.

Traube, E. (1986) *Cosmology and Social Life: Ritual Exchange among the Mambai of East Timor*, Chicago: University of Chicago Press.

5 Challenging the moral order
Water, kinship and war

In Chapter 3, we encountered oral histories of the region relating to trade and kinship exchanges with islands to the north of Baucau. According to one of the tellers, Major Ko'o Raku, the colonial period on the north-east coast began with the arrival of the Portuguese, followed by a period of Dutch rule and finally the return of the Portuguese. Augmenting the inter-regional marriage exchanges and trade of gold discs, coral necklaces and swords,[1] the period of Dutch rule was characterized by the trade of ceramic plates for sandalwood and beeswax.[2]

According to Major Ko'o Raku, in contrast to the first two colonial periods, the later return of the Portuguese signalled the end of marriage exchanges between the people of Baucau and their 'outside' interlocutors from across the sea. With the threat of Portuguese military intervention and other colonial measures now in place, the swords, coral necklaces and marriage partners eventually stopped coming (cf. Correia 1944: 299–301; Belo 2011: 133–134). While the Portuguese were also intent on securing sandalwood,[3] this time they introduced forced labour, the payment of taxes, and the routine whipping and beating of people. They also established a formal education system. While some Timorese were educated to middle primary school, a minority, mainly the sons of the local rulers, were educated to high school level. Towards the end of the Portuguese rule (1974), a critical event took place. Major Ko'o Raku reports that the Portuguese sent seven Timorese sons overseas to study. On their return these men[4] formed political parties[5] and all of them became key political figures during the Indonesian occupation. The three largest of these parties, Fretilin,[6] UDT[7] and Apodeti,[8] distributed party affiliation cards amongst the population. According to Major Ko'o Raku these new party political identities created a kind of division amongst the rural people that they had never experienced before. It divided families and challenged the pre-eminence of house-based alliances based on marriage exchange relations.

As we have seen in the previous two chapters, oral histories such as this continually foreground and prioritize continuities and changes in kinship relations and alliances between houses. It is unsurprising then, as we will see below, that threats to this established moral order of exchange (first by the Catholic Church and later by the colonial administration) were the catalyst for many of key momentous events recorded in local histories. It is important to stress, however, that the anti-colonial and anti-Christian sentiment in these stories is not a result of the presence of outsiders per se, but of the culturally disrespectful excesses exhibited by them. In all of these stories, water and the associated hydrosocial cycle features as a part of local resistance. It is a key enabler of both war and peacemaking. As such, this chapter and those that follow show how distinctive regional narrative genres around the agency of water are adapted and developed across the colonial interface and how these narratives and associated practices continue to recalibrate relations into the present.

In this chapter I chart the interconnections between the colonial-era stories of three Timorese interlocuters: the 'magician' Joao Lere of Wani Uma, the resistance hero Dom Boa Ventura of Manufahi and the colonial collaborator Nai Leki of Bahu. Within this historical period (circa 1512–1940s) we also chart the decline in the power of the great Kingdom of Luca and the subsequent emergence during this period of a new regional geopolitics centred on north coastal ports (see Map 5.1).

It must to be noted from the outset that ritual and political leaders of communities across the Baucau Viqueque zone date the Portuguese arrival in their communities to 1512 and that this period is frequently associated with the arrival of the Portuguese priest Padre Antonio Tavares.[9] While both this 'discovery' date and the historical figure of Tavares are key elements of the Western historiography of Timor (see Gunn 1999; Hägerdal 2012), there is much conjecture in particular about where this priest actually travelled during his sixteenth-century sojourn from Solor to Timor (see McWilliam 2007: 225). This chapter continues the task of (re)telling these and other stories outside of the confines of Western historiography, drawing from local accounts and lifeworlds further insights into these events and the high drama of local political relations.

In different ways all of the protagonists found in the stories below display one or more of the familiar tropes of characters found in 'true tales' across the region: the ignorant ancestor; the too smart prophet; the jilted husband and the trickster leader. Yet collectively these characters share another important characteristic. They are all themselves either 'outsiders' or in close contact with outsiders, and for this reason they are themselves prone to be involved in transgressions which challenge the moral order. While in the independence era the figure of the anti-Christian and anti-colonial prophet Joao Lere is elevated as a champion of Timor's struggle against outside domination, from the early twentieth-century story in which he figures it is clear that he was, at the time, also considered by his own people to be dangerously powerful, smart, proud and, most troubling of all, addicted to radical change. His wildness had to be reined in and, for this to happen, he needed to be sacrificed. In contrast, the twentieth-century ruler of Bahu, a man known as Nai Leki, was also powerful, smart and addicted to change. His trajectory though was different. He survived the encounter by building alliances with foreigners (although largely through cultivating an ability to deceive them).

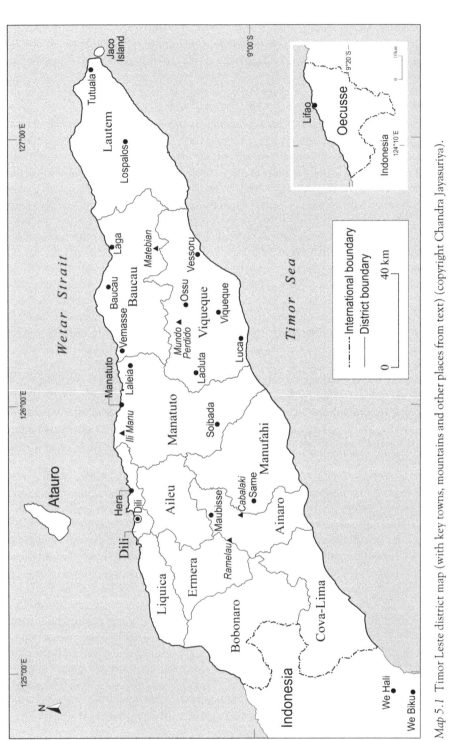

Map 5.1 Timor Leste district map (with key towns, mountains and other places from text) (copyright Chandra Jayasuriya).

The excesses of Joao Lere

While glossed as a magician, Joao Lere was a famous ritual specialist and local ruler (*liurai*) of Wani Uma who railed against the Catholic Church and the Portuguese administration. His actions led many to seek his downfall, but try as they may his death was only possible when he surrendered his own body to the authorities and gave them specific instructions detailing how to kill him. In the 1930s Baucau's colonial administrator, Armando Pinto Correia (1935: 108–110, 132–136), transcribed a story of Joao Lere. While the details of Joao Lere's socio-political connections and life are only partially recorded in this version, it is clear that this is a regionally significant story. One clue to this is Joao Lere's connection to the coastal cave and subterranean water source of Kai Hunu near Bundura [Ponte Bondura]. Associated in Correia's account with the most sacred house in the Baucau region, Oca Ba'i (W: 'sacred cave') in Baha-Kai-Lale (W: 'the hamlet in the forest'), this cave was the site of a regionally important pilgrimage involving the collection of holy water and a rainmaking ceremony (discussed further in the Conclusion). In Correia's account (in which all the local language terms are in Makasae) all of the Baucau sub-district savanna and wet rice growing communities are said to have participated in the pilgrimage.

Meanwhile, in the version of this story told to me in 2012 by the cave custodians and senior ritual and political leaders of Wani Uma, both the socio-political genealogy of Joao Lere and the extent of the community participation in this pilgrimage of holy water stretches to include people from the far east of Timor and the southern kingdom of Luca. The people of Wani Uma state that in the pre-colonial era the clans of Bundura region had jurisdiction to the west as far as Fatu Ahi (the hills above Dili) and to the east as far as Los Palos, as well as to the islands beyond. This, they say, was the time of the dark earth, when the people worshipped rocks and water. As we have seen in Chapter 3, the first peoples of the Baucau coastal zone intermarried with other arrivals to the region who brought with them the knowledge of gold, metalwork, irrigated rice production as well as a system of respectful exchange.

Throughout much of the colonial period, Luca was buoyed in its status as the ritual centre of the region through its alliances with the Portuguese.[10] Yet it later had its own power usurped by the rising influence of the trading ports and north coastal kingdoms of Vemasse and Laleia/Manatuto. The story of Joao Lere traces this period of colonial encounter, missionary activity, trade and rule in the east. Joao Lere is characterized by his own people as *matenek liu* (too clever/wise/powerful) with extraordinary powers, including the capacity to make the sea waters rise up and the earth crumble into the sea. At one point in his story, he even attempts to split the island in two, leaving the area from Bundura to the far east under his control and the other half of the island to the Portuguese occupiers.

Sometimes referred to today as the anti-colonial resistance hero of the east, Joao Lere has a complicated socio-political genealogy. His father was from (or came via) Luca. His mother, who in some accounts appeared from the sky, is also

110 *Challenging the moral order*

Figure 5.1 Re-construction of Wani Uma *umo oe* (W: ruling political house), October 2013.

said to be a female ancestor of the celebrated 1970s nationalist hero Vicente Reis (Sahe). In this and other accounts we can infer the reason for Sahe's own *matenek* (powerful knowledge) was a direct result of his connection to Joao Lere, whose own writings (recorded first on the walls of caves and later in a book) he is said to have obtained from its keeping place in a Wani Uma sacred house in the 1970s (see Figure 5.1). Like Joao Lere, Sahe's mission was to free the Timorese from imposed foreign rule. After Sahe's death in the early Indonesian resistance era, the independence hero of modern Timor, Xanana Gusmão, is said to have accumulated powerful knowledge through his access to a secret case of Sahe's books which he read during the long years of his resistance and study in the Timorese jungle (Niner 2009: 69). While all three of these men, Joao Lere, Sahe and Xanana, received a formal education from Catholic missions, in the case of Joao Lere and Sahe these schools were located across the sea (in Flores and India for Lere and in Portugal for Sahe). It was to be Xanana, educated as well in the jungles of Timor, that ultimately triumphed in repelling the foreigners.[11] Below is a summary of the version of Joao Lere's story told to me by the Wani Uma ritual leader and 'historian of the dark earth', Moses Nai Usu:

> His father came we think from Luca. His name was No Mori. He was in Luca hunting birds with a blowpipe. When his golden arrow pierced a bird

Challenging the moral order 111

it flew off with the arrow to the peaks of Mundo Perdido. He followed it to there but it flew down to Leki Loi Watu [on the Baucau plateau]. Again he followed it, but it flew off through Hare Ite before arriving in Baha Kai Lale [between Caisidu and Wani Uma]. He followed it once more and in Baha Kai Lale he encountered a woman called Maria weaving cloth (*tais*).

No Mori asked the woman if she had seen a bird pierced by an arrow. At first she said she had not, but No Mori said to her '*Noi*, you must lie to me. If you tell me the truth, I will only keep the arrow, you can keep the bird to cook.' Then Maria admitted she had found a bird pierced by a golden arrow and had put it in the house.

She fetched the bird and arrow and No Mori gave her the bird to cook. Later No Mori asked Maria to go inside to fetch him a drink of water. Then No Mori secretly placed a cigarette inside the bamboo hollow of Maria's cotton reel.

After he had drunk the water, No Mori announced he must leave. He returned back through Leki Loi Watu [W: 'Leki Loi's rock'] where he looked back and saw that Maria had begun to weave the cloth again. When she did this the cigarette fell from the bamboo hollow.

She said, 'I have found something sweet smelling'. She decided to light it with her fire flint and as she did so lightening suddenly struck in the sky.

A week or so after this she realized she was pregnant. All we know was she smoked a cigarette and became pregnant.

When the baby was born she gave him the name Kai Ho'o Wau Bubo Leki Loi Wau Bubo. The child was a huge eater. When he was born he cried and straight away ate ten pots of rice. Whenever he cried, he would eat ten pots of rice. It was always like this.

Eventually his [maternal] grandfather Kai Dau Naha Dau also assisted Maria in the task of feeding the child, but the food supplies were still not enough.

He grew up eating all of his uncle's food, yet his real father took no responsibility for the child. When he was grown he said to his uncles, 'In gratitude to all my family, now I must feed you'. He began to cook and placed a chicken in a pot and later divided this into many pots. But when it was placed in the other pots the chicken meat transformed into the meat of pigs, goats and buffalo.

After this he went off to school in Larantuka [Flores]. In the morning he would leave the house for school and return in the afternoon. He would travel to school by crocodile. When he had finished his schooling, he and his uncles went to the fields to make swidden and fencing.

At this point his mother said to his uncles that they must kill him because he eats too much. His uncles agreed and tried to kill him by felling trees on him but he simply carried them off on his shoulders.

When they returned home that afternoon his mother asked 'Did you kill that child?' His uncles replied 'we killed him but he didn't die'. Next they tried to kill him with a large rock but the child, whose magic was so strong,

112 *Challenging the moral order*

simply caught the rock. The child who was also known as Degu Tina (W: 'dark cooking') was unable to be killed. Because of this they decided to send him off to school again, this time to India. He set off to school (travelling by eagle to India) but was quickly home again already knowing everything. This child was also known as Joao Lere.

By the time Joao Lere had reached the peak of his revealed and acquired knowledge and power (*matenek*), the Portuguese had arrived in Timor. They and Joao Lere were set to oppose each other. The remainder of this story relayed to me in 2012 concurs in many respects with the one told to Correia in the early twentieth century. In order to demonstrate his prowess and control over the land and the sea, the young Joao Lere decided to divide the land by calling forth the waters from the sea. His mother warned him against these actions, which involved the forbidden act of opening a sacred western door to the sea in the Kai Hunu cave (known as *Odamata Losi-Tasi*). So instead, he decided to open the door to the east. When he did this, he found a tobacco pipe (which was also manifest as a golden snake) belonging to his 'magician' uncle who was away in the far east in Tutuala. With the assistance of a pair of giant bellows (W: *tuha*), Joao Lere lit the pipe and began to smoke it, as he did so fire from the force of the bellows began to spread across the area. His uncle in Tutuala saw the smoke rising from Mamau-Tuha (the 'place of the bellows') close to the Kai Hunu cave. He leaped across the land from Tutuala to Laga to Dasu Buinau (a hill and 'place of divining justice' in Seisal), finally alighting near Bundura where the fire was raging out of control. He quelled the fires, but given the proven recklessness of the young Joao Lere, his uncle returned to Tutuala with him under his care. It was in Tutuala that Joao Lere was discovered by a priest who was returning to Dili and ordered the young man to carry his many possessions to a nearby port. While the priest set out first on horseback, by the time he had arrived at the port Joao Lere and the bags were already there. Joao Lere had used his magic to move the items through the air, but he hid these powers from the priest, telling him a team of porters had carried them. Next the priest set off for Vemasse but again when he arrived there, Joao Lere and his possessions had again arrived ahead of him. This happened as well on the next stage of the journey to Fatu Ahi (between the ports of Hera and Dili). By the time he reached Fatu Ahi the priest realized the extent of Joao Lere's magical powers (*matenek*). Returning to Portugal, he relayed this story and discussed Joao Lere's threat to Portuguese power. The priest then returned to Timor as a bishop and a plan was made to kill Joao Lere. The colonial authorities seized him, tied him up and threw him from a boat into the middle of the sea. But before they got back to shore, Joao Lere was there still alive. After this they tried many times to kill him, but he would never die.

In the end Joao Lere told the authorities that if they wanted to kill him they needed to bring some black palm fibre, rice stalks and a salt basket from Wai Wono (near Bundura) to the port town of Manatuto. He then instructed them to put these together on top of a flat rock. Following this, at four o'clock in the

Challenging the moral order 113

afternoon he sat atop the rock playing a bamboo flute. He instructed them to set alight the fibres and as the fire burned he continued to play the flute (calling forth his *dai* or ancestral spirit). He played until the evening and then suddenly the smoke of the fire rose in a single column and he disappeared. All that was left on the rock was one large goat dropping. After his death Joao Lere's (magic) basket was carried by the wind from Manatuto all the way to Kai Hunu, where it turned into a rock known as Watu Tege on a nearby coastal shelf platform (see Figure 5.2). The wind signalled its imminent arrival to his mother who ran to the shore and began to sing a song:

Loi Kere Kuru Lale	Loi Kere Kuru Lale
He Watu Tege, Bali Watu Tege	I am waiting for the basket, waiting for the basket
Watu Tege Bunini	The owner of the basket
Kii-Leki Kuru-An-Leki-Kuru.	Kii-Leki Kuru-An-Leki-Kuru.

According to the people of Wani Uma it was Joao Lere's own uncles who had told the Portuguese that they must kill him. They feared his reckless and excessive powers and told the colonial authorities that if they did not kill him he would come to rule the land and drive out the Portuguese. They locate these events in the time of Padre Antonio Taveiro (Tavares) who they say arrived in

Figure 5.2 Watu Tege (Joao Lere's basket) and Bundura coastline.

114 *Challenging the moral order*

1512 (as noted above, the historical record tells us that he was the first missionary who arrived in Timor from Solor in 1556. See McWilliam (2007: 225, 233)). But in their telling of Joao Lere's life story these events span a long historical period which includes the time of the Dutch and a time of 'civil war'. Along the way Joao Lere and his various namesakes were first pitted against a priest, then a bishop and then the Portuguese government. While all of these outsiders are also present in the version of the story told to Correia in the 1930s, in this telling Joao Lere is characterized as a threat to the power of the rival king of the port of Vemasse and it is he who urges the Portuguese governor to kill Joao Lere.[12] Downplaying such power dynamics between local rulers, today the people of Wani Uma assert that it was the coming of *agama* (I: religion) that killed Joao Lere in order that this religion could rule Timor.[13] Indeed the hilltop site in Manatuto where Joao Lere was killed now contains a chapel dedicated to Santu Antonio (many other *lulik* sites in the region are also now dedicated to a Catholic saint). Despite this colonial Catholic transformation, when people from Baucau familiar with the Joao Lere story pass by the site of his death near the main road in Manatuto they still pay their respects by placing an object (a rock or a cigarette) in their mouth and throwing it on the ground in the direction of the site.

Meanwhile the site near remote Bundura where Joao Lere's uncle alighted as he leaped back from Tutuala to put out the fires is known as Dai Kele Fatin (W: 'the foreigner's footprint'). While Joao Lere was said by Pinto Correia (1935) to be descended from Timorese and foreign parentage, the elders of Wani Uma state that this site is known as the foreigner's footprint to disguise its real meaning and power. Like Joao Lere, his uncle was a powerful 'magician' from Wani Uma house of Wata Huu Ana[14] and his influence stretched as far as Tutuala where his footprints are also found. Meanwhile they say another footprint connected to Joao Lere can be found in Lifao (the first colonial capital in Oecusse).

According to Major Ko'o Raku's version of the Joao Lere story, Joao Lere was the son of a man that came mysteriously from across the sea (he specifies this to be Larantuka) by way of We Biku We Hali through Luca to Matebian and finally Baucau. Joao Lere's father arrived from across the sea with a group of eight contemporaries who were equally *matenek*.[15] As a result of their superior *matenek* (cleverness/wisdom/power) all were eventually killed by the Portuguese. The source of this group's *matenek* and great power was '*natureza*' (W: *namu degu, namu rema, ria luli*; M. *mu'a gamu, mu'a usa, mu'a falun*) or the dark world most commonly associated with lands from across (or under) the sea. This powerful lineage drawn from *natureza* and the sea is also signified by the fact that after Joao Lere allowed himself to be killed, he returned to his wife's side in the form of a snake (*talibere*). His wife, however, then shrieked in fright, leading Joao Lere to disappear forever from this world. In this account, Joao Lere was the last in a long line of powerful rulers who could metamorphose into their *dai* (in this case, *talibere* the ancestral snake). Killed by the Portuguese, their dark earth power was usurped by that of a new nominally Christian moral order. Yet like his *dai* in the hydrosocial cycle, Joao Lere (*lere* = to clear) symbolized the path of life and death (see Conclusion). In death, this legacy was honoured by the construction of a powerful sacred house in Baha Kai Lale linked to the coastal cave of Kai Hunu whose underground waters are, like Joao Lere, connected to Luca (a centre with unrivalled ritual communication with the sea).

Meanwhile, as we saw above, it was also Joao Lere's sacred house complex which housed his book of writings (written in Chinese, Arabic, Malay, French, Dutch and Portuguese). It was from reading these books that the nationalist hero Vicente Reis (Sahe) gained his real *matenek* (cleverness, wisdom and power). In this sense Joao Lere also opened another path: the path for others to cultivate their *matenek*, to combine the darkness of the past with light of the new, and ultimately achieve Timor's independence.

The fall of Luca and the rise of Vemasse

According to Antonio Vicente Marques Soares (pers. comm. 2006; cf. Soares n.d., 2003: 45–53), a Timorese historian and elder from Uma Tolu, Lacluta in Viqueque district, prior to the colonial era the island of Timor was divided into three kingdoms. These comprised the apical ritual centre of We Biku We Hali on the south-west coast near the current international border (see Map 5.1), Sombai centred in Punjan (Kupang) in the west and Luca on the south-east coast. The jurisdiction of the latter stretched from the far east to Maubara in Liquica and included the islands of Wetar, Alor, Kisar and Leti (all of which the Portuguese later traded with the Dutch).[16] Luca and We Hali had strong historical, political and ritual links and according to Soares this culminated in a colonial era accord between the two in 1712. At the River Masin Babulu ('the salt of Babulu') which runs along the present-day border, both rulers faced each other in the river and took a sacred oath. This oath proclaimed that from now on Luca would govern the (Portuguese) east side of the island and We Hali would govern the (Dutch) west side. When there were incidents of *karau nakfera* (ET: 'the rampaging buffalo'), a metaphor for the kingdoms being in serious conflict and crossing boundaries, it was agreed that the two kingdoms would come together to broker peace and stability. In 2012, I was told this story in narrative verse by the ritual leader (*lia na'in*) of the ruling house of Luca. In this story the kingdom of Luca is synonymous/linked with We Biku and Luca's ritual pair the kingdom of Viqueque (once known as Ai-Sahe) is synonymous/linked with We Hali (for the full narrative see Appendix 2).

Almost 150 years before the formal colonial division of the island in 1859, this agreement effectively anticipated East and West Timor. However, Soares also states that it was in 1702, a year after the Portuguese established their first seat of government in Lifao, that the local rulers of the east were called there to make an oath accepting Portuguese rule. This was followed by another oath-making ceremony in the central eastern kingdom of Soibada in 1703 (Soares 2003: 89; see Map 5.1). The rulers pledged to govern under the umbrella of the Portuguese flag and the colonial government pledged to respect Timorese

116 *Challenging the moral order*

traditions, laws and customs. In the centuries that followed, while the Timorese people continued to adhere to a belief in the divine power of their rulers, inevitably with the extension of colonial power and presence beyond Lifao and later Dili, these regional indigenous kingdoms began to be 'corrupted' and lose both their power and autonomy (and, as we have seen, their *matenek* rulers). By 1832 Luca and We Hali were embroiled in a war which led to the demise of We Hali (Soares 2003: 56).

As specific alliances were forged and broken between rulers and the colonial powers, indigenous systems of exchange and alliance increasingly became aligned with 'tribute' payments to 'foreign' rulers (cf. Forman 1978). Oral histories recount how these products, including rice, maize, beeswax candles, woven cloth and palm fibres, were important in the indigenous and colonial systems of tribute, exchange and power relations. In these exchanges, kingdoms such as Luca returned to their 'vassals' the symbols of the right to rule such as sacred gold discs (*belak*), headdress (*kaebauk*), sacralized betel nut (*bua malus*), sacralized waters and, eventually, the Portuguese sceptre (*rota*). Indeed, according to Forman (1978), this merging of indigenous and foreign systems of exchange and alliance was an integral element of the political and moral transition to Portuguese rule. Forman also argues that there was by the late nineteenth century a 'dovetailing' of the indigenous (Makasae) asymmetrical alliance system with 'the distribution of rank and title in the Portuguese colonial administration', to the extent that 'native exchange ideology afforded a sense of legitimacy to the form of hierarchy to which became attached to it' (1978: 110).[17] In exchange these rulers were expected to provide protection for their 'loyal' subjects.

Meanwhile Baucau, a place of minor political importance until the early 1900s, was prior to this time under the rule of Luca. As we have also seen in oral histories in Chapter 4, at some point Luca lost its power and its rulers retreated back across the mountains in shame.[18] Another oral history told in the Baucau village of Bahu recalls the fate of a despotic ruler called Dom Bastiao (Sebastiao is a name synonymous in the east with colonial-era rulers from Luca). Around the same time as the colonial capital was moved from Lifao to Dili (1769), this ruler's interference with a succession of young women in Baucau led to the local population taking the extraordinary decision to bury him alive. A trap was set and he fell in, to end his days buried with his slaves deep in an underground crevice south-west of Wai Lia in central Baucau.

Following the formal divisioning of island Timor between the Dutch and the Portuguese in 1859, in 1862 Governer Alfonso da Castro divided Portuguese Timor into eleven districts. While the formal administrative boundaries were new, according to Soares, the boundaries were drawn up in consultation with political and ritual leaders across the east of the island and largely followed the existing sacred border agreements between the kingdoms and sub-kingdoms. One such agreement was said to have occurred early in the colonial period between the houses of Loi Leki in Wailili and the emerging 'autonomous' kingdom of Vemasse. This story centres on a spring called Wai Lotu (which is today connected to the five branch houses of Loi Leki) and provides a local

Challenging the moral order 117

account of the arrival of Portuguese rule (in the form of a *rota* which they say they received from Vemasse in 1512). While both Wailili and Vemasse had received ruling sacra in the past from Luca, the people of Vemasse were now in possession of sacra (*rota*) given to them directly by the Portuguese in Lifao. As a result of these changing political dynamics, the Wailili rulers from the houses of Loi Leki house were called to the coast to make an agreement about the division of political authority under (symbolic) Portuguese rule. Following a ritual which proved the 'stupidity' of the indigenes of Loi Leki (and hence the political superiority of the rulers of Vemasse) the houses of Loi Leki carried the *rota* from Vemasse east to other kingdoms as far away as Baguia.[19] This sacred oath created two new houses – Uma Meti (the ruling house of the sea) in Vemasse and Uma Lari (the secondary house of the mountains) in Wailili. As with the sacred oath made between the springs of Wai Husu-Wai Lewa and Wa Lili-Wai Wa (see Chapter 4), from this sacred agreement the people of the salty waters of Vemasse (ET: *we masi(n)* = salty water) and the spring of Wai Lotu (W: 'small water') in Wailili exchanged ritual names. Until this day certain houses from Vemasse are said by the elders of Loi Leki to have the rights to the fruits of the land around Wai Lotu and in the past to have come to offer annual sacrifices to the ancestors of the spring.

Dom Boa Ventura and the waters of Baucau

By the time the Portuguese Governor Afonso de Castro took his decision in 1862 to organize the territory into districts, Baucau was within the territory of Vemasse and was recognized as a kingdom within that district. Timor's famous resistance-era bishop, Dom Carlos Belo (himself a son of Baucau), has written a book documenting colonial era local rulers of Timor and records the first king of the kingdom of Baucau as Dom Manuel Caetano Delegado Ximenes. Appointed by the Portuguese in 1884, Dom Ximenes hailed from the Jurisdiction of Laleia (França 1897: 235, cited in Belo 2011: 131). He swore allegiance to 'all the governors in this district of Timor' and to 'maintain the respect of my kingdom for the Catholic faith and to pay the *finta* (tax) that is ordered and give men [*auxílio*] for war and workers for public duties upon request' (Belo 2011: 131–132).

In 1891 the Portuguese Bento da França described Baucau as a kingdom of 2,000 persons (*almas* = souls) and 250 Christians (França 1897: 34–35, cited in Belo 2011: 330). Belo (2011: 133) records a second king of Baucau Dom Francisco da Costa Freitas (a son of the king of Vemasse) who was appointed in 1900 by the governor José Celestino da Silva. This king ruled in Baucau from a house near the spring of Wai Lia. The house, still known as Uma Liurai ('the Ruler's House'), was also the site of the first chapel in Baucau town. In his *Dicionário Chorográphico* (1903: 18), Rafael das Dores offers the following description of Baucau:

> The seat of a military command center, on the north coast of the island and to the east of Dilly, being a suco of Vemace, it was some time ago elevated

118   *Challenging the moral order*

to the status of kingdom, but remained a very insignificant one at that. There is a hamlet (*povoação*) of the same name on the northern flanks of the great mountain at a high elevation above sea level, with abundant water and a wonderful climate, such that some governors resided there for long periods of time, and some administrators went there to recover from illness or to get fresh air, which has developed the area, having a comfortable house of residence for the governors, a church and a parish, and a fort with a small barracks. If on the coast, from where one ascends via a precipitous track which is almost vertical in parts, there were a good anchorage, the place would be more frequented by visitors, but because the disembarkation is most difficult and even dangerous, this part will never be appropriately taken advantage of for a sanatorium, unless a regular road is built that links it to Dilly. Just a few small hamlets make up this tiny kingdom, in each one of which there are perhaps a dozen souls, and it seems to me that it will revert to the kingdom that it used to be a part of. It produces vegetables, and some tobacco, but only enough to cover local consumption.

(Cited in Belo 2011: 331)

A third ruler of the kingdom appointed in 1905 is recorded as being Dom Manuel dos Reis da Costa, and was from a house of Bahu. Given the title lieutenant colonel, he resided at the coastal hamlet of Hare Lai Duro (Belo 2011: 133). By this time, as the Portuguese presence had expanded, many ruling houses had been pushed out and relocated to the fringes of the town.[20] The coastal area of Hare Lai Duro was popular site of relocation as it also enabled local houses to avail themselves of the benefits of the busy colonial era interregional trade. However, Belo (2011: 133) writes that the colonial authorities soon began to take objection to the inter-island trade, in particular that of ongoing marital relations with the Dutch (and Protestant) controlled island of Kisar. As a result, this third ruler of Baucau was imprisoned by Governer Celestino who also gave orders that the ports of Baucau be closed to embarkations from the island of Kisar (Belo 2011: 133–134). In these accounts we can see a clear correlation with Major Ko'o Raku's narrative (see above) which blames the now severed relations with Kisar on the lack of Portuguese respect for local fertility-giver, fertility-taker traditions of exchange and reciprocity. A colonial connection between Kisar and Baucau was re-established in the 1920s (cf. Correia 1944: 299–301), but this exchange no longer had the depth of connection established through previous inter-island fertility-giver, fertility-taker relationships.[21]

It is clear from historical accounts that from the time of 'first contact' in the sixteenth century, shifting alliances and even insurrection between indigenous and colonial rulers was the norm across island Timor (Hägerdal 2012; Pélissier 1996; Gunn 1999; Ramos-Horta 1987: 19). Yet by the late nineteenth century the ferocity and extent of these rebellions by many local kingdoms in the east towards their Portuguese masters was increasing apace. Elsewhere in the district, Belo (2011: 273–274) reports that the people of Quelicai in the mountains of

Challenging the moral order 119

Matebian were the last to be 'pacified'. Battles involving troops loyal to the Portuguese from Vemasse, Baucau and Ossu quelled rebellions in Quelicai in 1892, 1904 and 1912 (Belo 2011: 273–274). Historians in general suggest that the cause of these increased insurrections and heightened resistance was an ever harsher Portuguese taxation regime, particularly the doubling of a head tax. Meanwhile some other historical accounts also draw attention to an emergent anti-colonial, even nascent nationalist, movement, inspired as well by alliances with other outsiders, including the Chinese (cf. Gunn 1999: 175–190; Pélissier 1996; Soares 2003: 88; Ramos-Horta 1987: 19). The most famous of these insurrections against colonial rule is known as the Manufahi rebellions. Taking place in a series of uprisings from 1880, the insurrections ended in 1912 after the defeat of the local ruler Dom Boa Ventura. Today, in the new nation of Timor Leste, Dom Boa Ventura is officially regarded as Timor's first nationalist hero.

By the early twentieth century the rulers of Baucau were aligned with the Portuguese. *Moradores* or second line troops of Baucau had already engaged in battles to pacify those elsewhere who resisted Portuguese rule (Belo 2011).[22] As we will also see below, according to Major Ko'o Raku by the turn of the twentieth century the indigenes of Baucau town realized that if they were to rule the region they needed to collaborate with the *malae mutin* ('white foreigners', referring here to the Portuguese). Meanwhile, many of the remote mountain kingdoms of the Baucau district opposed the Portuguese and wanted to drive them from Timor. Dom Joao Vicente Paulo, the first ruler of Baucau's ancient village of Boile to receive the *rota* from the Portuguese (cf. Belo 2011: 138; da Costa *et al.* 2006: 43) played a key role in organizing the *moradores* to carry out attacks on the hostile mountain kingdoms. These battles, which included taking part in quelling the Manufahi rebellions, continued for decades, until the people of Baucau town and their allies finally triumphed in a battle against the kingdom of Berecoli. According to Belo (2011: 274) this final pacification was brokered in 1930 by Nai Leki or Major Carlos da Costa, a traditional ruler from Ro'ulu in Bahu and by then Portuguese administrator of the sub-district of Quelicai.

Yet in contrast to stories of tax rebellions or incipient nationalism, in more localized indigenous tellings the Dom Boa Ventura series of rebellions is expressed somewhat differently. According to Major Ko'o Raku, the Boa Ventura insurrection was triggered, as with many Timorese wars, by the betrayal of a marital alliance.[23] Taxation and nationalism do not figure in this account, which occurred after a visit to the house of Dom Boa Ventura by the administrator from Dili. A faithful party to local compacts with the Portuguese colonists, Dom Boa Ventura had organized his subjects to grow cotton and other crops. At this time he was hosting a visit by the administrator who had come to inspect the region. However, while Dom Boa Ventura was out during daylight hours overseeing the fields, this man repeatedly entered the private rooms of the house and engaged in sexual relations with Dom Boa Ventura's wife. Alerted to the happenings, on the Dom's return the administrator was encircled by a large party of men as he emerged from the bedroom. The administrator's penis was cut off and put on a plate, after which it was delivered by a messenger to Dili

120   *Challenging the moral order*

and presented to his wife. Alarmed, the Dili administrator's wife sent immediately for support from the administrator of Baucau who rallied together the *moradores* of Baucau's second line regiment. These troops came together as a force known as '*Companhia Loidua*' and were under the command of Joao Paulo Vicente. Along with the village of Loidua, it drew together warriors from the villages of Bucoli, Wani Uma, Tirilolo, Caisidu, Caibada, Buruma, Sialale (Bundura), Boile, Macadai, Ro'ulu, Ana Ulu, Maukali, Diwake, Buibau and Samalari. While in 2010, I was told by Major Ko'o Raku that these troops went willingly to support the Portuguese in Manufahi, three years later he qualified this by stating that the expedition had set out on the premise of assisting the Portuguese to locate the Dom who had somehow become lost. It was not until they arrived in Manufahi that they realized they had been lied to by their Portuguese masters. By then it was too late to withdraw and the battle had begun (as we will see below, this seemingly revised account can be understood in the context of the state-organized 100-year anniversary celebration in 2012 which commemorated the uprising of the nationalist hero Dom Boa Ventura).

Whatever their intention in setting out for Manufahi, the oral histories of this period in Baucau recount that the loyal troops of '*Compania Loidua*' were successful in their campaign, returning to Baucau with many enemy heads. These were subsequently buried in a forested area not far from the centre of Baucau town (cf. Belo 2011: 136). Some members of '*Compania Loidua*' returned to Baucau in the possession of slaves: vanquished men, women and children of Manufahi. The descendants of these people subsequently settled in local villages.

In 2012 the independent nation of Timor Leste held a 100-year anniversary celebration to commemorate the Dom Boa Ventura uprising. It was expected that each district of the new nation would send a delegation. A few days prior to this event, Major Ko'o Raku was hurriedly called to the Baucau district administrator's office and asked if he could attend as the senior ritual representative of the district. Due to its pivotal role supporting the Portuguese in the Manufahi uprisings, Baucau had much unfinished business with the people of Manufahi and it was perhaps because of this that no other ritual leader from the district was brave enough to lead the delegation. This is Major Ko'o Raku's account of what transpired:

> I was called to the new town and asked if I would go to Same [Manufahi] (see Map 5.1). I said I would, but first we needed to sacrifice a white chicken and pray to *gituba ginana* [the springs or 'other worldly' portals from where the water flows forth]. We did this and read the liver of the chicken. The reading was not good. I asked the district administrator to find and bring me another chicken. We repeated the sacrifice and this time I prayed to the ancestors of Tirilolo, Bahu and Caibada. The liver reading was still bad. I ask him to look for another chicken. This time I prayed to the ancestors of Fatumaka Leten and Fatumaka Kraik [including the villages of Wailili, Gariuai, Loidua, Buibau and Samalari]. From this point the liver

readings began to improve. [I was told he also called out the name of the place in Baucau where the decapitated heads of the vanquished had been buried].

I called out in these prayers that our ancestors had committed sins, that we were now going to Same to redress this and make peace. Only after I had spoken these words, did I receive the positive reading from the chicken liver. I then made another offering to the ancestors with the corn and we were we able to leave for Same.

In the end it was a good result. No one in our party died either in Same or on the way. This was lucky because a prayer recited by another ritual leader who went from Baucau was not good. When we arrived in Same he called out the names of the three mountains Ramelau, Cabalaki (near Same) and Matebian. He called out that they were in a younger sibling–older sibling relationship. But this was the wrong prayer, he didn't even call out the name of Baucau. We needed first to acknowledge Baucau's role in the war, in particular the names of the springs from where our warriors received their power and to call out the names of the villages from where these warriors came. That night the other ritual leader from Baucau who went with us [himself an independence-era administrator within the district] became sick, he lost the feeling in half of his body. I gave him some [traditional] medicine and told him that the cause of his ailment was that his prayers had not been done correctly; they had not been addressed to the correct door, the springs or *gituba ginana*.

Major Ko'o Raku explained that when he arrived in Manufahi he called out in his prayers to the *gituba ginana*, the springs of Wai Husu-Wai Lewa (which as we have seen are connected by sacred oath to the springs of Wai Lili-Wai Wa and through this Fatumaka Leten and Fatumaka Kraik). When in 1912 *Compania Loidua* had set out for Manufahi they had first made offerings and prayed to these springs and asked that these ancestral waters give them the power to overcome their adversaries. They had carried some of this water with them into battle. In 2012, Major Ko'o Raku and his party had also carried with them a bamboo length filled with water drawn from the springs of Wai Husu-Wai Lewa. Once in Manufahi they had carried out a ritual offering ceremony and had roasted a goat and a rooster over the fire. They had prayed and said that if the acts of their ancestors were wrong then they were there to ask for forgiveness to cleanse these sins, and compensate the descendants of the fallen with these offerings and the sacred water. The next day at the official ceremony ground Major Ko'o Raku made an offering of two coral necklaces (M: *gaba*) and a golden breast plate at the feet of the newly erected statue of Dom Boa Ventura. With these two ceremonies, he concluded, he had 'paid' for the sins of Baucau's warriors. When they returned to Baucau they did so via the Manufahi River where they ritually washed the sins of their ancestors down to the sea. It was only after this ceremony that Baucau was able to once again enter into a sibling relationship with the people of Cabalaki and Manufahi.

122   *Challenging the moral order*

The delegation stayed until the end of the formal proceedings and returned home via the south coast and Viqueque. The direction of this return journey was chosen in order to pay their respects to those kingdoms from the eastern region who had fought together with Dom Boa Ventura – eight leaders of 1,007 men from Berecoli, Laga, Baguia and Quelicai. Major Ko'o Raku explained that 'we don't know what happened to them. Some were taken to be killed or imprisoned by the *malae mutin* (Portuguese). We don't know'.

Nai Leki's triumph

By 1914, after centuries of local alliance-making with, and uprising against, their foreign rule, the Portuguese used the occasion of the defeat of Dom Boa Ventura to decisively intervene and install a new generation of leaders at the helm of 'kingdoms' across the island. By this stage, many higher level kingdoms had effectively devolved power to the level of the village and, as remains the case today, village or *suco* heads were commonly referred to as *liurai* – rulers or kings. These new leaders needed to fulfil two criteria: they were obliged to take an oath of allegiance to the Portuguese and they had to come from a groomed and educated local elite (who were usually associated with a ruling house). This new class of rulers became known locally as *liurai kalsa* ('the kings in trousers'). In many cases, these new rulers deposed the *liurai lipa* ('the kings in sarongs'). At the same time, as noted in Chapter 2, the arrival of Portuguese into the region also triggered a process whereby many ruling houses voluntarily forfeited aspects of their leadership role to others. While the former ruling houses retreated with their ritual knowledge back into the darkness, the newly created 'political houses' were obliged for their part to stand up alongside and speak to the foreigners. Even when the process of power transfer between houses was consensual, rearranging ruling lineages (and with it rights to land and resources) was always a transgressive act. In the cases where these transgressions were not consensual, they remain as underlying tensions in the governance of many rural villages. In some instances, of course, it was the sons of the *liurai lipa* who became the *liurai kalsa*. As we will see below in these cases, without recourse to an alternative lineage, the present-day effects of these processes on custom and ritual life are even more disruptive.

In Baucau in the early twentieth century a son of one of the ruling houses of Bahu, Nai Leki (also known as Major Carlos da Costa Ximenes), was drafted into Portuguese administrative ranks. During his career he served in several administrative roles across the district, including the prestigious post of administrator of the mountainous *posto* or sub-district of Quelicai in the 1930s. In 1934 it is recorded that he accompanied the Baucau Administrator Armando Pinto Correia on an official visit to Portugal (Correia 1935: 256; Belo 2011: 134). He died in 1948, a few years after much of Baucau town had been destroyed by Second World War aerial bombing. It was Nai Leki, along with other indigenous leaders of early twentieth-century Baucau, who was said to have enticed the Portuguese in to establish a town by the ancestral spring of Wai Lewa. By the time of Nai Leki's death in 1948, Baucau was a 'Portuguese town' with stately buildings and promenades, an emergent culture of its own, and a lively economy driven largely by the activities of the resident Chinese traders who had set up shop around Wai Lewa (see Figure 5.3).

In 1930 the district of Baucau is recorded to have had 76,482 inhabitants of which sixteen were from Portugal, three from other colonies, twenty-one from 'other localities', while 148 were 'foreigners' (Figueiredo 2004). 'Foreigners' refers to the Chinese residents, mostly from Macau, some of whom, according to their descendants, had arrived in the Baucau region in the nineteenth century. Correia (1944) records that there was in the town a class of women called '*nonnas*' who were either of Chinese descent or somehow associated with the Portuguese administration. Other girls who would come in from outlying areas to be educated and would also be initiated into this 'town culture', which included highly coveted skills of Portuguese cookery, cake decorating and needlework. It was in this refined milieu that Nai Leki announced on his death bed that his people, from Bahu's Ro'ulu hamlet, should now adopt Portuguese ways and leave behind them the traditions of the past. The apical Ro'ulu sacred houses, Uma Liurai and Uma Loi Leki, had been destroyed during the Japanese occupation. Despite their ritual power and significance for Baucau, the present-day ritual leaders of Ro'ulu say they feel bound by Nai Leki's request and at the time of this interview in 2012 these houses remained un-reconstructed.

Figure 5.3 Old Baucau market and irrigation channel feature, built during the colonial administration of Armando Pinto Correia (circa 1930s).

124 *Challenging the moral order*

In Major Ko'o Raku's telling of this history, at some point during these early twentieth-century counter-rebellion campaigns, the *malae mutin* (Portuguese) in Baucau were so low in morale that they retreated back to Portugal to regroup. When they did so they took with them Nai Leki or Major Carlos da Costa. On their return to Baucau, these officials and Major Carlos visited the Portuguese outpost of Macau.[24] In Macau, Major Carlos made a sacred agreement between himself as the ruler of Bahu and the Portuguese he had met in Macau. Introducing himself as a native of a place called Posto Wai Lewa (the sub-district of Wai Lewa), he explained to them that, 'At my spring I have a fruit tree (*ai-tobal*) whose fruit falls to the ground as silver and gold'. This tale was intended to entice these *malae* to visit the region and augment the Portuguese settlement of the town. The story worked and they too made the long journey from Macau to become a part of the permanent and by now significant *malae* population.[25]

The sacred agreement made during this visit to Macau had also been a way of cementing the relations between Nai Leki and his hosts. As we have seen in other intra-local contexts such oath-making was formalized through an exchange of names. Likewise in this instance, Posto Wai Lewa exchanged names with Macau and became Waukau. A Waima'a poem recording this exchange is called '*Kulu ana de ana Waukau*' ('A little breadfruit born to the land of Waukau'):

Kulu ana de ana Waukau-Makau	The little breadfruit is born of Waukau-Makau
Kulu ana de ana Makau-Waukau.	The little breadfruit is born of Makau-Wakau.

The metaphor is one of a single breadfruit tree with grafted branches producing two separate lineages. The relation between Portuguese Macau and Waukau was now one of siblings and the Portuguese were said to have later changed the name of Waukau to Baucau.[26] By the 1930s Major Carlos or Nai Leki had become the most important indigene in the Portuguese administration of the Baucau district and, as we saw above, in his role as *Chefe de Posto* in Quelicai he is credited with pacifying the district. Yet despite joining the ranks of the local Lusophone elite he was known to carry with him wherever he went a particular *lulik* (sacred) object: a torn piece of cloth which had belonged to the great magician Joao Lere (Correia 1935: 136). An anecdote which suggests that Nai Leki's own cleverness (*matenek*) was a critical factor in ensuring the Portuguese development of Baucau (indeed by the 1930s the area was already becoming known as Timor's second 'city'). Yet this cleverness came at a cost to his people: the ways of the dark earth were to be left behind, with his people requested to move forward into the future following only the path of the *malae mutin*.

Discussion

Forever striving 'to place themselves in historical context, tapping into diverse kinds of memory sources in a self-defining act', many of the stories told in this chapter resonate with indigenous narrative strategies elsewhere (Abercrombie 1998: 10–11). At the same time, in their encounters with colonial outsiders, the Timorese desire for power and knowledge is clearly marked by a preference for relationship making. In these indigenous worlds, outsiders are seen as both the harbingers of new knowledge and as central for the exchange of goods and the building of relations. It is the excesses and transgressions of these outsiders and their frequent failure to live up to their characterization as 'potential affines' (Gow 2001: 307) that leads inevitably to a breakdown in these relations. For example in his intensely embodied betrayal, Dom Boa Ventura is portrayed as a loyal party to the alliance, pushed to retaliate by the excesses of an ultimately disrespectful colonial regime. Joao Lere meanwhile epitomized the fearsome power of *dai* (which, as we saw in Chapter 2, can also mean *malae* or foreigners) and their true home in the dark earth, and ultimately this power too was excessive. Yet Joao Lere's cleverness, wisdom and power (*matenek*) sourced from the sea and *natureza*, was in his death also able to be appropriated by Nai Leki, Sahe and through him the independence leader Xanana.[27]

The stories of Joao Lere's magic, the Manufahi Wars and Nai Leki's wooing of the *malae mutin* all feature the power and unpredictable agency of water. While in Joao Lere's case the waters of the 'other world' accessible through the Kai Hunu cave had the fearsome potential to rise up and repel the Portuguese, they also became a source of blessing for pilgrims from across the region. This recognition of the other-worldly power of water was, as we have seen in earlier chapters, at the heart of Luca's ritual compact with sea and Joao Lere was himself a son of Luca. Yet like Joao Lere's demise, Luca was eventually repelled from the region, triggering as well a 'retreat' of the waters which had previously gushed forth from Baucau's springs. It is also clear that the ancestral power of these springs, while depleted, still remained. Nai Leki was able to successfully portray these waters as a source of 'other-worldly' magic and wealth and drew the *malae mutin* into an alliance with the indigenous rulers of Baucau. In doing so he took a risk and became a servant to a type of 'trade' with the *malae* (W: *dai*) which propelled him and his people some way into the light (cf. Gow 2001: 307). Similarly these same waters were the source of power for the warriors of Baucau who defeated Dom Boa Ventura and the resistant kingdoms of Matebian. Both of these actions ensured a prominent role for Baucau in Timor's future. At the same time as this alliance of local houses with a new class of *ema matenek* ('clever and powerful people') brought with it a change in governance arrangements with ongoing ramifications, there also remains a firm sense of obligation and indebtedness to the ancestral domains which made this all possible.

126 *Challenging the moral order*

Notes

1 While Major Ko'o Raku asserts that this trade began in the dark earth period, he also suggests that it was contemporaneous with the Dutch presence along the north coast (for another account of this era, see McWilliam 2007). The sixteenth century is noted for the heightened presence of Makassan seafarers along the north coast but it is possible these stories may also refer to a much earlier contact period between people from island Timor and elsewhere in the archipelago (see Chapter 3).

2 Hägerdal (2013: 241) mentions Dutch treaties with the Waima'a and the Kingdom of Ade in present-day Vemasse. Other historians record fragments of these stories (Gunn 1999; Hägerdal 2012; Soares 2003; Belo 2011; Spillett 1999).

3 Observing the booming international spice trade in the early sixteenth century, a Portuguese official in Malacca called Tome Pires famously wrote that God had created Timor for sandalwood, Banda for nutmeg and the Moluccas for cloves (Adnan 2009: 355).

4 Asserted by Major Ko'o Raku to have been Vicente Reis (Sahe), Mari Alkatiri, Ramos Horta, Rogerio Lobato, Abilio de Aruajo, Fransisco Lopes and Xavier Amaral.

5 Major Ko'o Raku records these as Fretilin, UDT, Apodeti, Travalista and Kota.

6 *Frente Revolucionaria do Timor Leste Independente.*

7 *Uniao Democratica Timorense.*

8 *Associacao Popular Democratica Timor.*

9 Stories of this priest (often asserted to be a bishop) occur in local narratives across the east. In most accounts he is said to have had, or tricked people into believing he had, power over the sea or nature (see also Hicks 2004: 6; Spillett 1999: 289–306). The historical record tells us that Tavares was the first missionary who arrived in Timor from Solor in 1556 (see McWilliam 2007: 225, 233).

10 Although this alliance was at times fickle and plagued by revolts (see Gunn 1999; Belo 2011; Hägerdal 2012). See also endnote 16 in Chapter 2.

11 The story of Joao Lere resonates with Traube's (2007) account of a Mambai narrative tradition featuring a Christ-like figure and prophet of the light known as Tat Felis. Felis arrives in the area with local missionaries and is persecuted by local rulers. Traube's Felis has a similar story of illegitimate parentage as Joao Lere (Felix's father Joseph also disappears) and like Joao Lere he survives repeated murder attempts. Yet in the Felix narrative, Timor's first president, Xavier Amaral in 1974, took on a name Mau Bere (which belonged to Felix) without knowing its owner and hence without formalizing the exchange. It was this transgressive act which triggered the civil war and the Indonesian invasion. Ultimately the Mambai people suffered and died to pay back with their own bodies the debt for Felix's own betrayal and suffering. Unlike Felix, a prophet of the light, the source of Joao Lere's *matenek* is located in the depths of the dark earth.

12 Key centres mentioned in the Joao Lere narrative were all colonial trading ports Hera, Manatuto, Laleia and Vemasse (the latter was also known in the early colonial period as Ade). The historical sources recount that between the 1500 and 1700s the people of Vemasse were already engaged in trade with Dutch, Chinese, Macassans and were beginning to establish relations with the Portuguese. Trade wars were commonplace (Gunn 1999; Belo 2011; Hägerdal 2012; McWilliam 2007).

13 Indeed the Kingdom of Vemasse was to become closely aligned with the Portuguese and the Catholic Church. A chapel was built in Edan (Ade) in 1748–1752 (Soares pers. comm. 2012) followed by one in Vemasse in 1775 (Soares 2003: 46). The latter was a lavish affair built by Governor Caetano Lemos Telo de Menezes to maintain good relations with the *liurai* (rulers) of Vemasse and Baucau (Soares 2003: 46). According to Soares, Edan (Ade) was established in the late sixteenth century after the Portuguese outpost in Solor was attacked and some residents moved to settle in Edan. Edan is a Galoli word meaning where the salt and fresh water meet (Soares pers. comm. 2012).

14 The present-day custodians of Joao Lere's sacra.

15 The others are specified to be all *liurai* known as Dom Lere, Dom Paulo, Dom Buibere, Dom Girimau, Dom Jeremias, Dom Joao, Dom Lifao and Dom Alariku.

16 Alor paid tribute to Likusan (Liquica) until the late 1800s (Gunn 1999: 150).

17 These ranks and titles included *Dom, Dona, Brigadeiro, Coronel, Tenente Coronel, Capitao, Major, Ajudante* and *Chefe*.

18 In the late 1700s the colonial record tells us that Luca lost its jurisdiction over Venilale as a consequence of a failed rebellion against the Portuguese known as the 'War of the Madmen' (Belo 2011: 336). Luca itself had oscillated in support of the Church, alternatively allowing baptisms, at other times (it is claimed) ordering or carrying out the murders of priests (see Belo 2011: 310; Gunn 1999: 76; Hägerdal 2012: 31–32; Soares 2003: 56; Spillett 1999: 289–306).

19 In this story, a man and a dog were taken from Wai Lotu to Vemasse where they were decapitated in order to determine towards which party their heads would roll (the rulers of Wailili or Vemasse). As each party took their position at opposite poles from the site of the decapitations the Liurai of Vemasse chose the low ground. The heads duly rolled towards him and he earned the right to rule. Wailili tellers of this story laugh raucously at the apparent stupidity or backwardness of their forebears.

20 Correia (1935: 272) notes that within twenty years the Timorese elite in Baucau lost most of their 'prestige, fortune, and authority'.

21 Later in 1937, Jose dos Reis da Costa, the Portuguese-educated son of the imprisoned king from Hare Lai Duro, was appointed the new king of Baucau. In 1933, he was invited by the Administrator Pinto Correia to join the colonial entourage to visit Vonrelli, the capital of Kisar (Belo 2011: 134). He died, and with only an uneducated son to succeed him, no further kings were appointed in Baucau (Belo 2011: 135).

22 Correia (1935: 58) writes that '[t]he Timorese, especially those from Baucau, reveal a strong predilection for militarism. *Sucos* [villages] of *moradores* surround the town of Baucau'.

23 Likewise Luis Cardoso's (2000: 5) 'unofficial narrative' of Dom Boa Ventura told to him by his father in the 1960s recalls that the Boa Ventura rebellion was instigated by the actions of a Portuguese military commander who had become entranced by the 'fair skinned' wife of Boa Ventura. Not being able to bear the thought of her being married to a 'native' he set out to save her from such transgression. Boa Ventura then retaliated.

24 Until the 1890s Baucau and other districts were administered through Macau. In 1934 Nai Leki travelled with Baucau Administrator Armando Pinto Correia and a Timorese delegation to an expo in Portugal (Correia 1935: 256).

25 Major Ko'o Raku also relates the story of a leader called Noko Loi from Defa Wasi in Baguia who similarly tricked the *malae* into settling in Baguia by telling tales of the gold associated with its spring.

26 This account of the origins of the name of Wau Kau is disputed by others.

27 According to the elders of Wani Uma, a ritual specialist from Joao Lere's house prophesized the Indonesian invasion in 1974 and it was this that led Sahe to take Joao Lere's book.

References

Abercrombie, T. (1998) *Pathways of Memory and Power*, Madison: University of Wisconsin Press.

Adnan, A. (2009) *Portugis dan Spanyol di Maluku*, Jakarta: Komunitas Bambu.

Belo, D. (2011) *Os Antigos Reinos de Timor-Leste*, Baucau: Edição Tipografia Diocesana Baucau.

128 Challenging the moral order

Cardoso, L. (2000) *The Crossing: A Story of East Timor*, London: Granta.

Correia, A. (1935) *Gentio de Timor*, Lisbon: Agência-Geral das Colónias.

Correia, A. (1944) *Timor de Lés a Lés*, Lisbon: Agência Geral das Colónias.

da Costa, C., da Costa Guterres, A. and Lopes, J. (eds) (2006) *Exploring Makassae Culture*, Baucau: Publicacoes Matebian-Grafica Diocesana Baucau.

Dores, R. (1903) *Apontamentos para um Dicionário Chorográphico de Timor: memoria*, Lisbon: Imprensa Nacional.

Figueiredo, F. (2004) 'Timor: a presença Portuguesa (1769–1945)', unpublished MA thesis, University of Porto.

Forman, S. (1978) 'East Timor: Exchange and Political Hierarchy at the Time of the European Discoveries', in K. Hutterer (ed.) *Economic Exchange and Social Interaction in Southeast Asia: Perspectives from Prehistory, History and Ethnography*, Michigan Papers on South and Southeast Asia No. 13, The University of Michigan, 97–112.

França, B. (1897) *Macaue Seus Habitants, Relaçoes com Timor*, Lisboa: Imprensa Nacional.

Gow, P. (2001) *An Amazonian Myth and its History*, Oxford: Oxford University Press.

Gunn, G. (1999) *Timor Loro Sae: 500 Years*, Macau: Livros do Oriente.

Hägerdal, H. (2012) *Lords of the Land, Lords of the Sea: Conflict and Adaption in Early Colonial Timor, 1600–1800*, Leiden: KITLV Press.

Hägerdal, H. (2013) 'Cycles of Queenship on Timor: A Response to Douglas Kammen', *Archipel* 84: 237–251.

Hicks, D. (2004) *Tetum Ghosts & Kin: Fertility and Gender in East Timor*, Illinois: Waveland Press.

McWilliam, A. (2007) 'Looking for Ade: A Contribution to Timorese Historiography', *Bijdragen tot de Taal-, Land- en Volkenkunde* 163(2/3): 221–238.

Niner, S. (2009) *Xanana: Leader of the Struggle for Independent Timor-Leste*, North Melbourne: Australian Scholarly Publishing.

Pélissier, R. (1996) *Timor en Guerre: Le Crocodile et les Portugais (1847–1913)*, Paris: Pélissier.

Ramos-Horta, J. (1987) *Funu: The Unfinished Saga of East Timor*, Trenton: The Red Sea Press.

Soares, A.V.M. (n.d.) *Hanek Matan Au Kenuk Tis no Saen Rai Lamak Tasan*, unpublished manuscript.

Soares, A.V.M. (2003) *Pulau Timor: Sebuah Sumbangan Untuk Sejarahnya*, Baucau: Edicao Tipografia Diocesana Baucau.

Spillett, P. (1999) 'The Pre-colonial History of the Island of Timor Together with Some Notes on the Makassan Influence in the Island', unpublished manuscript, Museum and Art Gallery of the Northern Territory, Darwin.

Traube, E. (2007) Unpaid Wages: Local Narratives and the Imagination of the Nation', *The Asia Pacific Journal of Anthropology* 8(1): 9–25.

6 Water relations
The embodied politics of ritual and irrigated rice production

Across the Baucau Viqueque zone, spring water is critical to the way that people relate to one another and their ancestors. This chapter traces the importance of spring water and associated spirit ecologies to the production of wet rice and examines the complex political fluidities and continuities in local livelihood practices across time and space. To do this it investigates the foundational moral economy and variously embodied beings under whose auspices irrigated rice production is enabled and local water politics play out.

While most of the anthropological work on agrarian practices in Timor Leste has focused on swidden agriculture, wet rice is also a crop that has been long produced in the favourable agro-ecological niches of this particular zone. The timeline of the introduction and spread of rice agriculture across Timor has not been determined (but see Chapter 3 and also Oliveira 2006), nor have there been any studies of the history of indigenous irrigation practices. A few minor mentions in early twentieth-century colonial-era sources and a late colonial-era study by Metzner (1977) provide only fragmentary evidence about the history and trajectory of indigenous irrigation in the region.

In a paper first published in 1949 [1977] the Dutch anthropologist Onvlee described the customary system of rice irrigation and ritual in an area of Sumba, an island to the immediate west of Timor (see Map 1.3). He noted that in this region of Mangili there were ancient rice paddies and water channels whose management was encompassed in a ritual built around the metaphor of wife-giver and wife-taker relations (or 'fertility-giver' and 'fertility-taker' relations). These irrigation channels were divided into male and female conduits which at two points crossed each other's path. At one of these points a hollow wooden log served as an aqueduct for the female water to channel through. Periodically this log needed to be replaced, necessitating a pilgrimage of the clan houses associated with the rice fields to the forest of a neighbouring wife-giver group. In this forest they would retrieve a suitable 'bride log'. Onvlee writes: '[a]quiring this wooden bride thus activates the traffic between two groups whose relationship is significant to the whole society' (1977 [1949]: 155). Symbolizing and activating actual marriage relations, this resource and gift exchange ritual also enabled the water to flow down male channels to fertilize the female land of the rice fields below. According to Onvlee this ancient system reproduced not just

130 *Water relations*

marriage relations but also 'reflections and manifestations of the interdependencies of cosmic forces which make all life possible—the very forces which give this human activity its background and meaning' (1977 [1949]: 160). When he wrote this piece in 1949 the system was threatened by the construction of a modern dam in the area. While Onvlee remarked that this might auger well in some respects for economic development, he worried that this would 'also augur the dissolution of a way of life', which would 'force us to ask: What other bedrock can this culture now build on? Into what shall it root?' (1977 [1949]: 163).

While I do not know the answers to these questions in the context of the Mangili Dam in Sumba, the questions are pertinent to the status of similar ways of life linked to practices of irrigated rice production in the Baucau Viqueque zone. As noted in other 'resource' contexts across Timor Leste (see McWilliam and Traube 2011; Palmer and Carvalho 2008; McWilliam 2005; Ospina and Hohe 2001; Carvalho 2011) in the post-independence era a 'renaissance' is occurring in the region in relation to a range of ritual economy and resource regulatory practices, including water sharing and blessing rituals (see also Figure 6.1). Continuing a close reading of the socio-cosmological significance of water, this chapter turns its attention to both the everyday practices and the ritual politics associated with irrigated rice and assesses the past and present challenges facing this mode of production. Tracing the ways in which this suite of rituals

Figure 6.1 Community spring water and agricultural fertility ritual, Lekitehi, Maubisse.

Water relations 131

evolved as a way for local populations to communicate to themselves about themselves and their relationship to their environment (Rappaport 1999), irrigated rice production practices and their associated ritual politics are shown to be simultaneously ways of encoding and communicating core moral values and of mediating and negotiating the changing relations which embody them.

Aside from the few with the luxury of a public service job and salary, their own business or employment in the Catholic diocese, most of the population of Baucau town and surrounds continue to be semi-subsistence farmers. Focusing in the latter part of the chapter on irrigated rice production in Baucau's marine terraces, I explore the range of complex socio-ecological variables which impact on the agricultural use and management of water resources in this particular karstic zone (cf. Urich 1989). I argue that even in this urban environment the spiritual ecologies associated with diverse practices of irrigated rice production remain relevant, and demonstrate that along with its agro-ecological salience, it is because of the deeply embodied religious connection between water and all beings that such practices remain to varying degrees extant.

The mixed agricultural economy

While traditional wet rice production is confined to areas with appropriate agro-ecological conditions across the Baucau Viqueque zone (Metzner 1977), it is integral to the regional subsistence economy and is mixed in with numerous other crops such as maize and tubers and practices of hunting, foraging and fishing (see also Blust 1976; Ormeling 1955; Pannell 2011).[1] Inter-regional trade and marital exchanges meant historically that the products of this polymorphous economy were in constant state of flow from place to place (Forman 1978). Products such as rice, maize, beeswax candles, woven cloth (*tais*) and palm fibres were important to both indigenous and colonial systems of tribute, exchange and power relations.

Depending on the ecological niche(s) the seasonal livelihood calendar in the Baucau Viqueque zone has traditionally included: successive periods of land clearing and burning followed by the planting and harvest of crops in dryland fields (*toos*); preparation, planting and harvest of irrigated rice and other crops; grazing of livestock; hunting of wild animals such as birds, civet cat, boar and deer; tending to 'plantations' of areca nuts, a variety of palms (for coconut and palm wine harvest and building materials), fruit trees and climbing vines; harvest of forest products including timber, 'wild' root vegetables, bamboo, fruits and honey; freshwater and intertidal zone fish trapping and marine foraging; and, in some coastal areas, salt production (see Figure 6.2).[2] Both women and men participate to varying degrees in all of these activities,[3] which in the past were all 'traditionally' enabled and religiously sanctioned through individual or collective recourse to localized agricultural rituals (Friedberg 1989; Forman 1981; McWilliam 2002; see Chapter 6). Under Portuguese rule (1540–1975) there was also extensive inland deforestation of sandalwood, teak and other hardwoods and establishment of coffee, coconut and other plantations. The

132 *Water relations*

Figure 6.2 Roadside vegetable stalls and sellers, Logo Bere spring, Mundo Perdido.

Portuguese also actively encouraged the increased production of maize, irrigated rice and other vegetables such as cassava, sweet potato, pumpkin and peanut (Shepherd 2013).

Local rice farmers from across the Baucau Viqueque zone state that irrigated rice pre-dates the arrival of Portuguese into their region. Across the zone I have been told stories of the first irrigated rice crops which emerged from the ground after two siblings prepared the *natar* (irrigated fields). In these stories, most commonly an old brother ties up his younger sibling and drags him around in the mud until rice emerges from the earth (suggesting that crop germination is dependent on the interaction between the (male) body and the (female) land. Cf. Lazarowitz 1980; Forman 1980, 1981). The first swidden maize fields were prepared in a similar manner (cf. Barnes 2013). It is perhaps because of this that maize and rice are said to be related to each other in an older sister–younger sister (*bin-alin*) relationship, a relationship in which the progenitors are human beings.[4]

As we find in the creation stories of many agricultural communities in the region, in the remote south coast village of Irabi (M: 'sacred water') in Watu Carabao, Viqueque the creation of the origin community and ruling house is linked to ancestral sacra emerging from the spring (see Map 2.1). According to the spring custodian, Armindo da Silva, in the distant past a woman of this house entered the underground world hidden beneath the spring and married with its crocodile king. The pair had two sons who continue to live in the spring, one who transformed into a fish and the other into a crocodile. As a result of the power of this spring and its associated sacra, waters from Irabi were carried across the region enabling marriage and creating the right to rule in other communities (these stories stretch as far away as Laga on the north coast). At some point a son of Luca, from the south coast sub-kingdom of We Soru (Vessoru), arrived in Irabi and married a daughter of the spring's custodian, creating a long-term ritual and political alliance between Irabi and We Soru. While the area is home to both Makasae and Naueti speakers, Makasae is used in the ritual language associated with the spring, suggesting that Makasae has a longer presence in the region.[5]

Another story relating to this spring tells of the time when it began gushing forth buffalo (cf. Hicks forthcoming). While the population feared this would create catastrophic flooding eventually a large male buffalo emerged and its body blocked the exit path. These buffalo became a central part of the ancestral inheritance of the people of Irabi[6] and a critical enabler of the wet rice production associated with the spring. As with other areas in the zone, irrigated rice production is said to precede the Portuguese presence and some indigenous wet rice varieties, such as a red rice known as 'fuu ga', are still planted there. The waters from the Irabi spring and the river into which it runs are shared by local rice farmers through a traditional process known as *fiar malu* (trusting in each other/respect). In more recent times, demographic changes and the in-migration of Makasae and Naueti speakers from the surrounding areas has also led to the need for a 'water controller' (M: *ira kabu*) to oversee the process of water distribution between fields.

Farmers carry out sacrificial offerings each rice-growing season to the custodians of the spring water. The yield from each harvest determines the type and quantity of animals sacrificed. A highly successful harvest requires the sacrifice of four animals (a chicken, a dog, a pig and a buffalo) in a ritual known in Makasae as '*diki*'.[7] After the annual rice harvest, the arrival of the monsoon signals the time to plant other crops such as maize, potatoes, cassava and yam (*kumbili*).

The springs of Loi Hunu

North-west of Irabi at the southern base of the Mundo Perdido range is the village of Loi Hunu where the creation narratives of local springs are also linked to the development of irrigated rice production (see Map 2.1). A past Liurai of Loi Hunu, Fransisco da Costa Guterres relayed the following story to me:

> One day an old man called Loi Hunu and his dog called Bui Lua were roaming the forest uplands where the man had been tending to his swidden. He and his dog entered a cave looking for bats to hunt and eat. The old

134   *Water relations*

man managed to kill many bats and filled his bag. But his return out of the cave was then blocked by a sudden flow of water. During the next seven days he could not exit and he ate all of the bats and even his clothes. Then a python came along. The python said to the old man: 'Loi Hunu come with me and I will take you to the sea, I will take you out of here'. But a black eel came along and told Loi Hunu not to do this: 'It will eat you on the way', the eel said of the python. With that the python continued on its way. Then a huge white eel came along and asked Loi Hunu to go with him. The black eel again warned against it, 'It will cast you off on the way' it said of the huge white eel. Then the black eel said 'If you get on my back I will take you back above ground'. They set off on a long journey. They found a small hole leading to the surface and Loi Hunu kicked at it, enough so that the eel's head could emerge. They gave this small hole in the ground the name Bui Lua (the name of Loi Hunu's dog). The man and his dog continued on down through the underground channels until they saw more light. The old man gave a big kick and the water poured forth onto the ground above.

Given the length of time he had spent underground, Loi Hunu's family in the upland area presumed him to be dead and had already carried out his burial proceedings. Meanwhile in the place where he emerged from the ground, a woman from the nearby hamlet of Ira Daba had come to draw water. She saw the man and his dog and became scared. She ran home to tell her family. Prior to Loi Hunu's emergence at this spring, the waters had been only meagre, now it had become a large water source. The people of Ira Daba came and took Loi Hunu home with them. They fed him and gave him something to drink and he recounted his story.

In this story of Loihunu's underground travels, we can see much similarity with the Wai Lia story from Baucau encountered in Chapter 4. Eventually, a thriving rice-growing community grew up around these springs which were known collectively as Loi Hunu. Each year this community would carry out rituals to give thanks to the ancestors of the spring. This spring water flowed as well into the Viqueque river from where it flowed to irrigate larger rice fields. The rice farmers from these downstream areas would bring rice as offerings for the ceremonies carried out at Loi Hunu springs. In the mid twentieth century, the colonial authorities negotiated with the people of Loi Hunu for the right to pipe water from the smaller spring of Bui Lua to Viqueque town. Following this each dry season the Viqueque authorities would bring sacrificial animals to the Loi Hunu springs.

During the Indonesian occupation the sacred house by the main spring, which had been built in honour of the ancestor Loi Hunu, was burnt down. Also lost in this fire were the sacra, 'the plates and spoons', which were used to 'feed' and activate the power of the ancestral spirits of the spring. Despite this setback the community continued, as best as they were able, to make annual sacrifices at the spring. They requested that the Indonesian authorities in

Viqueque pay an annual monetary contribution or '*sumbangam*' (I) to assist with the purchase of animals for these sacrifices. The authorities complied and they too would attend the ceremony. However, during the turmoil of the independence vote in 1999 and the population upheavals that followed, these ceremonies ceased. By 2008, the water was seriously diminished in the springs and the village head of Loi Hunu decided to organize a ceremony to restore the water's flow. This was done and the water began, at least for a period, to flow again (see below).

In 2012, I interviewed another local elder, Filomeno Da Camara, who had as a young boy been adopted by Dom Fransisco da Costa, a famous modernizing ruler of Ossu in the early twentieth century (see Shepherd and McWilliam 2014 for an account of this ruler). He explained that while his own and other local families still made the required offerings at the springs, others did not:

> Before everyone made offerings at their associated springs, but then the war and occupation began. Before when people made their offerings it was because they needed water for their rice fields, they believed in the power of their springs, rocks, trees, metal objects and other sacra. They would offer chickens, pigs and dogs to the spring. At Loi Hunu the names of the water custodians who first made these offerings were Gari Arvo and Leki Ruo. It was not [the uplanders from] Osso Rua that came to make these offerings at the springs, but Gari Arvo and Leki Ruo. Now Gari Arvo's descendants make the offerings and have the jurisdiction over Loi Hunu. However Osso Rua wants to dispute this and they say that it is part of their jurisdiction. But they are far away.

The story of the underground travels of an uplander to the springs of Loi Hunu is disputed by this local elder. He stresses that while these uplanders may now be claiming their rights in the area, these people from the neighbouring kingdom have never and do not now come to Loi Hunu to carry out these sacrifices:

> The springs here are not secure. People are fighting over them. Many people have now settled in this area. Legends from the past I don't believe, they tell them to try to take over the place. It was the government (in Indonesian times) who moved people to the roadside areas, now these people are stamping their feet and saying it's their land.
>
> I said to these people, 'people don't dig water from the land'. God gave this gift to the world. It's nature (*natureza*). It wasn't because someone kicked a hole in the ground. The old people just made up stories.[8]

Despite his scepticism towards the local spring creation narratives (particularly in the context of disputed post-independence land rights), Filomeno Da Camara does affirm the need for the local populace to make offerings to these springs whatever the challenges and obstacles:

136 *Water relations*

At Bui Lua they offer black chickens and black dogs. This was once done four times a year [after the first sowing and then harvest of both rice and maize]. However in the Portuguese times we had to pay too much tax and as a result we only were able to make offerings once a year. We paid all kinds of tax: head tax, livestock tax for buffalo and horses. Sometimes we had to work for free. We would only make our offerings in these circumstances prior to the time of harvesting rice. We would pray and call out the names of the ancestral places and rice fields so that the rice would grow well. But now these fields are abandoned. In the past we dug only earthen water channels and in the independence era these have been destroyed by landslides. Now people have moved in and built houses on areas formerly used to plant rice.

As we saw above, despite calling into question the authority of the creation stories associated with particular springs, Filomeno Da Camara makes it clear that this obligation to carry out sacrifices to the ancestors of these springs remains, whatever the difficulties, a crucial element of the right to control land and resources.

Each community will have their own particular customs and ritual practices for their respective springs (and these practices are, like narratives, often contested). Elsewhere in the Mundo Perdido region, some rituals processes entail the 'feeding' of local palm wine to the ancestral eels of the spring. This ensures the ritual cooling of their temperaments ('*fo matak malirin ba sira*') and encourages them to 'open' the flow of water to irrigation channels. Where it is the case that the associated rice fields are extensive these irrigation channels are overseen by water-controllers or *ira kabu*. The role of the *ira kabu* is also said to long precede the Portuguese presence in the area (see below pp. 143–145).

While little has been written about indigenous irrigated rice production in Timor, early twentieth-century Portuguese agricultural records are one source of information.[9] For instance in 1914, it was reported in the *Boletim de Comercio, Agricultura e Fomento da Provincia de Timor* (BCAeF) that the expansion of production in the traditional rice-producing kingdoms Manatuto, Laleia and Baucau was proceeding apace, connected to a 1912 decree to coercively force the planting of rice, so that the 'import of this cereal may be dispensed with' (BCAeF 1914(7): 478). Production was to be increased through (coercive) attention to 'methods of cultivation, which have to be transformed through the dissemination of the plough', in particular where expanses of land 'are naturally or easily irrigable' and amenable to 'two harvests per year' (BCAeF 1914(7): 478).

There can also be gleaned in this reportage at least some colonial-era recognition of a pre-existing indigenous culture of irrigated rice production. For example, it was reported in Baucau in 1914 that '[d]elaying sowing to greater or lesser degrees is a tactic that the *indigenas* use to coordinate with when there is more or less rain and less rats. There are less rats in June' (BCAeF 1914(7): 427). Yet, despite indigenous approaches to lessening these attacks by pests, it

Water relations 137

seems that rats were increasingly a problem for the colonizers. Hence, as well as their efforts to expand rice production, there is some discussion of the high cost of arsenic 'to combat rats' (BCAeF 1914(7): 44–45, 1915(2): 220). Meanwhile a report from an infantry lieutenant in Baucau in July 1914 concluded that 'the maize harvest is abundant and the rice looks pretty good … but in the last few days the rats have destroyed quite a lot, with some fields unlikely to yield a single grain' (BCAeF 1914(4): 190).[10] In 1915 the same infantry lieutenant reports that 'after so much effort on the part of individual plantation owners, the indigenes and the commanders, rice and coconut were relentlessly attacked … we can't get rid of these plagues' (BCAeF 1915(2): 220). While the causes of these plagues are not stated, they were clearly accompanied by an unprecedented intensification in the production of wet rice in the northern coastal zones (including an increase from the traditional practice of one crop to two crops of wet rice per year). Elsewhere in the archipelago, indigenous irrigation and rice cropping cycles have been reported to control and deny breeding habitats for pests (cf. Lansing 2007 [1991]; Winarto 2011; Maat forthcoming; Iskander 2007: 129; Urich 1989). When these practices were replaced with modernizing irrigation and rice-growing practices the damage caused by pests to these crops was unprecedented (Lansing 2007 [1991]). We can only hypothesise that in early twentieth-century Timor, the apparent increase in pest blighted crop production was somehow connected to the breakdown of extant local methods of irrigation and cropping cycles (see below).

While colonial irrigation interventions in the period also clearly built on indigenous irrigation channels (Correia 1944: 255, 261; Duarte 1930: 312), the attendant indigenous belief systems regulating the use of these channels were ignored or suppressed. One report from the wet rice zone of Manatuto noted the recalcitrance of indigenous ritual leaders who sought to control or suppress the supply of water to a particular irrigation channel (and presumably particular fields).[11] The colonial response in this case was swift, circumventing the ritual intervention by rapidly expanding the extent of the irrigation system so as to 'ensure enough water for the cultivation of all the lands of Manatuto' (BCAeF 1915(2): 229–231). Rice cultivation, it was added, would now be 'done properly since the use of the plough is gradually becoming a habit (literally "entering their customs") of the indigenes' (BCAeF 1915(2): 229–231).

We now return to the north coastal zone of Baucau and examine what clues there are to the history of the present-day irrigated rice production.

Irrigated rice production in Baucau

In Chapter 3, we encountered stories telling of the arrival of irrigated rice and metalwork to Baucau's coastal area. In Chapter 2, we traced the journeys of ancestral eels moving through the landscape. In one case, these eels emerged from a spring and transformed themselves into people moving the entire spring from the slopes of Mundo Perdido to Wailili on the edge of the Baucau plateau. In another story from Wai Husu in Baucau town an ancestral eel dug

138 *Water relations*

underground channels from Luca to Baucau and emerged from the spring making irrigated rice production possible.

In the ritual poetry recounting these watery journeys the custodians of waters from the inland zones call out to the populations on the coast, warning them: 'the controller of the water [M: "*ira kabu*" or W: "*kabu wai*"] has descended, when you see him you must not kill him'. The regional hydrosocial cycle is underpinned by ancestral eels who journey from 'the other world' (in many cases said to be enabled by the ritual centre of Luca) and forge subterranean channels criss-crossing the landscape. In cases where these pathways have for some reason become closed, downstream rice-growing communities know that they must send their ritual leaders inland to negotiate with the custodians of these water resources and ask them and their *dai* (the eels) to re-open the waters. In this sense these ancestral eels, which are synonymous as well with *tal-ibere*, are the original '*kabu bee*' (or water controllers).

The development of irrigation channels and new rice terraces

In contrast to these underground journeys of ancestral eels, the above ground irrigation channels now leading from Baucau's Wai Lia spring to the coastal rice fields of Bahu, Caibada, Tirilolo and Buruma are associated with the narratives of three brothers, Wono Loi, Tai Loi and Leki Loi (who, as we saw in Chapter 4, are alternatively autochthonous rulers of Baucau or invaders from the south). However, in Major Ko'o Raku's account of the development of above ground irrigation channels it was three brothers, Leki Sae, Wono Sae and Wali Sae from Makadiki Baka Hoi south of the central ranges, who initiated the construction of a network of irrigation channels stretching many kilometres from Wai Lia and Wai Husu to the sea. The expansive irrigated fields created as a result became the domain of various hamlets and households with each new terraced field being named after the farmer who created the bunds (*kabubu*) of the fields. These larger-scale irrigation networks expanded extant small-scale irrigation channels connected to particular fields and springs (see Map 4.1 for a depiction of the major irrigation channels currently flowing from Wai Lia and Wai Husu).

In contrast, the Wani Uma telling of the development of Baucau's irrigation channels focuses on the arrival of Tai Loi, Leki Loi and Wono Loi and the beginning of Bahu's monopoly over the marine terrace zone's irrigation waters. The story is recounted thus:

> In the beginning Bahu sent the waters down this way. This was done by *marui masara*. Marui masara is not a person, it is a snake [from Luca, synonymous here with eel] that married a person. It was he who opened the pathway for water to emerge down here. He tunnelled beneath the rocks and so emerged the underground channels. It is him we call *marui masara*, he is not a person, he is a snake with wings. He dug the underground channels and the water followed his tail down to the sea. We never paid for it to

Water relations 139

go down to the sea. But things are different now. After they built the irrigation channels we gave Bahu rice fields [to 'pay' for the water]. The *Liurai* (ruler) of Bahu has them until now. He eats and drinks for free. We also gave fields to the *Wai Kabu* [W: water controller] from Boile.

Hence while ancestral eels (*marui masara*) dug the subterranean water channels from Wai Lia to the sea (emerging along the way at smaller springs and creating the possibility of irrigated fields), this free flow of water was impacted on at some point by the construction of above ground irrigation channels leading from Wai Lia and for which Wani Uma were now expected to 'pay':

> Now about the water channels above ground. We call that Tai Laku Wai Dala. This is also about eels and about shrimps. They say this water belongs to Boile and Macadai [Bahu] but it really belongs to Wani Uma and Buruma. Those others were just smarter than us.
>
> After the arrival of Wono Loi, Tai Loi and Leki Loi [who they say arrived in the *tempu monarchia*, the time of Luca] the real custodians of the water were forced to buy our own water. We ignorant and stupid people didn't know. We gave rice fields to them down by the sea. This land belonged to Buruma and Wani Uma. The others lived at the waters source [at Wai Lia and Wai Husu]. But they just took this water, took it over. In ancestral times we all owned the water together, but the others came back smarter and they took over.

While the arrival of rulers from 'Luca' signals a critical development in irrigated rice production, as we have seen in Chapter 5 the Kingdom of Luca's power eventually also declined in the region. In the late nineteenth century, colonial rulers from Vemasse and Laleia increased their influence over the houses of Baucau and three of Bahu's sacred houses (Boile, Macadai and Wabubo) received their authority in the form of the *rota* (sceptre) from these new rulers. As these irrigation channels developed under the auspices of early twentieth-century Portuguese colonialism, another elder tells how the villages of Tirilolo and Buruma demanded that the water flowing from Wai Lia be formally shared with them through the water channelling process. This demand was made with reference to the founding sibling relationship that the three brothers, Wono Loi, Tai Loi and Leki Loi, had created between the villages.

The history of such changes during this period elsewhere in the Baucau district is demonstrated in the following account from the Wai Daba spring in Berecoli:

> What is important here is water. Our forebears were able to produce fields, rice and plantations because of this water. Our rice fields are old. In monarchical times before the Portuguese arrived we already had them. We had no buffalo or horses, we would prepare the fields by dragging rocks through them. We would make a place and tie a rope to a piece of limestone and

140 *Water relations*

drag it around to make the soil muddy. There were no animals. And there were only a small amount of rice fields. These original rice fields were all named. When the Portuguese arrived [in the early twentieth century] they were recorded in a book of tax records, but when our sacred house was burnt down [in the Indonesian era] that book was lost.[12] In the past my aunt who married a Chinese in Baucau would pay the tax for this land. Her husband worked with the Portuguese administrators and he would collect the tax for them. The Portuguese sent only the children of the rulers to school – this was a kind of politics. If this hadn't been the case we would all be smart by now. Berecoli is the heart of the Waima'a lands which stretched from here to the top of Matebian and across to Vemasse. While now these lands are largely dominated by the Makasae, it was the Portuguese that carved up the land.

While in this account an autochthonous connection to the land and waters is asserted, it is also clear that artefacts, such as taxation records, from the colonial encounter are also now a critical part of this story. Similarly, although the institution of the *kabu bee* (M: *ira kabu*, W: *wai kabu*) is said (without exception) to precede the Portuguese presence, the term *kabu* is most likely derived from the Portuguese *noscabo*, a lowly ranked military officer (cf. Barnes 2011). Hence in Baucau town in the early twentieth century the figure of *kabu bee* is remembered as a fearsome town crier who brandished a whip and called out the orders of the village heads (*liurai*) regarding the irrigation schedule and the cleaning of the canals. During this period the three *liurai* of Bahu, Caibada and Tirilolo would come together to decide the irrigation schedule over the following three-year period. The *kabu bee* would enforce this schedule.

Elsewhere in the 'new world', studies of long-standing irrigation communities in the American south-west show how the indigenous and non-indigenous *acequia* communities of the region are built on refashioned Islamic irrigation law first brought to the region by the Spanish colonial settlement in the 1500s. As Rodriguez (2007: 3) argues: '[a]cequias appropriated and transformed whatever irrigation structures and practices were operating among the Pueblos in the Upper Rio Grande Valley at the time of European contact'.[13] Such examples draw our attention to the inter-relationship and adaptive capacity of customary governance systems which encountered and continue to dynamically co-exist with colonial-era practices.

Extant practices of irrigated rice production in Baucau town

By the late 1960s, when the geographer Joaquim Metzner carried out fieldwork in the Baucau-Viqueque region, karst springs were the basis of the local rice production in the fields below Baucau town. While Metzner makes no mention of the rituals carried out at these springs he does note that in Baucau and surrounds agricultural production was dominated by what he termed an 'archaic' form of irrigated rice cultivation. In the lands directly below Baucau town he

Water relations   141

documented a tradition of double cropping terraced fields (*natar*) with an annual crop of rice, followed by one of maize, sweet potato or onion (Metzner 1977; cf. BCAeF 1918(4): 456). These fields were fed by two large spring complexes: Wai Lia located in the centre of the town itself and Wai Husu in Teulale just below the town proper. Metzner's description of the local rice ecology as 'archaic' referred to the following processes: the fields are fed by nutrient-poor spring water, with equally poor calcareous soils continually hardened by a field preparation method involving the trampling of mud by horses or buffalo, and into these rock-prone fields of largely unimproved soils are planted indigenous rice species returning low yields. Yet despite what he terms an 'archaic' process, Metzner did comment that one cannot fail to be impressed by the local 'display of ingenuity' (1977: 136) in regard to the terracing of the rice fields. In addition, he writes that:

> Owing to the constant water the terraces from Baucau village down to the sea are intensively cultivated [for a variety of crops] throughout the year. Thus apart from similar sites on the eastern and western escarpment of the Baucau plateau the region around Baucau village is certainly one of the most privileged agricultural zones of the Baucau-Viqueque area which, because of its near level platforms, is particularly suited for wet rice cultivation.
>
> (Metzner 1977: 25–26)

He reports briefly too on a series of man-made clay and mud water channels which branch out from the town's springs in order to feed the rice fields at some distance to the east and west and down to the sea (see Map 4.1).[14] He mentions in this regard the role of a figure 'assigned' by the 'local peasants' and known in Tetum as the *Kabo-be*, which he translates as the 'village official in charge of distribution of water for wet rice fields' (1977: xix). Despite this he says there are frequent quarrels over scarce water supplies. Rights to *natar*, whilst inheritable, were, in his opinion, more like a permanent usufruct than ownership and there were sometimes quarrels over seemingly abandoned paddy fields (1977: 147).

These practices described by Metzner are extant, if somewhat precarious, in Baucau today. The agrarian system embedded in the landscape continues to feature a scattered network of individually owned dry and wet agricultural plots transferred through inheritance or marriage. Such agricultural holdings and 'transactions' are recorded via story and specific naming practices and upheld through ritual practice.[15] Collective labour in fields is enabled by house-based marriage exchange networks and produce and money are distributed and redistributed through these inter-linked groups. Communal grazing of buffalo, goats and horses across these lands remains the norm, as does the shared planting and harvest of wet rice among aligned house-based groups (sometimes for payment and sometimes for meals). Little in the way of state agricultural support is offered to Baucau's marine terrace rice farmers and they have struggled to

142   *Water relations*

maintain their network of irrigation canals and restore their depleted stocks of livestock and machinery in the independence era. These difficulties are compounded by the drift of youth to Dili, creating a shortage of agricultural labour, particularly for the planting and harvesting of irrigated rice. Similarly, cheap government subsidized rice imports and an emerging preference for small-scale market gardens are shifting farmers' efforts away from wet rice production in this zone. As a result in some years, even when water is available, some fields may not be planted at all.

In the fields that are planted many rice cultivars are now sourced from imported varieties (which are theoretically higher yielding and faster growing). Some indigenous cultivars remain, particularly red rice varieties. In contrast to the river-fed plains around the Seisal River (see Map 4.1), rice in the marine terrace zone is usually grown only for household and ritual consumption. Due to the high cost of agricultural inputs it is also mostly produced by organic farming methods. In a few areas, mechanized rice threshing has become more widespread as the machinery has been distributed by international agricultural organizations.

Post-sowing and post-harvest rituals continue to punctuate the rice-growing calendar of most (see below). Horses and buffalo are still preferred to puddle fields although there is an increasing use of hand-tractors in some larger less rocky fields (tractors were for a period distributed to farmers' 'co-operatives' by the Timorese Ministry of Agriculture). In some areas there remain in place prohibitions against iron machinery such as ploughs, tractors or threshing machines entering fields. These prohibitions are applied to fields which were first opened by the ancestors and which remain central to a house's ongoing ritual exchanges with ancestral spirits. In such cases machinery may only be admitted to these fields after the permission of the ancestors has been requested and granted at rituals carried out at the relevant sacred house (many of which also continue to be constructed without the use of iron, including nails). The reasons for such prohibitions are twofold: first, these materials were not used by the ancestors[16] and, second, ancestral beings and nature spirits are in general averse to metals (this is why pregnant women may be advised to place an iron nail in their hair in order to ward off the unwanted attention of malevolent spirits).[17]

Across the marine terrace zone, rice is irrigated by a network of mostly earthen but sometimes lime-lined or concreted canals reaching from major springs while lesser springs have shorter earthen canals feeding smaller areas. In the case of the irrigation channels leading from the Wai Lia and Wai Husu springs there is one annual communal irrigation cycle for rice production. This also enables livestock grazing in the fallowed fields outside of this cycle. In some areas in this zone, two crops of rice may be grown annually. In such cases, the second crop remains outside of the communal irrigation cycle and must be fed by alternative irrigation waters. As described below, the annual irrigation cycle is enabled by the creation of irrigator groups whose individual members usually also have access to smaller springs as alternative, if less reliable, irrigation sources. The water controller and the irrigator groups from Baucau's marine

Water relations 143

terrace zone have no formal relationship with the district agricultural department, which concentrates its limited resources on working with more 'modern' irrigation co-operatives in the plains and river valleys (cf. Thu 2012).

Traditional irrigation co-operatives

To enable their cultivation of the terraced fields around Baucau town, water-sharing farmers come together in cross-village co-operatives to appoint irrigated rice water controllers known as *kabu bee* (or *wai kabu* in Waima'a and *ira kabu* in Makasae). These people enforce and police the annual allocation of water between sections of a particular water channel and between the rice farmers themselves. Each land-owning village will have several *kabu bee* appointed at a meeting of the community of rice farmers connected to one particular channel. As Bahu is the older brother in the sibling relationship between the villages these irrigation co-operatives will meet to appoint the various *kabu bee* at the Bahu village head's office. The water allocation for the annual rice-growing season rotates each year between the various channels and villages and is determined by meeting of the village and sub-village heads in consultation with *kabu bee* and the rice farmers.

The position of the *kabu bee* is held until retirement or ousting due to a failure to properly fulfil their responsibilities. Payment for their services is made up by the collective contribution of a small portion of the rice harvest from each of the farmers in that area. The *kabu bee* is responsible for organizing the irrigation co-operative to painstakingly clear and clean the several kilometres of water channels which feed into the shared named blocks of rice fields.[18] These water channels are fashioned from mud, clay, rock, lime and, in some places, reinforced with concrete. Annual repairs include cleaning away grasses, tree and vegetation roots and rehabilitating channel wash outs with mud, rocks and whatever other materials are at hand (see Figure 6.3). At the same time the work team will close off the many smaller water diversions to non-rice-growing areas.

The *kabu bee* also co-ordinates the rituals for water dividing and sharing. Meanwhile water 'opening' ceremonies are carried out by particular ritual leaders at springs and these rituals ensure the ancestral spirits will send the waters down the channels to the rice fields. Immediately or shortly after this ceremony to send the waters, a water sharing/dividing ceremony will take place at the fork in the main water channel above where the rice fields are to be irrigated in that year. During this ceremony, which involves ritual leaders, village and sub-village heads, the *kabu bee* and the male and female community of rice farmers, a goat will be sacrificed.[19] The ritual leader will invoke the ancestral names of Wono Loi, Tai Loi and Leki Loi, amongst others, in order to receive and give thanks for the water. The names of other ancestors connected to the named blocks of rice fields below the water division will also be invoked so that they in turn will receive the water. The water in the channel is divided by the placement of rocks in the middle of the water channel. The measuring of this

Figure 6.3 Annual irrigation channel repairs overseen by the *kabu bee* (water controllers) from Bahu and Caibada (Jose da Costa (right) and Enrici da Costa).

division will be done by the *kabu bee* with the village heads and subheads witnessing that the placement reflects the pre-agreed division. Next to the rock division will be placed a wooden stake hung with small branches, the public signal that water-sharing arrangements are in place and that from now on no one other than the *kabu bee* is authorized to make changes affecting the water irrigation. Anyone that does will be penalized with the fine of a goat or, in extreme cases, will have the water supply to their fields shut off.[20] Following the water-sharing ceremony a communal feast is held in the rice fields nearby.

Democratically elected, the office of the *kabu bee* is essentially secular. While he is directly accountable to the rice co-operative members he is also in some respects an agent of the village or sub-village head. However, it is also clear from the process outlined above that his own and the irrigation co-operatives' work cannot be carried out without the active support, participation and religious knowledge of local ritual leaders, as well as the living human custodians of the springs. In some communities with less extensive irrigation channels the spring custodian will carry out these tasks of water allocation and dispute resolution.

Once irrigation waters are received by each individual rice farmer they too will carry out rituals in their own rice fields. The most important of these are those carried out when the 'body' of the rice first forms and again after harvest

Water relations   145

when the 'first rice' is transported back to the farmer's sacred house. This rice must be transported back to the sacred house by a female member of the lineage.[21] This ritual, known in Makasae as *rau wai* ('good blood'), culminates at the house in the ritual washing of house members' bodies with water collected at the spring associated with the house. After this ritual, water from any of the springs which has fed the fields will be collected and sprinkled over the remainder of the rice before it too is carried home.

All of these planting, harvest and water-sharing practices and rituals are believed to be critical to the growth and fertility of rice crops and individual lineages. As we saw in Chapter 4, these ritual practices and relationships also extend upwards from the marine terrace zone to the custodians of the underground water on the Baucau plateau. A further component of the relationship between the *ria p'obo* (W: 'wet ground') and *ria mhare* (W: 'dry ground') communities is said to be the contribution to the house of Ledatame Ikun of one *lata*[22] of unmilled rice per rice farmer. The *kabu bee* is charged with collecting and delivering this 'tribute'. The gifted rice is then consumed by Ledatame Ikun in the ritual feasts for their twice annual ceremonies alternatively celebrating the harvest of rice and maize. Ritual leaders from Bahu are also invited to attend these feasts. The Ledatame ritual custodians of the water say that they do not demand this tribute, stressing rather that these are *gifts* which the coastal rice farmers choose to make. While it is unclear for how long this particular practice has been carried out it seems that the process has always been done under the auspices of the village of Bahu. The elders of Wani Uma state that:

> Recently the Liurai of Bahu asked us to take 50 *lata* (tins) of rice to Darasula. But we at Wani Uma have never gone there to do this. The smart people go. We ignorant and stupid people just follow what they say.

Ritual politics, ancestral names and bodies

While they are largely marginalized from the administrative village politics of the area, Wani Uma elders also make it clear that the political houses of Baucau today lack the true knowledge of the underground ancestral journey from the plateau to the Wai Lia spring. The true ancestral name and origins of the man who emerged from the spring is said to be concealed by the ritual prayers associated with the spring. They explained it to me thus:

> The water in Baucau really belongs to Wani Uma and Buruma because it was they that arrived first in the region. When they arrived they created the water sources. The man that emerged from Wai Lia was a son of Kelikai [Quelicai] who had come and married a woman from Ledatame. It was he who fell into the water after he tied a salt basket containing ash around his dog's neck and followed him to the water. The problem is that the name of this person was 'hidden' by the family of the woman who found and married him. If you know this story and the correct ancestral name when you recite

146 *Water relations*

> this prayer at the spring the buffalo will just fall down dead and the water
> will flow forth vigorously. There is no need to kill the buffalo with a knife.
> The so-called custodian of the water cannot do this. Only the ancestors of
> the Rikainena Primeru [a house of Wani Uma] knew this correct story.
> When the new rulers ('*ema matenek*') came along they changed Cai Bada's
> name to Tai Loi but the buffalo would not die. Calling the names Leki Loi,
> Wono Loi the buffalo still would not die. Only Rikainena Primeru could
> recite the prayer correctly and make the buffalo die.

In this claim made by the elders of Wani Uma it is clearly acknowledged that
while the village of Bahu may be clever (*matenek*) and has benefited from its
alliances with newcomers, they are not the 'true' holders of knowledge about
relationships connecting this spring to other places. This Wani Uma claim to
'true' knowledge is both an assertion of ritual precedence and a claim to pre-
eminent rights in both land and water in the area.

Meanwhile the present-day custodian of the Wai Lia headspring in Baucau is
the house of Wai Mata Buu (W: 'the Custodian of the Spring') in the village of
Bahu. As a result of disruption to these rituals in the second half of the twentieth century (this is discussed in Chapter 7), the present-day (Makasae-speaking)
custodian of Wai Mata Buu has, by his own admission, limited knowledge of the
ritual prayers (and stories) associated with the spring.[23] Nonetheless it was his
ancestor who emerged out of the spring seven generations ago and married a
woman from Macadai (as we see throughout this book, seven is a number with
particular ritual significance across the region, and in order to keep to this patterning some clans will only recount seven generations (Hicks 2004: 79)). The
full name of the hamlet where the house of Wai Mata Buu is located is Macadai
Wai Mata Buu. For the people of Macadai in Bahu this reflects the fact that the
original ancestor of Wai Mata Buu emerged in the waters of Wai Lia and subsequently in-married (*kaben tama*) into the woman's house in Macadai. This
absence of a 'proper' marriage exchange process between the fertility-takers and
the fertility-givers (in this case from the husband's family to the wife's family[24])
enables Macadai to also claim a role as the rightful custodian of the waters of
Wai Lia. However, this version of events is disputed by Wai Mata Buu and the
elder brother house of Ledatame Ikun who maintain that an exchange of buffalo
and other goods did eventually take place. In another account, the Bahu house
of Boile Komu claim to have adopted the original ancestor of Wai Mata Buu (in
this account it was women and men from the house of Boile Komu who rescued
him at the spring) and to have arranged the marriage and exchanged the appropriate goods with the house of Macadai. Through this account Boile Komu is
able to assert its own older sibling connection to the Wai Lia spring and story.

Given the present-day challenges surrounding the organization of large-scale
community rituals at the spring (see Chapter 7), what is also notable about
these many versions of the one story is that they now lack a collective forum for
deliberation and negotiation. Nonetheless despite the lack of ritual knowledge
of the present-day custodian of Wai Mata Buu and the various 'truth' claims

relating to custodial relationships, when ceremonies of whatever scale are held at the spring, Wai Mata Buu's 'bodily' presence is central to activating the mutuality of relations (or co-beingness) between human and non-human water custodians. It is his body that provides the path to this diversely manifest ancestral realm and only together can these 'bodies' activate the fertility and flow of the irrigation waters.

Discussion

It is evident that there are a range of challenges facing the politics and practices of traditional irrigated rice production across the zone. At the same time there is also great continuity in the frameworks through which rights to rice fields and water continue to be envisioned and enabled. These relations are dynamic and open to reinterpretation via both the telling of stories and the ritual practices associated with them. Many of these place-based practices have also long been engaged with formal colonial governance processes and interventions. Through this all, honouring ancestral and marriage exchange relations clearly remains a central consideration in the local configurations of rights and responsibilities and to the success of the rice irrigation and harvest (and all revolve around 'gift giving' in exchange for fertility) (cf. Hicks 2004).

Nonetheless in the complexity of people's relationship to place and each other, it is often the case that the stories of ancestral and human relations connected through water never quite add up. Despite all the tellings of the parts, the whole remains elusive, a sort of hovering 'absent presence' (Traube 1989: 340). As Traube writes, local people:

> do not necessarily try to order parts into a whole, and so to understand how everything hangs together, but rather content themselves with a faith that things do indeed cohere, and that the source of that coherence lies in the past ... an untold remainder.
>
> (Traube 1989: 340)

There is thus an ever present tension in these narratives between elusive 'true', complete or 'trunk' knowledge and partial 'tip' knowledge. The point of the latter, writes Traube, is to 'reinscribe paradigms into narrative sequences' (1989: 341) and such narrations are an 'interpretative act by which individuals at once give meaning to their own socially lived experience and construct their identities in relation to their audiences' (Traube 1989: 339).

Also exploring the constant assertion of and search for 'true words', in the highlands of the Manatuto district Bovensiepen (2012: 57) pays close attention to the paradox of 'dynamic processes' and the ways 'through which villagers sought to establish the notion that these words exist in a timeless sphere external to the human body'. Later, by drawing together an analytical distinction between essentialist (timeless) and inter-subjective (negotiated) notions of knowledge, she argues that:

148 *Water relations*

> In a particular context, these two notions can *seem* opposed, but one element of this opposition ('trunk' knowledge) always also contains its opposite ('tip' knowledge). Hence, at one level, these two poles can appear opposed, even though, at a different, preceding level, the two opposites (trunk and tip) are encompassed by a greater original totality (the trunk).
>
> (Bovensiepen 2012: 70–71)

Yet it can be argued from the material presented in this chapter that also significant to such knowledge politics, is the fact that attached to these words are ancestral names and to them actual bodies: the bodies of the dead and the bodies of the living. It is, then, this continuity between the living and the dead that is the greater original totality. In this way knowledge is never something external to the body, it is critically embodied and relational, relying on the co-being and constant 'participation' of particular bodies which connect the dead to the living (and the not yet born). Such continuities apply equally to the bodies of named objects, the sacra used to feed the ancestors of springs and sacred houses (this is discussed in Chapter 7).

In the politics surrounding such knowledge negotiations and ritual practices, Traube concludes that what matters more than the telling of these stories is the presence of knowledgeable ritual leaders at events, those who could tell, but choose not to. Yet what is also evident, particularly in the context of twentieth-century disruptions to local livelihoods and ritual practices, is the centrality in this 'absent presence' of those who may no longer be able to tell (in either narrative or prayer) but whose own socially inscribed 'body' constitutes a critical part to the whole. In such cases what matters is the attributes of their bodily presence, forming as they do a conduit between the storied world of the living and the ancestral presence of the *dai* (cf. Tsintjilonis 2004; Viveiros de Castro 2012). Hence while the words of the living enliven the world, it is essentially the spiritual ecology of the 'collective body' of the custodians of the waters (living and dead, humans and non-humans) which transmute its life force, forming a contiguous link to a greater whole. This link, activated through water and ritual, ensures that such practices remain embedded in a constant process of communication, negotiation, debt and obligation with the ancestral realm.

As in the past, this world of relational, always embodied knowledge is challenged in the independence era by other frameworks of land and property relations. As we will see in the next chapter, eliding the ongoing significance of 'participation' and the intergenerational flow of life (fertility) between marriage exchange alliances, the living and the dead, humans and non-humans, these powerful, 'other-worldly' frameworks seek to solidify boundaries demarcating individuals and groups, land and property. While these changes are embraced by many, others are more fearful. Across the Baucau Viqueque zone, elders pose similar questions to that of Onvlee over half a century ago in Sumba: 'What other bedrock can this culture now build on? Into what shall it root?' (1977 [1949]: 163). It is to this question that I turn my attention in the final chapter.

Notes

1 By the late twentieth century, in many localities factors such as war, population growth and modernist agricultural ideologies had all contributed to a lessening of the hunter-gatherer aspects of this economy.

2 Correia (1935: 113) gives an account of a similar range of activities in the Makasae seasonal calendar.

3 Women are usually responsible for the sale of non-subsistence produce at local markets and roadside stalls.

4 Schulte Nordholt (1971: 271) describes a myth of the Atoni in which two brothers known as Sonba'i kill their sister and chop her body into pieces. From her limbs sprout crops.

5 We saw on the north coast that the arrival of (returning) peoples from across the sea was connected with the emergence of rice agriculture (Chapter 3). During research carried out by Susana Barnes in the nearby kingdom of Babulu, local Naueti speakers suggested that their ritual language contains many 'old' Makasae words, the meaning of which is not clear (pers. comm. 2014).

6 The last remaining descendants of this herd were lost during the Indonesian occupation.

7 A lesser ritual involving the sacrifice of a dog, a chicken and a pig is known as *saba lesa*.

8 As a result of his adoption by Dom Fransisco, Filomeno Da Camara was educated to class four in Ossu's elite missionary college. This was not a common occurrence for local men of his generation and something for which he is understandably proud.

9 It is not known exactly how long irrigated rice has been grown for in Timor. According to Soares (2003: 144), irrigated rice was introduced (or at least significantly expanded) by the Portuguese in Timor by Governor Jose Alcaforado de Azevedu e Sousa in 1816 with assistance from Javanese irrigators. The longevity of irrigated rice expansion can also be inferred by Silva who writes that:

> [i]n Timor, the cultivation of rice is done under more diverse conditions. Here and there, one notes the influence of practices used in neighbouring islands, where the population knows how to cultivate rice with skill. It is very likely that immigrants of various origins have taught something [to the Timorese], just as it appears that the Japanese took advantage of the agricultural lowlands [presumably for rice] ... The region in which rice cultivation is most advanced is, undoubtedly, Viqueque, on the plains of Luca.
>
> (1956: 104)

10 In addition to this many buffalo were dying (BCAeF 1914(4): 190), possibly due to the increasing pesticide use (cf. Urich 1989).

11 Manatuto farmers say that Manatuto once had similar indigenous irrigation practices and rituals as those described below in Baucau town. Land in the senior landowning groups in Manatuto is passed through the matriline.

12 This book of records is important in the context of a current dispute over rights to particular rice fields between the custodians of the land and waters and the descendants of others from Quelicai. In the early twentieth century, the latter were 'invited' in (through sacred agreement with a *liurai* from Quelicai) to farm in the area.

13 This body of irrigation law brought to New Mexico from Spain was an adaptation of Islamic law brought to the Iberian Peninsula (both Spain and Portugal) during the north African occupation of the area (an occupation that lasted some 700 years until being expelled by the Conquistadors in the thirteenth century). This body of law was subsequently adapted by the new Christian rulers of the Peninsula and eventually taken to the New World in the late fifteenth century (Rivera and Glick n.d.).

150 *Water relations*

14 Duarte (1930: 312) also notes the existence of indigenous irrigation channels and a programme of government improvement and management. Correia (1935: 255) refers to masons lining irrigation channels near Buruma with limestone. While some irrigation channels were previously earthen, others appear to have been fashioned from bamboo (BCAeF 1918(4): 459).

15 A minority of areas, such as fields close to Gariuai village and the Fatumaka Agricultural College, had their (fertile) agricultural lands surveyed and registered through Indonesian-era cadastral surveys.

16 This preoccupation with ancestral processes of rice production is perhaps linked to the point made by Forman that '[r]ice itself was not sacred to the Makassae, but only that which was ritually produced and processed' (1981: 105, 106; cf. Iskander 2007: 119).

17 There are many local spring narratives which recount the danger of disclosing to the ancestral realm the living's use of metal fishing hooks (cf. Hicks 2007, forthcoming). In many of these myths power objects retrieved from springs via the 'dark world' emerge from the springs in the first instance as vegetative substances such as gourds and vines. Only later, after the sun has risen, do they transform into wealth such as gold, swords and buffalo.

18 Failure to participate incurs a fine, usually a goat, although if a farmer or landowner (with labourers) is unable to participate a representative can be sent or alternatively a contribution can be made to feed the working team of men.

19 Depending on the size of rice fields each rice farmer contributes a small sum of money ($1–2) for this sacrifice.

20 Non-participation of rice farmers in the water-dividing ceremony may also attract the fine of a goat.

21 A similar set of harvest rituals is described in detail by Correia (1935: 92–98, cf. 64).

22 Timorese use bulk not weight measures '*Lata* = 20 litre oil tin equiv 12.8 kg of unmilled rice' (Metzner 1977: 129).

23 At spring ceremonies these ritual prayers are narrated by others (notably Major Ko'o Raku).

24 See Chapter 1, endnote 9.

References

Barnes, S. (2011) 'Origins, Precedence and Social Order in the Domain of *Ina Ama Beli Darlari*', in A. McWilliam and E. Traube (eds) *Land and Life in Timor-Leste: Ethnographic Essays*, Canberra: ANU E-Press, 24–46.

Barnes, S. (2013) 'Gift Giving and Gift Obligations', paper presented at 7th EuroSEAS Conference, Lisbon, July 2013.

Blust, R. (1976) 'Austronesian Culture History: Some Linguistic Inferences and their Relations to the Archaeological Record', *World Archaeology* 8(1): 19–43.

Boletím de Comercio Agricultura e Fomento da Provincia de Timor [BCAeF] (1914–1918).

Bovensiepen, J. (2012) 'Words of the Ancestors: Disembodied Knowledge and Secrecy in East Timor', *Journal of the Royal Anthropological Institute* 20: 56–77.

Carvalho, D.A. (2011) 'Ritual Sira Kona ba Jestaun Bee Nudar Aplikasaun Matenek Local iha Timor Leste', in D.A. Carvalho (ed.) *Matenek Lokal Timor Nian*, Jakarta: UNESCO, 70–83.

Correia, A. (1935) *Gentio de Timor*, Lisbon: Agência-Geral das Colónias.

Correia, A. (1944) *Timor de Lés a Lés*, Lisbon: Agência Geral das Colónias.

Duarte, T. (1930) *Timor: Ante-Camara do Inferno?* Lisboa: Famalocao.

Forman, S. (1978) 'East Timor: Exchange and Political Hierarchy at the Time of the European Discoveries', in K. Hutterer (ed.) *Economic Exchange and Social Interaction in*

Southeast Asia: Perspectives from Prehistory, History and Ethnography, Michigan Papers on South and Southeast Asia No. 13, The University of Michigan, 97–112.

Forman, S. (1980) 'Descent, Alliance and Exchange Ideology among the Makassae of East Timor', in J. Fox (ed.) *The Flow of Life: Essays on Eastern Indonesia*, Cambridge, MA: Harvard University Press, 152–177.

Forman, S. (1981) 'Life Paradigms: Makassae (East Timor) Views on Production, Reproduction, and Exchange', *Research in Economic Anthropology: A Research Annual* 4: 95–110.

Friedberg, C. (1989) 'Social Relations of Territorial Management in Light of Bunaq Farming Rituals', *Bijdragen tot de Taal-, Land- en Volkenkunde* 145(4): 548–562.

Hicks, D. (2004) *Tetum Ghosts & Kin: Fertility and Gender in East Timor*, Illinois: Waveland Press.

Hicks, D. (2007) 'Younger Brother and the Fishing Hook on Timor: Reassessing Mauss on Hierarchy and Divinity', *Journal of Royal Anthropological Institute* 13: 39–56.

Hicks, D. (forthcoming) 'Impaling Spirit: Three Categories of Ontology in Eastern Indonesia', in K. Arhem and G. Sprenger, *Animism in Southeast Asia*, Routledge.

Iskander, J. (2007) 'Responses to Environmental Stress in the Baduy Swidden System, South Banten, Java', in R. Ellen (ed.) *Modern Crises and Traditional Strategies: Local Ecological Knowledge in Island South-East Asia*, New York: Berghahn Books, 112–132.

Lansing, J. (2007) [1991] *Priests and Programmers: Technologies of Power in the Engineered Landscape of Bali*, Princeton: Princeton University Press.

Lazarowitz, T. (1980) 'The Makassai: Complimentary Dualism in Timur', unpublished PhD thesis, State University of New York.

Maat, H. (forthcoming) 'Commodities and Anti-Commodities: Rice on Sumatra 1915–1925', in F. Bray, P. Coclanis, E. Fields-Black and D. Schaefer (eds) *Rice: Global Networks and New Histories*, Cambridge: Cambridge University Press.

McWilliam, A. (2002) 'Timorese Seascapes: Perspectives on Customary Marine Tenures in Timor Leste', *The Asia Pacific Journal of Anthropology* 3(2): 6–32.

McWilliam, A. (2005) 'Houses of Resistance in East Timor: Structuring Sociality in the New Nation', *Anthropological Forum* 15(1): 27–44.

McWilliam, A. and Traube, E. (eds) (2011) *Land and Life in Timor-Leste: Ethnographic Essays*, Canberra: ANU E-Press.

Metzner, J. (1977) *Man and Environment in Eastern Timor: A Geoecological Analysis of the Baucua-Viqueque Area as a Possible Basis for Regional Planning*, Canberra: The Australian National University.

Oliveira, N. (2006) 'Returning to East Timor: Prospects and Possibilities from an Archaeobotanical Project in the New Country', in I. Bacus and V. Pigott (eds) *Uncovering Southeast Asia's Past*, Singapore: National University of Singapore, 88–97.

Onvlee, L. (1977) [1949] 'The Construction of the Mangalili Dam, Notes on the Social organsiation of Eastern Sumba', in P.E. De Josselin de Jong (ed.) *Structural Anthropology in the Netherlands: A Reader*, The Hague: Martinus Nijhoff, 150–163.

Ormeling, F. (1955) *The Timor Problem: A Geographical Interpretation of an Underdeveloped Island*, New York: AMS Press.

Ospina, S. and Hohe, T. (2001) *Traditional Power Structures and the Community Empowerment and Local Governance Structures Final Report*, Dili: World Bank.

Palmer, L. and Carvalho, D.A. (2008) 'Nation Building and Resource Management: The Politics of "Nature" in Timor Leste', *Geoforum* 39(3): 1321–1332.

Pannell, S. (2011) 'Struggling Geographies: Rethinking Livelihood and Locality in Timor-Leste', in A. McWilliam and E. Traube (eds) *Land and Life in Timor-Leste: Ethnographic Essays*, Canberra: ANU E-Press, 217–239.

152 Water relations

Rappaport, R. (1999) *Ritual and Religion in the Making of Humanity*, Cambridge: Cambridge University Press.

Rivera, J. and Glick, T. (n.d.) *The Iberian Origins of New Mexico's Community Acequias*. Available at: http://taosacequias.org/Documents/GlickRivera409.pdf (accessed 20 August 2014).

Rodriguez, S. (2007) *Acequia: Water Sharing, Sanctity and Place*, Sante Fe: School for Advanced Research Resident Scholar Book.

Schulte Nordholt, H. (1971) *The Political System of the Atoni of Timor*, The Hague: Martinus Nijhoff.

Shepherd, C. (2013) *Development and Environmental Politics Unmasked: Authority, Participation and Equity in East Timor*, London and New York: Routledge.

Shepherd, C. and McWilliam, A. (2014) 'Divide and Cultivate: Plantations, Militarism and Environment in Portuguese Timor, 1860–1975', in F. Uekotter (ed.) *Comparing Apples, Oranges, and Cotton: Environmental Histories of the Global Plantation*, Chicago: University of Chicago Press, 139–166.

Silva, H.L. (1956) *Timor e a Cultura do Café*, Lisbon: Ministério do Ultramar.

Silva, H.L. (1964) *Programa de Desenvolvimento Agrícola 1965–1975: Comunicação no 47*, Lisbon: Missao de Estudos Agronomicos do Ultramar.

Soares, A.V.M. (2003) *Pulau Timor: Sebuah Sumbangan Untuk Sejarahnya*, Baucau: Edicao Tipografia Diocesana Baucau.

Thu, P. (2012) 'Negotiating Displacement: A Study of Land and Livelihoods in Rural East Timor', unpublished PhD thesis, Australian National University.

Traube, E. (1989) 'Obligation to the Source: Complementarity and Hierarchy in an Eastern Indonesian Society', in D. Maybury-Lewis and U. Almagor (eds) *The Attraction of Opposites: Thought and Society in the Dualistic Mode*, Ann Arbor: University of Michigan Press, 321–344.

Tsintjilonis, D. (2004) 'The Flow of Life in Buntao: Southeast Asian Animism Reconsidered', *Bijdragen tot de Taal-, Land- en Volkenkunde* 160(4): 425–455.

Urich, P. (1989) 'Tropical Karst Management and Agricultural Development: Example from Bohol, Phillipines', *Geografiska Annaler Series B, Human Geography* 71(2): 95–108.

Viveiros de Castro E. (2012) 'Cosmological Perspectivism in Amazonia and Elsewhere', *Master Class Series 1*, Manchester: HAU Network of Ethnographic Theory.

Winarto, Y. (2011) 'The Ecological Implications of Central Versus Local Governance: The Control over Integrated Pest Management in Indonesia', in M. Dove, P. Sajise and A. Doolittle (eds) *Beyond the Sacred Forest: Complicating Conservation in Southeast Asia*, Durham, NC: Duke University Press, 276–302.

7 Independence and the (re)negotiation of customary relations[1]

Like the rest of post-independence Timor Leste the spectre and expectation of development looms large in Baucau, the municipal hub of the east and the nation's second largest city.[2] Yet in this 'in desperate need of development' economy, less discernible to the unacquainted is the fact that the customary processes of exchange and inclusive sociality tracked in the pages of this book are equally enmeshed in complicated relationships with the formal state and capitalist sector. In this chapter I explore the renaissance of custom in Baucau town and surrounds and its many challenges. I begin with a discussion of the issues which confronted customary water governance in the late twentieth century and then examine the independence-era reassertion of ancestral identities and relationships. Through all of this I shed light on the multiple ways these worlds are being (re)negotiated 'cleaving' together and apart with powerfully discursive alternative practices and relational materialities (Lavau 2013). I also examine the ways in which the substantial resources invested to build community-based water supply systems and carry out hydrogeological research have to date elided substantive consideration of the complex socio-ecological variables impacting on the use and management of water resources in this particular karstic zone.

During my fieldwork for this book, the Timorese government (in association with USAID) was developing new land and property laws and trialling a process of land registration to further demarcate property and create secure land markets, particularly in urban areas (Rede Ba Rai 2013; Fitzpatrick *et al.* 2012). Another part of the bureaucracy was working with international advisers to draft new national water laws and policies (Jackson and Palmer 2012). This meant that as local peoples were embracing their freedom to reconstitute their ancestral traditions and invigorate relations among themselves, they were also drawn into processes which sought to define land and resources through new systems of abstraction, legibility and value. Despite the land registration trial being limited to urban Baucau, the consequence of this discursive intervention across the zone was that a new emergence was underway: '*agora rai folin iha*' ('now the land has a price'). The immediate effect of the new laws was to enhance the power of the state to 'purchase' long-term leases or expropriate lands for development (Rede Ba Rai 2013; Stead 2014). Such a powerfully

154 *The (re)negotiation of customary relations*

discursive set of practices overlaid existing relational processes with new tensions. In Baucau, the result has been disquiet, simmering anxiety and even violence between local residents, neighbours and families. Sub-village heads say they are now called to intervene and mediate in an unprecedented number of local property disputes.

At the same time as new land titling processes are being trialled, made legible and passed into law, district administrators and their national level counterparts eagerly encourage and plan for development and international investment in the district. Village heads are asked to support particular development visions often prior to community 'socialization', and this inadequate 'consultation' leaves many villagers uninformed and embittered. District administrators meanwhile are hopeful that new national political administrative laws will drive a municipal makeover. Amidst this milieu of aspirational rhetoric and weak consultation, national and international aid agencies roll out a bewildering and repetitive suite of 'global best practice' development programmes aimed at improving wellbeing, livelihood capacities and local governance (cf. Peake 2013; Shepherd 2013).

In all this planning for economic development, to deliver services, to build local capacity, to create jobs and wellbeing, the formal sector continually ignores or underestimates the extant capacities for active economic engagement, social and environmental governance which is manifest in the customary economy. While some customary practices may be recognized in rural development initiatives, this recognition is routinely dichotomized against urban enclaves such as Baucau which are imagined to harbour only remnant traditions (see ARD 2008; Costin and Powell 2006). Yet the discursive sidelining of the customary economy and attachments to place does not mean that they go away. As we saw in the previous chapter, customary understandings of exchange and 'inclusive sociality' are very much ongoing concerns in both rural and urban areas. To understand both the commitment to, and the halting re-emergence of, such ritual relationships in the independence era, below I examine the succession of late colonial 'developments' that have impacted on Baucau's water supply and customary governance.

Late colonial development in Baucau

As we have seen in previous chapters, in twentieth-century Baucau the sacred house complexes clustered around the springs of Wai Lia were incrementally destroyed or moved elsewhere as the colonial presence in the town became entrenched. The rice fields in the immediate vicinity of the Wai Lia spring also slowly disappeared, replaced with government and church buildings, shops and roads. Yet in the late 1930s the ritual processes at Wai Lia spring were still vibrant events, comprising annual house-based rituals and the larger 'one in seven year' ceremonies involving villages from the wider region. Each dry season around August, ritual prayers and ceremonies would commence and continue for seven nights, feeding the spring's custodial *dai* (manifest as large eels) and culminating in a celebration of song and dance involving groups of young men and women. After this the water would begin to flow. While Pinto Correia, the administrator of Baucau in the 1930s, does not report specifically on these rituals, he does note that '[l]*ulic* are the springs of Cai-Bada, of Baucau, of Uai-Líli, of Loi Dua and of Uai-Cana [Venilale], *lulik* are all the streams, the trees that sink their roots into them, and the eels that live in them' (1935: 63). He also notes that '[i]n the spring of Uai Tequi, of Bucoli … the custom persists to gift the eels who lives there, rice and grated coconut' (1935: 63). He reports that once in Baucau '[w]hen a European sergeant accidentally killed a *lulic* eel that lived in a well near the water fountain [see Figure 5.3], a wave of terror spread among the *indígenas*' (1935: 63–64). He noted that '[i]t is forbidden to drink palm wine [*tuaca*] at the spring of Baucau' (1935: 67).

During the Second World War the town was occupied by the Japanese and bombed by the Allies. Much of the town's population fled to the hills. When life returned to normal in the post-war era, the suite of rituals connected to the Wai Lia spring decreased in frequency and magnitude due in part to a new colonial tax placed on the slaughter of animals (cf. McWilliam *et al.* 2014). By the 1960s a municipal water pumping station had been constructed at the site, forming the basis of the town's piped water supply (see Figure 7.1). Meanwhile on the plateau, a Chinese-Timorese market gardener from Baucau town had 'discovered' the underground water source at Wai Lia Bere and had dynamited

Figure 7.1 Wai Lia pump station and Wai Lewa spring and grave, Baucau.

156 *The (re)negotiation of customary relations*

the cave in an unsuccessful attempt to extract water for agricultural development. This explosion destroyed the seven distinct channels of water flowing inside the cave. Around the same time an international airport was constructed on the edge of the Baucau plateau (see Map 4.1).[3]

In the late 1960s, an incident at a market-day cockfight in Baucau town led to a violent altercation between people from the plateau and others from Baucau. Soon after this the waters at the Wai Lia spring ran dry. Angered by the lack of respect shown to the people from the plateau by the townsfolk, the plateau custodian of these waters had intervened (either physically[4] or spiritually) to shut off the town's water supply. Hearing this rumour, the town's colonial administrator was so incensed that he sent an armed convoy of cars to arrest those responsible. A group of men from the hamlet of Buburaga were arrested and detained in the Baucau police station. The administrator stated that they would not be released until the water flowed again. Eventually the plateau custodian of these waters descended and convinced the administrator that as he was not God, he was not in control of the water supply and the prisoners should be let go.

By the late twentieth century the water supply at Wai Lia was intermittent at best. The Indonesian occupation had also severely disrupted the conduct of ceremonies at Wai Lia. Due to the ongoing armed conflict, the majority of people from remote villages were now resettled in Baucau's 'new town' area (Budiardjo and Liem 1984: 81). This burgeoning 'new town', an Indonesian administrative centre, was on the plateau edge above the Wai Lia spring. This growing city desperately needed more water. In order to facilitate this, in the 1980s the Indonesians tried to construct a large-scale water extraction facility at Wai Lia Bere on the plateau. This triggered a large explosion and the project was abandoned.

Armed conflict, death, the widespread burning of sacred houses, forced relocations and highly restricted population movements meant that relations between houses and communities across the region were now severely disrupted (cf. McWilliam and Traube 2011). In addition, while many of the local ritual governance traditions were familiar to the Indonesian occupiers (shared as they are with local populations across the archipelago), the privileging of the Indonesian state's own political and economic agenda, the destruction of many sacred houses and a ban by the military on large-scale gatherings of Timorese for political reasons meant that customary rituals were unable to be properly carried out. Fear and suspicion pervaded relationships at all levels. Yet as this repression eased in the mid 1990s, a young custodian of Wai Mata Buu (the custodial house of the Wai Lia spring) was able to reconnect with Ledatame Ikun, the older sibling house on the plateau. Once reunited Wai Mata Buu reconstructed his own sacred house in the hamlet of Macadai Wai Mata Buu some distance below Wai Lia in Baucau.

By the late 1990s the water at Wai Lia had dried up again completely. Panicked by the lack of water, in 1998 the town's administrators sought out the village heads and the custodians of the Wai Lia spring to seek a resolution.

The (re)negotiation of customary relations   157

Eventually money and, more crucially, Indonesian military permission was given for the village heads and ritual leaders to organize a large 'one in seven year' ceremony at Wai Lia. The respective ritual leaders of the four villages of Bahu, Tirilolo, Caibada and Buruma were called together and an approach was made to Ledatame Ikun, the custodians of the water on the plateau. A small ceremony was held at Wai Lia Bere, and in August 1999 a large collective 'one in seven year' ceremony was carried out at Wai Lia. While following this ceremony the water flow returned to Wai Lia, initially it was not strong. This was attributed to the fact that the Indonesian authorities had insisted that the sacrificed buffalo was killed according to Islamic principles (strung up from a tree and slaughtered) rather than being slain directly into the spring water as was the custom.[5] It was not until the Indonesian occupiers finally exited Baucau in late September 1999 that the waters of Wai Lia really began to flow again.[6]

The exit of the Indonesians was not the end of the water governance troubles at Wai Lia. In September 1999 the village head and traditional political ruler of Bahu[7] also left Baucau. A long-time collaborator with the Indonesians, he had feared for his life and fled across the border to West Timor where he remains. This, and other absences, added further challenges to the independence-era governance of the spring. Another issue impacting in particular on the organization of large-scale 'one in seven year' ceremonies (an ideal rather than actual period of time), is the fact that conducting these rituals takes an immense investment of time, community co-ordination, livestock and money.

In contrast to these larger-scale community rituals, rituals linked to particular houses are a less problematic undertaking. In the early independence era many Baucau house communities began reconstructing or renovating their sacred houses (da Costa et al. 2006; Loch 2007).[8] This process continues and the resurgence and reconstitution of these material forms and practices is everywhere evident, reinvigorating as well house-based marriage alliances and their accompanying life cycle rituals. On the whole these house-based alliances are private matters and remain outside of the purview of formal state institutions and practices of governance.[9] Nonetheless ritual leaders do make a link between the vibrancy of these house communities and their potential to eventually reconstitute broader community rituals such as those held at Wai Lia.[10]

In the past large ritual gatherings at Wai Lia (and other springs) were overseen by local political leaders. Yet most large-scale public ritual gatherings in Baucau today are devotional acts of procession, prayer and song connected to Catholicism (see Figure 7.2). One is now more likely to find political leaders in church reading psalms to their subjects during Sunday Mass, than overseeing rituals seeking agricultural fertility, community prosperity and harmony at springs.[11]

Catholic syncretism

As in other places, across the region the Catholic Church has cultivated and inserted its own presence at spiritually potent sites, particularly mountain tops,

158 *The (re)negotiation of customary relations*

caves and springs. While for local people there is no necessary disjunction between these largely animist and Catholic processes of worship and devotion, a seemingly syncretic relationship often belies a history of simmering unease, even hostility.[12] Intervening early on to groom the children of locally prominent houses for the priesthood, since the 1930s much of the land around the Wai Lia spring has belonged to the Church. Over the years it has become the single

Figure 7.2 Procession of Santu Antonio, Baucau.

The (re)negotiation of customary relations   159

biggest landowner in Baucau and at some level the town today continues to operate like a medieval bishopric. Its various businesses and entrepreneurial priests control and direct much of the formal economic activity in the town and play a critical role in maintaining civic functions and infrastructure in the post-independence era. It has now constructed a new teacher's college and Centre for Bakita (the Black Madonna) near the site of the long since destroyed apical sacred house complex in the hamlet of Waukau. In 2012, when another of the most important houses connected to the Wai Lia spring complex was being renovated, a controversial decision was taken by some family members to move it from its location and rebuild it closer to a nearby Catholic grotto. An elder of the house, a now retired Catholic priest, explained to me that the rebuilt house was now an *oma lisan* (M: a house of tradition) and no longer an *oma lakasoru* (M: a ritually powerful sacred house). The house he said was now *mamuk* or spiritually empty. This was not the view held by all members of the house and the renovation was a source of much inter-familial tension.

Tensions between Catholic and animist traditions was also evident in another happening at the spring of Wai Lia in 2010. At the time, sporadic neighbourhood violence and fighting between 'local' and 'in-migrated' youth in the centre of the old town was taking place in the marketplace near Wai Lia. Along with the frequent fights occurring in its vicinity, the area's neglected appearance was perceived by some to be the result of the local community's failure to respect the 'sanctity' of this critical water source (many now living in this area had only recently migrated to the town from elsewhere). This led to a decision by local Catholic priests to erect a statue of the Madonna at the foot of the spring's overhanging cave. This, they believed, would reinforce the sacred qualities of the area and encourage mindful meditation as people came to light candles and pray to Our Lady (*NOSSA SENORA*). The young Timorese priest, who was leading this particular initiative, supposed that the erection of the statue would have no impact on the *lulik* qualities of the spring. In their reconfiguration of the site, he and his work team had taken care to demarcate places both for animist ceremonies and for Catholic rituals centred on the Madonna. Having both traditions operating in the same grounds would, he surmised, make the area doubly sacred, creating a powerful protective aura.

This syncretic solution, however, was not the view held by the ritual custodians for the spring. For them, the initiative, which began without their knowledge or involvement (although the priest did discuss it with the village head), was a dangerous and risky undertaking. Whilst most were reluctant to speak out against the Catholic Church of which they themselves were members, they were highly anxious about the potential ramifications of the initiative. It was not known, they said, how the ancestral *dai* or custodian of the spring (*bee na'in*) would react to the placement of the statue in its dwelling place. *Dai* (as we saw in Chapter 2) comprise a mixture of benevolent and malevolent forces, and are known to be unruly and quick to anger. The ritual custodians were certain of one thing: the two spiritual essences – the Madonna and the *bee na'in* – could not co-exist, because a saint and a potentially malevolent spirit cannot inhabit

160 *The (re)negotiation of customary relations*

the same space. Should this be imposed upon them, the almighty power of the Christian God would overcome the *bee na'in*, most likely driving it away (cf. Bovensiepen 2009; Allerton 2009). What they were unsure of was the reaction of the *bee na'in*. Where would it go? Would it seek retribution in the form of sickness befalling the ritual custodians, whose task it is to feed its appetites and protect the water source? Even more worrying for the ritual custodians was the possibility that it would lead to the complete drying up of the spring water. Given that Wai Lia is the headspring of the town's water supply, this eventuality would deprive the entire town and dependent agricultural fields of water.

The ritual custodians were convinced that the only way forward was for the statue's erection to be halted while all parties came together to discuss a resolution. One of them explained that this must involve a large-scale communal 'one in seven year' ceremony held at the spring. Bringing all those involved together in such a way would, they insisted, provide the proper forum to ask the *bee na'in* whether it would accept the will of the Church. If this was not done, the ritual custodians continued, the benefits of a recently improved flow of water to the spring (an outcome they attributed squarely to their own post-independence ritual renaissance of house-based and collective water increase ceremonies) could all be squandered. In the end, while the concrete platform for the Madonna was prepared, the statue was never erected and the project is now derelict and abandoned (see Figure 7.3). Yet, in my last interview with a senior

Figure 7.3 Baucau's Wai Lia spring and cave with unfinished *Nossa Senora* project at rear and author in foreground.

The (re)negotiation of customary relations   161

ritual custodian for the site in 2013, it was suggested that if the Church continued its 'obstructionism' the next 'one in seven year' ceremony may have to be moved to another ceremonial site altogether.

The rocky outcrops above Wai Lia are now crowded with the unchecked construction of Indonesian-era dwellings and ramshackle street-side market stalls crowd the spring's perimeter. Contamination of the site and its waters are of increasing concern for the city's water supply administrators as stall holders (who are mainly from elsewhere in the district) often use its semi-fenced grounds as a refuse site. Many of the newer permanent dwellings above it are also occupied by people from elsewhere, part of the Indonesian-era legacy of rural to urban migration. Indeed this intra-district migration has meant that over time many people from the origin houses of Baucau have felt increasingly marginalized. The expansion of the town upwards to the 'new town' on the escarpment edge has also effected previous customary agreements pertaining to village boundaries (see below). These contested land issues have been inflamed by the discourse of new land and property laws which prioritize long-term occupation rights over ancestral connection and precedence.

Independence-era water supply in Baucau town

Giving the city's burgeoning size, following the violent withdrawal of Indonesian troops and damage to the city's infrastructure, water in Baucau became an even more urgent development issue. Built on karst limestone foundations at an elevation of 300 metres the town has potentially abundant water resources, yet the present water infrastructure remains woefully inadequate. The water pump station at the Wai Lia spring was established in the 1960s on gravitation principles. It has over the years expanded to include uphill water pumps, distribution reservoirs and pipes which service Baucau's new town. The spring yields on average 25 litres of water per second which is vastly inadequate for the growing urban demand on supply. Yet even in Indonesian times sub-standard water infrastructure meant that the city was also dependent on the services of twelve water trucks.[13] The latest upgrades to the pump station system were carried out under the United Nations Transitional Administration (UNTAET) in early 2000 with Portuguese funding. Water from the Wai Lia complex is now pumped uphill several days a week to storage reservoirs feeding the domestic water supply of the ever-growing 'new town' (see Figure 7.4). While the delivery of this water to businesses and houses in the new town remains problematic, the seasonal and otherwise intermittent nature of the spring flow (see endnote 6) can also have serious ramifications for the water available in the old town. Diverting water and pumping it to the new town means many residents in the old town are then without piped water at those times. The government's water and sanitation department operates on an inadequate budget, lacking resources to address the myriad of water management and supply issues which the city faces. In addition to large-scale infrastructure limitations, the department also struggles to deal with smaller-scale issues such as pipe leaks and illegal connections by residents.

Those at the end of the pipe networks receive little, if any, water. Meanwhile the town's piped water is drawn from the same waters that feed the irrigation channels below Wai Lia.

As urban water needs expand so too does the demand placed on the existing infrastructure. While most government services, businesses and households have some access to the city's piped water supply, for the reasons stated above, this supply is usually inadequate and often infrequent. Some businesses and residents in the cave-studded hillside of the old town are fortunate to be able to also tap springs within their own properties. Meanwhile some residential areas in the new town have been without a piped water supply for the entire independence era. In the old town disruptions to the water supply to irrigation channels lead to disgruntlement, and some say sabotage, on the part of farmers who are also dependent on this water.

Those who can afford it pay private water tankers to deliver tanks of water collected at one of the downstream springs (see Figure 7.5).[14] Poorer residents in the new town buy water from the water tanker owners by the drum for fifty cents in the wet season and two dollars in the dry season. While in the wet season people are also able to collect rainwater, in the dry season a small family may spend $15–20 per month on water, a substantial percentage of average household incomes. At the very end of one of the water pipes lies the Baucau hospital (the country's second largest) whose water supply, intermittent at best, was at

Figure 7.4 Escarpment edge houses and water pipes on the way from Wai Lia to Baucau's new town.

Figure 7.5 A privately owned water truck refilling at Wai Lua spring, Baucau.

the time of writing broken and awaiting the construction of an alternative piped route. In 2013, the budget enabling water purchasing at the Baucau hospital was drastically reduced, affecting the availability of water in the hospital and forcing many patients to bring their own water in plastic containers.

In the UNTAET period (1999–2002) there were plans by international donor countries to reconfigure the water supply and distribution system but no action was taken. Since then urban water masterplans for Baucau have been proposed (but not yet enacted) in 2004, 2009 and 2014 by Asian Development Bank consultants. Since 2010 the Timorese government in collaboration with Australian government aid and technical assistance has carried out a series of scientific surveys to map and better understand the region's karst hydrology with the aim of improving the city's water supply system. This research is discussed below.

Groundwater research and policy development

From January–June 2011, an international hydrogeologist advising the National Directorate for Water Control and Quality (DNCQA) carried out a series of dye tracing and monitoring activities in the karst environs of the Baucau plateau (Furness 2011). The results of the experiments found no traceable connection

164 *The (re)negotiation of customary relations*

between the water in the Wai Lia Bere cave and water in the Wai Lia spring in Baucau. Rather the water from Wai Lia Bere cave was shown to flow (in this period at least) through the Wai Lia Mata cave then north-east to the springs of Wailili.[15] Water analysis from waters drawn from the Wai Lia spring showed that this water had a mean age of 2,000 years (and it was noted that scientifically proving the origins of this water would be an almost impossible task).[16] After carrying out a helicopter mounted electromagnetic survey to establish the likely direction of groundwater flow in the area (see Map 1.2; Furness 2012; Wallace *et al.* 2012), the hydrogeologist hypothesized that the waters feeding the Wai Lia spring were in the main sourced from rainfall recharging groundwater in a zone between the Baucau airport and Baucau's new town (see Map 4.1).

In 2014, the results of these experiments and their conclusions about Baucau town's groundwater resources were made available on the Internet via a fact sheet published in Tetum by the DNCQA (Direccao Nacional de Controlo e Qualidade de Agua n.d.). While the custodians of Wai Lia Bere had, at the time of writing, not been briefed on the research outcomes from the dye tracing experiment, they remained sceptical about the experiment's results. According to their own observations the water source in Wai Lia Bere flows at its strongest in the early dry season (from May onwards) and it was only after this that waters from Wai Lia Bere reached Wai Lia in Baucau (usually around August). By placing the dyes in the waters of Wai Lia Bere in January (and only monitoring the flows in downstream springs until June) they believed the experiments had missed this crucial part of the seasonal cycle.

Similarly, in contrast to local understandings of the interconnections between the Mundo Perdido range and the Baucau plateau (see Chapter 2), past and present geological surveys conclude that the much older limestone formations of the Mundo Perdido region and the younger limestone formations of the plateau are in fact separated by an impermeable rock formation (cf. Audley-Charles 1968; see Map 1.2). As noted above, the scientific understanding of the plateau's hydrogeology was further elaborated by the 2012 electromagnetic survey which mapped likely groundwater pathways through the limestone and identified potential sites close to Baucau where it might be possible to drill for water.[17] To obtain a more precise understanding of these potential sites further targeted electromagnetic surveys were conducted in late 2014 by the DNCQA with the support of Australian Aid and CSIRO Australia.[18] This research revealed further the complexity of the Baucau Aquifer, where depending on the location, groundwater flows in several different directions, via different flow pathways. This groundwater may be seasonal or represent many years of accumulation. While actual drilling for this water has been hampered for various reasons, once located it is hoped this water will become the basis for Baucau's urban water supply and reduce or halt the need to pump water uphill from Wai Lia. As this scientific research continues, the potential impact on other springs in the region of extracting this water from the karst aquifer is something which will need to be further considered and evaluated.[19]

While there has been a significant investment made to physically map the subterranean water pathways of the Baucau plateau, developing an understanding of the social context in which these water resources are understood, accessed and managed has not to date been prioritized. As a result the DNCQA lacks a formal understanding of the local hydrosocial cycle and the ways in which increasing urban demands for water place pressure on the local agro-ecology. The Tetum fact sheet on Baucau's water resources prepared by the Ministry of Public Works, with support from Australian Aid, assures the public that scientific surveys have been carried out to understand local hydrology. While it states that this research has yet to locate a new water supply, the fact sheet gives the impression that the community should place their trust in the process and government decisions in relation to the water supply issue.

In 2011 international advisers and their Timorese counterparts in the DNCQA carried out a community consultation process on developing national water laws and policy. This process in most cases involved district consultations with a group of district and sub-district administrators, village heads and community leaders. The discussions during each of these consultations were summarized in Tetum and later translated into English. The Tetum notes from the Baucau consultation convey the overwhelming concern of those present to recognize and formally engage with the role of the ritual custodians of the water (the *bee na'in*). Water custodians were identified as having the ability to give and withhold water (although there were a variety of views on the appropriateness of this in the democratic era). In the group discussion about water extraction from Wai Lia spring complex those involved stated that the government should provide money for rituals at the spring. This, they said, would ensure the supply and proper management of the water. However, the subsequent English translations of these notes do not clearly articulate these sentiments. Given that the international advisers involved in drafting these initial water laws and policies did not speak Tetum, it is unclear to what extent they were able to engage with the community views and concerns emanating from this consultation process. Hence in this case, despite their dutiful consultations and struggling with the DNCQA's own national level resourcing and capacity issues, such complex socio-cultural understandings of the hydrosocial cycle in Baucau were once again largely elided. However, in subsequent community consultations in 2014, carried out when developing Baucau's proposed urban water masterplan (2015–2030), the ongoing assertion of these customary priorities (see also Palmer 2010, 2011) did result in some acknowledgement of the need to address and engage with the sensitivities surrounding Baucau's urban water use and the customary economy.

Similarly over the last two years the national Water Resources Law and Policy drafting process has substantially revised the approach taken to the need for community consultation on socio-cultural aspects of water when structuring water resources management. It is now anticipated that in areas where there is likely to be competing demands on a water resource, a water resources plan may need to be developed. Such a process would require an integrated approach with

166 *The (re)negotiation of customary relations*

detailed community consultations to identify socio-cultural aspects of the water and traditional management of the water resources. It is anticipated that these laws and policies will be finalized in 2015.[20]

Community managed water supply systems

Despite the fact that international donors have directed significant resources at the sector, water programmes and projects have to date struggled to achieve sustainable results in both urban and rural areas. In the rural areas, the model of water supply management adopted by the development industry in Timor Leste (and indeed elsewhere in the world) has been based on community participation (Schoffel 2006; McGregor 2007). One of the reasons for this was the structural limitations of developing much needed state-operated water and sanitation services (including lack of technical capacity and operating funds) (Schoffel 2006). In 2006 the Asian Development Bank published a consultant's report titled 'Timor-Leste: Community-Managed Water Supply and Sanitation' (Schoffel 2006). Interestingly the findings of the report were scathing in their analysis of the effectiveness of what is considered internationally to be a model of 'best practice' community participation in water supply management (Schoffel 2006: 1). In contradistinction to most critics of the failure of community based development in Timor Leste, the report concludes that the issue is not one of a lack of community education (which, it is usually argued by proponents of the model, can be addressed with the investment of more time and follow-up resources) (Schoffel 2006).

The report does not discuss the existence of customary water user groups, their governance processes or indeed locally enforced practices such as sanctions. Rather, Schoffel concludes that the model of community participation, planning and management was itself the problem. In all community water projects surveyed in Timor Leste, Schoffel found that despite the assumptions embedded in the model, there was no evidence that people in these communities will 'voluntarily obey collectively agreed rules to equitably share, pay for, and take care of common property without sanctions to enforce the rules' (2006: 11). Hence the report concludes that:

> piped water supply systems are unlikely to be sustainable in any circumstances in Timor-Leste without an established and qualified institution that is empowered by the state to manage them; carry out repairs and maintenance, collect user fees, and impose regulations on use and sanctions on abuse.
>
> (Schoffel 2006: 15)

In contrast to the above report, another report funded by the Asia Development Bank does mention the significance of traditional beliefs, customs and practices to the management of Timor's water resources (Costin and Powell 2006). At one point it briefly reports on concerns about the high rate of project

The (re)negotiation of customary relations   167

failures, associated problems with newly configured water users' groups and the need to better understand the influence of 'tradition' at this interface (Costin and Powell 2006: 85). It also states however that 'the influence of "traditional" beliefs and practices associated with water use and allocation in urban environments is largely invisible to most residents, if they exist at all' (Costin and Powell 2006: 72). Yet, as is clear from the government's own water resource consultations, even in the country's second largest urban centre of Baucau, local concerns about the need to address issues of customary use and allocation of water remain central.

While issues of system scale and the allocation of resources are critical to the long-term effectiveness of both state-operated and community-based water supply systems, it is also the case that preparedness to engage with local politics and expectations of custom and tradition around water are important. In a minority of cases, where for particular reasons the ritual obligations of the custodians of the water do underpin aspects of the piped water supply management system, both rural and urban residents report a high level of satisfaction with the system and its capacities for conflict resolution. These of course are not matters without precedence. We have seen in the previous chapter, how in various localities across the region the need to create piped water supply systems drew successive colonial administrations into the ritual cycle of particular springs.[21] In the independence era the expectation that the government administration will contribute to these ritual events remains. In Baucau, given the ongoing dependence of the town's water supply on Wai Lia, it is expected that the government will participate in this ritual cycle by supplying the buffalo and money required for the large 'one in seven year' ceremonies. While outsiders may see this as cynical opportunism, for ritual leaders this is simply a necessary component of a dynamic and socio-ecologically responsive tradition.

It also needs to be acknowledged that aside from government support and recognition there are many factors which impact on the current efficacy of these customary governance systems. Below I highlight some of the complexities of customary relationships to land and waters and the challenges that these pose to the development of appropriate governance mechanisms.

Ritual dynamism

As there is a need for particular human bodies to be present at rituals, the absence of ancestral sacra can also create challenges for the present-day custodianship and management of springs. This is the case with the ritual governance of Wai Lakulo, the head spring in the spring water complex of the village of Wailili. As we saw in Chapter 4, Wailili and its spring complex was once an important ritual centre. In the twentieth century the Catholic Church arrived and erected a grotto at the site known as Bo'o Dai (W: sacred) where ritual offerings were made to the Wai Lakulo. Then during the Indonesian occupation sacred objects associated with the spring were said to have become lost. These sacred objects, collectively named Baha Kura Mesa Baha Dala Hitu (comprising

168   *The (re)negotiation of customary relations*

a coral necklace, a sword, a gong and a spear) are needed to properly carry out the rituals at the spring of Wai Lakulo.[22] In the ancestral past, these sacra were carried every year by the custodians of the waters who would enter the spring and travel up its underground chasms calling the waters forth and searching for its origins. They would travel for seven days and seven nights and, while they never reached the source, after this yearly ritual the waters of Wai Lakulo would always flow well. While subsequent generations of custodians carried out their rituals beside rather than entering the spring, they would always have with them the ritual sacra carried by the ancestors.

The story of the loss of the Baha Kura Mesa Baha Dala Hitu sacra is ambiguous. Once belonging to the house of Loi Leki, at some point during Luca's rule of Wailili they were transferred to a neighbouring house now belonging to the village of Gariuai (see Map 4.1). While the transfer of this sacra was not necessarily illegitimate, neither was it expected to be permanent. However, as this house has not yet returned the sacra to its rightful owners (and it seems are now unable to do so) many of the descendants of this caretaker house have prematurely died or become infertile. Meanwhile without the Baha Kura Mesa Baha Dala Hitu sacra the present Loi Leki branch house custodians of the water are also unable to make the full suite of ritual offerings to the spring at the time of their new maize and new rice harvest (these sacra are also referred to as 'the things concerning the dry (maize) and the wet (rice)'). The absence of this sacra also makes it difficult for them to reconstruct their sacred house (which was burnt down in the Indonesian era). While lost sacra may be replaced via the ritual blessing of new objects, these must be exact replicas of what they replaced (aside from needing to agree on the specificities of now long lost objects, as a result of the conflict era this is also difficult given the regional depletion of exchange objects, especially ritual swords of various varieties and embellishments). Loss of sacra is akin to the loss of a limb: while one can still function that function is greatly impaired. Beyond the sensitivity and enormity of the challenges confronting this house, it is clear that the intention of these elders in relaying these stories to me was to record their identity as the 'true' custodians of the water. In the context of regional water resource developments, it was also made clear that it is they who the government should consult in relation to developments at the Wailili spring complex.

Despite the hiatus in Wailili's once vibrant water rituals, the spring complex remains the acknowledged centre of ancestral power in the zone known as Fatumaka Leten and Fatumaka Kraik (upper and lower Fatumaka). This was publicly evident in 2013 when the village of Gariuai began negotiations with its neighbouring villages to enable a *tara bandu*, a seasonal prohibition ceremony, aimed at protecting its resources on the plateau and surrounds. The trigger for this particular *tara bandu* had been a tragic event several months before when one of the senior custodians of the Wai Lia Bere cave complex was found murdered on the plateau. The man had been tending to his buffalo in an area of sacred forest near Darasula and it is believed that those responsible for the murder were there to illegally cut timber. As we saw in Chapter 4, *tara bandu*-like events were once at the heart of

The (re)negotiation of customary relations   169

the ritual relationship between the communities connected to the springs of Wai Husu-Wai Lewa (Baucau) and Wai Lili-Wai Wa (Wailili). While this relationship is also dormant, a further aim of the *tara bandu* was to reinvigorate the ritual relationships existing within the domain of Wai Lili-Wai Wa which was once united under the house of Loi Leki (a domain now known as Fatumaka Leten and Fatumaka Kraik). The starting point for this ritual event was an ancestral 'mother' pole erected by the Wailili spring complex. 'Child' poles were then erected at specific localities where the outwardly migrating branch houses of the Loi Leki house had first settled. Although it was originally hoped that the villages of Tirilolo and Bahu (Wai Husu-Wai Lewa) would participate as witnesses to the event, they were not expected to be formally involved.

Locally enacted customary practices of ritualized prohibitions, glossed as *tara bandu* in the national language of Tetum, are known in Makasae as *lubu badu*[23] and similarly in Waima'a as *luhbu badu* (literally 'the prohibition pole'). While the practice is often referred to as 'seasonal or periodic resource harvesting restrictions' (Meitzner-Yoder 2005: 249), it can also be more broadly interpreted as a practice which regulates a range of place-based social and environmental relationships. Elevated as a tool for forest protection by the Portuguese at the turn of the twentieth century, over several decades the practice of *tara bandu* became the favoured 'indigenist ideology' supported by the state (McWilliam *et al.* 2014). This officially favoured status afforded to it as an indigenous 'environmental protection practice' has to some extent been reinvigorated in the independence era. Alongside a significant amount of community and non-governmental organization level embrace of the process (McWilliam *et al.* 2014), *tara bandu* has developed a profile as a 'traditional' mechanism which is garnering significant attention and traction in the development of formal resource management laws, many of which have been drafted by 'expert' foreign advisers (Jackson and Palmer 2012). In 2013 the Secretariat of State of the Environment was also supporting such rituals through small allocations of funding and in some cases the attendance of senior government members. *Tara bandu* it seems is increasingly valued by the state as a local mechanism 'to conserve and promote the environment and the preservation and sustainable use of natural resources' (Article 10 (2) of the Draft Water Resources Law, Ministry of Infrastructure 2012).

What is understood today as the *bandu* process is usually conducted at the sub-village or village level at locally specified intervals (ranging from months to years). While the ceremony is announced and co-ordinated by the local political leader (usually the village head), the law-making power emanates from the ancestral and ritual power of the sacred house or houses of one or more of the area's autochthonous or origin groups (in this case connected to a spring). Ceremonies are public events which announce the pre-agreed suite of prohibitions to the community and others present to witness the ceremony from outside. In the period preceding the event, outside guests will be formally invited and these may include political and ritual leaders from neighbouring communities, members of the clergy, government, police and civil society. The ceremony itself will be a multi-day event involving much preparation for the law-making

170   *The (re)negotiation of customary relations*

practices, specifically ritual speech, celebratory ritual dancing, drumming and singing, betel nut exchange, animal sacrifice (which animals and how many depend on the traditions and capacity of the village and the subject of the *bandu* itself), divinatory techniques including an augury based on these animals' internal organs and communal feasting. Prior to the feasting, the relevant ritual elders must also come together to share in the consumption of specially prepared foods, which are also symbolically shared with the relevant ancestral spirits of the 'houses', lands and waters. In most areas, following the ceremony large ritual 'mother' posts and smaller 'child' posts will be placed around the locale and hung (*tara*) with relevant symbols (usually skulls of the sacrificed animals, forest foliage and crop items) of the prohibitions (*bandu*) now in place.

A further purpose of this particular *tara bandu* was to honour the ancestral sites which link the lands of different sub-village and villages in this ritual domain. In these areas 'child poles' were erected, accompanied by ancestral prayer. In what can be read as both a strategic intervention and a reminder of significance of custom in the simmering independence-era disputes over land and village administrative boundaries in Baucau's new town, a child pole was placed in the town centre. Another 'child pole' was planned at an equally contentious site at the boundary zone between the villages of Gariuai, Bucoli, Bahu and Tirilolo. This ritual pole placement did not, however, go according to plan. Prior to even the placement of the pole a violent altercation flared between the people from the village of Gariuai and the people of Triloca, a new village created during the Indonesian era (see Map 4.1). Under the 'law' of this *tara bandu* Tiriloca was considered a 'child' village of Bucoli and Gariuai (villages which can be read here as representatives of the once paired domains of Wai Husu-Wai Lewa and Wai Lili-Wai Wa). The people now settled in Triloca considered that the *tara bandu* process was failing to acknowledge them as a village in their own right. The ensuing violence damaged a car and this case has now been referred for adjudication in the Baucau Tribunal. The incident has also had wider ramifications. Across the sub-district plans for other *tara bandu* have been placed in limbo while the Baucau sub-district administrator attempts to mediate boundary issues with all eleven villages in the sub-district.

While these tensions emerged as a result of a particular *tara bandu*, the disputed issues are a legacy of colonial and Indonesian-era administrative process. They are also, it is said, a result of the emerging 'development' value attached to these rural lands, and independence-era developments and development plans in the area have fuelled mistrust and suspicion between sub-villages and villages. In these difficult circumstances, independence-era attempts to secure resource regulation and village boundaries through either customary or formal agreement making are increasingly fragile. It is now said that people are killing each other over land.

Springs and national politics

Beyond an environmentally functionalist engagement with concepts such as *tara bandu*, the intricacies and independence-era complications of the customary

The (re)negotiation of customary relations 171

realm have to date remained largely unengaged by the formal policies and practices of national-level natural resource bureaucracies. In contrast, at the highest levels of Timorese politics there is at least tacit acknowledgement and engagement with custom. At this 'presidential' level, there is recognition of the need to 'payback' the debt to *lulik* and the customary realm and also to reinvigorate communication with the ancestors. During the 2012 presidential election campaign, a representative of the *lia na'in* from every district, including Major Ko'o Raku from Baucau, were brought to the national capital to preside over the presidential debate of the twelve candidates. The day before the nationally televised debate the *lia na'in* were gathered together to carry out a ritual calling for the ancestors of the earth and the sea and to bless and ritually cool the candidates and their supporters in the presidential campaign.[24] In a country where democracy is a new and challenging concept, this was seen as a critical (if somewhat tokenistic[25]) intervention to the broad acceptance of the process. Indeed, despite the grave fears of many national and international commentators, the 2012 presidential and parliamentary elections were largely free of violence.

During the campaign itself concern was heightened as the various candidates travelled from district to district on their respective campaign trails (see Figure 7.6). Perhaps given the 2006 civil unrest and 'ethnic' tensions between peoples from the east and west of the country (cf. Shoesmith 2007; Office of the United

Figure 7.6 Rally for Fretilin's 2012 presidential candidate in main street of old Baucau town near Wai Lia.

172 The (re)negotiation of customary relations

Nations High Commissioner for Human Rights 2006), there was a heightened degree of tension surrounding the 'youthful' Partido Democratico candidate Fernando 'La Sama' de Araujo's campaign visit to the Fretilin party stronghold of Baucau.[26] Being himself from the western region, to overcome any negative perceptions of a lack of affiliation to Baucau he was introduced to the crowd as someone with an intimate connection to the east. As a leader of the student clandestine resistance during the Indonesian occupation, it was explained to the crowd that his 'power' and victory in this struggle was also attributable to the many ceremonies which had been carried out in his name by ritual leaders at springs and other sacred sites across the east. As a result 'La Sama' was now permanently connected and indebted to the east of the country. Meanwhile during his campaign in Baucau, the Fretilin Mudanca candidate Jose Luis Guterres paraded through town in ritual regalia celebrating his status as the younger brother of the present 'king' of Luca. He was dressed in ritual regalia for the event by Major Ko'o Raku.

Another expression of high-level political engagement with the power of the custom in Baucau relates to the ex-prime minister, ex-president and ex-Falintil[27] Commander in Chief Xanana Gusmão. In 2004, as the then president of the new republic, he supported his former guerilla colleagues to carry out two large public ceremonies of thanks to the custodians of the water at Wai Lia Bere and Wai Lia (while it transpires that Xanana was represented by others at these events, the story is always told as if he himself was present). Buffalo provided by Xanana were slaughtered at Wai Lia and Wai Lia Bere, fulfilling a debt incurred as the result of the protection and power that these waters had afforded his Falintil fighters. It was Xanana's CNRT[28] candidate Taur Matan Ruak who eventually won the presidency in 2012.

Discussion

Across Baucau there is a renewed, if not always fulfilled, desire on the part of local populations to re-instigate a range of house and community 'resource' rituals. These rituals mark out connections across space and time and the limits of authority in particular contexts. The wishes of elders, often assisted by younger generations, to relay to me these highly personal experiences indicates also a desire on their part to have their stories told, to have their authority recognized as a part of the nation-building process. Yet as we have also seen, the water research and governance processes carried out in Baucau under the auspices of the state have been slow to engage with these narratives and the renaissance of ritual practices. Nevertheless, across Timor many communities have begun to make use of the 'power of spectacle', staging events such as *tara bandu* as public performances to be captured on film and radio by a burgeoning media interest in Timorese cultural traditions (see Palmer 2007; Palmer and Carvalho 2008; Barnes 2011). These events are also significant as the self-conscious expansion of the local political and ritual spheres into the national body politic. In these circumstances, local communities are seeking an active role in the

The (re)negotiation of customary relations 173

designation and management of their community lands and waters, and demonstrations of resource management capacities through practices such as *tara bandu* are highly important political interventions. From a local standpoint *tara bandu* is not just about conserving and promoting 'the environment and the preservation and sustainable use of natural resources'. Rather, as we saw above, it is more broadly interpreted as a practice which regulates a range of inter-community relationships. In this sense, there is no separation between a community's natural, cultural and economic resources. Yet as the state bureaucracy engages with practices drawn from the customary realm as uni-dimensional tools for environmental conservation, the social and political complexities which constitute both their 'traditional' and modern-day character is elided and the power of these events are potentially compromised (cf. Zerner 1994). As such activating these rituals as 'counter maps' in the identification of resources and their governance is a politically risky strategy, but one which local peoples have so far been willing to take, realizing perhaps better than most that negotiating the 'friction' (Tsing 2005) of material imaginations and practices is always messy and incomplete, dynamic and opportunistic.

Hence along with the persistence and re-emergence of local organizing principles, binaries and symbolic operators in 'town' life, this chapter has also made visible the internal challenges facing these complicated customary resource governance processes in the independence era. In the intricate power relations at work between relational spheres, the ritual politics of land are clearly tied to water and to associated sacred 'objects' which are themselves named and personified. While independence has brought with it a freedom to embrace long suppressed ancestral identities, their reassertion is often hampered by the absence of 'bodies' to properly mediate these connections. The presence of new governance 'bodies' is also something which must be contended with. These instances of loss and change often make it difficult for rituals to be carried out and even, in some instances, for sacred houses to be rebuilt. In some cases, the problem may also be that these objects or sites are now under the control of others or that the knowledge relating to specific rituals is now incomplete or lost.

Struggling with these internal challenges, in the post-independence era these house societies and their local spiritual ecologies are also subject to the imposition of a global grab bag of ostensibly apolitical and ahistorical land and resource governance arrangements (cf. Ernstson and Sorlin 2013). These challenges augment those created by the Catholic Church which has long sought to transform water from the 'sentient substance of [diverse] earthly vitality' to 'living water' symbolic of the Holy Spirit (Strang 2004: 91).[29] Seeking to 'connect and universalize' nature (Viveiros de Castro 2004: 476), both Catholicism and modern water governance processes effectively dematerialize water into an abstract substance which 'ceases to be particular to any place or group' (Strang 2004: 246). In contrast, the customary realm of *lulik* practice seeks to contextually 'separate and particularize' a related whole (Viveiros de Castro 2004: 476), understanding 'nature' as always emergent and sensitive to the particular configurations of relations which make substances and their transformation.

174 *The (re)negotiation of customary relations*

Developing the concept of ethnogeomorphology, Wilcock *et al.* write that reducing waterscapes to universalizing and technical scientific processes and 'assuming that others will adhere to that worldview, constitutes continued colonialism' (2013: 594). Indeed most governments assert sovereign authority over water on behalf of a citizen public and Western scientific rationalities are the 'common-sense' view that underpins national water resources management. Yet as Wilcock *et al.* make clear, Western science is equally as able as indigenous ontologies to embrace the notion of emergent, contingent land and waterscapes, mutually constituted across space and time (2013: 595). While such notions of continual emergence may not always be prioritized in modernist interpretations, a holistic reading of the findings of the groundwater research in Baucau illuminates karst water's complex and changing underground pathways as well as the time lags which influence its underground disappearance and emergence. These hydro-geomorphological understandings are, like those of many indigenous ontologies, based on the principle that 'contemporary adjustments cannot be known without a basis for seeing multiple timescales simultaneously' (Wilcock *et al.* 2013: 594). In this multi-time space, 'time is not linear, nor forwardly sequential, but, put simply multiple times are all happening at the same time. These multiscalar relations affect current relations' (Wilcock *et al.* 2013: 594).

Yet in local understandings, the frictions and co-becomings of these multiple materialities of water and its governance are not imagined as spaces of uncontrolled mixing. People refer in this sense not to dynamic co-existence, but to the need for measured co-existence. For example in local peoples' configurations the state, Catholicism and *lisan* (customary norms and practices) are understood as distinct, if somewhat ambiguous, entities: the state attends to the nation as a whole, the Church to the recently deceased; and *lisan* remains the basis of people's identity and inter-relations in the everyday and cosmological sense. While people are proud of the fact that their new nation's constitution recognizes the importance of their cultural identity, they also make it clear that house communities must be primarily responsible for fulfilling their ancestral obligation to these traditions. It is also clear that this aspiration for measured co-existence in diverse ontological assemblages is dynamic and, as with mythic understandings, can only ever be achieved (partially) via specific relational engagements, usually rituals.

By recognizing that customary relations are by necessity always becoming, emergent across multiple bodies and times, we can also see that the transformation and the renegotiation of power and ritual-political structures in postconflict Baucau is neither surprising nor novel (cf. Bovensiepen 2014a, 2014b). It is merely one aspect of the ongoing negotiation of relationality and autonomy which characterizes this vitalist framework of inclusive human and non-human sociality. While these complex local socio-ecological relations are enabled and directed by a moral and philosophical order which demands constant vigilance, in the modernist's illusory search for certainty these extant and very often ambiguous methods of meditating dissolution and chaos are simply overlooked (cf. Lansing 2006; McWilliam *et al.* 2014). Yet while universalist ideas of nature

The (re)negotiation of customary relations   175

are challenged by the particularity and 'excessive' relationality of these spiritual ecologies (and vice versa), it is because of its very dynamism and creativity that the hold of custom does not appear to be waning. Rather than seeking to supersede it, could it be that recognizing and legitimizing this sense of co-beingness and a moral order deeply embedded in the lifeworlds of kin-based economic exchange and ethical decision-making could be a catalyst for the engagement of community and the recognition of new economic and socio-ecological co-becomings in Baucau?

Notes

1 Parts of this chapter previously appeared in Palmer (2010) and McWilliam *et al.* (2014).
2 Population 21,000 (NSD and UNFPA 2011: 19). Since independence the capital Dili has close to 200,000 people.
3 The airport had (and has) the country's longest runway. In the 1960s and early 1970s aircraft travelling between Europe and Australia would land there to refuel. For this brief time, Baucau's lush spring groves and cooler climate saw it become something of a holiday destination for intrepid Australian tourists (cf. King 1963). The airport was used by the Indonesian military during the Indonesian occupation. At the time of writing it remains closed, although the local population expects that its re-opening is imminent.
4 It is believed by some Baucau residents that the custodians of the water on the plateau are able to enter the cave systems and manipulate and divert the water supply through particular underground channels (this is done via the use of woven palm fibres or, more recently, roofing iron) (see Palmer 2010).
5 The animal's blood flowing into the water is a sacred gift to the *dai* (ancestral beings) who return the gift by fertilizing the soils and protecting crops from attack by pests.
6 Baucau has a very marked wet and dry season. The dry season is generally between June and October each year. The average annual rainfall for Baucau town and surrounds is 1,300 mm, with more than three-quarters of this falling in the wet season. Up to 30 per cent of this rainfall is thought to contribute to groundwater recharge (Furness 2004). While I do not have access to 1999 rainfall data for Baucau, national data shows that the 1998/1999 wet season was a La Nina year during which average rainfall significantly increased. During La Nina years (an extreme 'wet' phase of the Western Pacific's El Nino-Southern Oscillation) the wet season on the north coast usually starts earlier and finishes later (Pacific Climate Change Science Program Partners 2011). Given that Wai Lia is said by locals to flow strongest from the early to mid dry season, it is possible that the stronger flow in late September 1999 may have also been a result of this increased annual rainfall. The rainfall data available for Dili shows that the periods of 1973/1974 and 1998/1999 had the (significantly) highest rainfall on record (Pacific Climate Change Science Program Partners 2011: 4). The El Nino-Southern Oscillation occurs at average intervals of up to seven years.
7 From the house of Wabubo which has a ritually paired relationship with the house of Boile Komu.
8 Known as *uma lulik* in Tetum, *oma falunu* in Makasae and *umo ba'i* or *umo luli* in Waima'a.
9 Given the difficulty of controlling it administratively, since the early twentieth century the Portuguese abolished the recognition of hamlet (*knua*) (and their associated sacred house complexes) from their political administrative structure. At the same time, the administrative level of the district, sub-district, village and sub-village governance were increasingly alienated from the ritual and political domain of sacred

176 *The (re)negotiation of customary relations*

houses (Soares pers. comm. 2006). This resulting disjunction between the ritual and political affairs of sacred houses and the political administrative domain explains much of the present misalignment or non-communication between ritual political and political administrative concerns.

10 These community rituals are also being reinvigorated at other regional springs. In 2009/2010 the spring community of Wai Mori Bere in Buibau (see Maps 4.1 and 4.2) reinvigorated their connection to the Wai Lia Bere spring and its custodians on the plateau (see also Chapter 4, endnote 14). During the Indonesian occupation the resident communities around the spring of Wai Mori Bere fled to the jungle, or had their lives otherwise disrupted by military occupation. As a result these spring rituals were severely disrupted and it is said the spring became dry for nearly two decades. In 2009 a ceremony was organized to make amends for this breach of ritual obligation. An offering of a chicken and a goat was taken to Wai Lia Bere and a sacrificial ceremony was carried out at the sacred banyan tree by the cave followed by a descent into the cave where 'mother water' was collected. This water (M: *ira falun*) was carried in a bamboo container along with seven bundles of betel chew to the Wai Mori Bere spring. There the sealed bamboo container of water was immersed in the centre of the spring. Following this a ritual invocation by the custodians of the water was carried out and the betel chew from the ceremony at Wai Lia Bere was spat into the water. Through this process the sins of the ritual obligation breach were cleansed and the ancestors were asked to accept the request that waters flow once more. After seven days the water began to flow. Later the water carried from Wai Lia Bere to Wai Mori Bere was ritually returned to its source on the plateau along with an offering of a pig and a goat for the sacred house of Ledatame Ikun. With the ancestral connection thus ritually re-established a further two ceremonies were required to cement this relationship into the future. The first was a ceremony at Wai Lia Bere in 2010 when a buffalo was taken to Ledatame Ikun by the Wai Mori Bere water-sharing community as a final payment for the past breach. The second required the water-sharing community of Wai Mori Bere to gather together for a large ceremony at their spring to '*ira gi gini*' (M: 'bang firm' or strengthen) the re-established relationship. At this latter ceremony a buffalo was slaughtered at the spring.

11 Estimated to have ranged from 15–30 per cent prior to 1975, the Catholic congregation of the new Indonesian province of Timor Timur (East Timor) grew to over 90 per cent during the occupation (1975–1999). This was mainly the result of the requirement in the Indonesian constitution (put in place under the anti-communist regime of President Suharto, 1966–1999) that citizens must ascribe to one of the world's five major religions: Islam, Hinduism, Christian Protestantism, Christian Catholicism and Buddhism. In the province of Timor Timur, the choice of the vast majority to become Catholic (rather than something else) was partly historical and partly due to the support the Church gave to the Timorese resistance during the occupation (Balthasar Kehi pers. comm. 2014).

12 During the colonial period, the ancestral sacra of many houses were 'taken away' by others for storage and safe keeping elsewhere. In a ruling house connected to Luca in Wailili, the traditional symbol of rule was at some point replaced with a statue of Our Lady (*Nossa Senora*). It is said that in subsequent decades this transgression led to the decimation of the lineage.

13 In 1999 these trucks were taken by the Indonesians when they departed. They have now been largely replaced by privately owned vehicles.

14 In 2014 the *bee na'in* for the spring, Wai Lua, where the water trucks now fill their tanks charged truck owners a levy of $1 per tank (a tank of water sells for US$12).

15 As we can see in Map 4.2, the local understanding of the flows of water from Wai Lia Bere also connects it to the springs of Wailili.

16 As we can also see in Map 4.2, the local understanding of the water flowing to Wai Lia is that it arrives via two distinct flows or channels – one is a deep underground

The (re)negotiation of customary relations   177

channel which continues through to emerge in the tidal spring of Watabo. The other channel, which is susceptible to 'manipulations' from the *bee na'in* ('custodians of the water'), flows closer to the surface and ends when it emerges in spring of Wai Lia (see also endnote 4 above).

17 Baucau's limestone reefs are thickest at the coastal areas with the thinner limestone formations of the Baucau plateau being underlain by impermeable clays. Wallace *et al.* (2012: 57) note that '[g]roundwater is principally near the surface in limestone Baucau plateau due to underlying impermeable clays. This restricts the potential storage of groundwater in the karst aquifer system'. Over a period of several years prior to 2012 many expensive wells had been sunk on the plateau by the government and private businesses. Each of them had come up dry.

18 Craig McVeigh pers. comm. 2014.

19 See Carvalho and Palmer (2012) for a discussion of similar complex socio-ecological hydrogeology issues in the far eastern zone of Iralalaru in Lautem. In 2010 Norway proposed a mini hydropower system at the Wai Lia spring in Baucau. The system would have resulted in spring flows being diverted away from communities that currently rely upon this water downstream of the spring. After community consultation and community concern, the proposal did not proceed (Craig McVeigh pers. comm. 2014).

20 Craig McVeigh pers. comm. 2014.

21 Similar ritual exchanges of piped water and animal sacrifices are reported to have occurred between the Indonesian military and the custodians of the water at the Aubaca spring near the Baucau airport.

22 Similarly at Wai Lia, the custodians of the house of Wai Mata Buu will bring with them sacred ancestral spears and swords to ceremonies carried out at the spring.

23 Also known as *lubu etena* (see da Costa *et al.* 2006: 94).

24 These *lia na'in* also appealed to the ancestors to ensure the prosperous future of the nation and particular focus was placed on securing the 'riches of the sea', specifically oil and gas.

25 Such ritual blessings should not, elders cautioned, be done at the expense of careful attention to the detail of ceremonial exchange. In a discussion about the presidential ceremony, one participating elder later explained that he and others had not been happy with what they saw as 'tokenistic' aspects of the ritual. In his opinion the ceremony which is known in Tetum as *'nahe biti'* or 'rolling out the mat', was compromised at the outset by the choice of mats themselves. By tradition, the woven grass mats used in the *nahe biti* ceremony should have been drawn from inside the host's sacred house, in this case the house of Motael in Dili. Instead the mats had been bought at a shop and carried in to the event by a police officer who, it was noted, unceremoniously rolled them out onto the ground. Each house has their own style of mat which needs to be respected. In the Ossu region these *lulik* mats are woven with a particular wetland grass (M: *popo kai*) which ensures the mat rolls out with a particularly elegant flow.

26 Although he was well into middle-age his campaign slogan was *'Foun sae mos bele'* ('the youth can also govern'), reflecting the fact that his party is an offshoot of the student resistance group, RENETIL (*Resistencia Nacional dos Estudantes de Timor Leste*, an organization for which he was Secretary General in the resistance era). Fretilin (*Frente Revolucionaria do Timor Leste Independente*) meanwhile, is thought of as the primary party of the resistance and for this reason is widely supported in Baucau.

27 *Forcas Armadas da Libertacao Nacional de Timor Leste.*

28 *Conselho Nacional de Reconstrucao de Timor.*

29 Strang (2004) is referring to the period of English history (between the sixth and sixteenth centuries) when pagan values and associations with water were being transformed by Christianity.

178 *The (re)negotiation of customary relations*

References

Allerton, C. (2009) 'Static Crosses and Working Spirits: Anti-Syncretism and Agricultural Animism in Catholic West Flores', *Anthropological Forum* 19(3): 271–287.

Association in Rural Development (ARD) (2008) *Ita Nia Rai (Our Country)*, Dili: ARD and USAID.

Audley-Charles, M. (1968) *The Geology of Portuguese Timor*, London: Memoir of the Geological Society No. 4.

Barnes, S. (2011) 'Origins, Precedence and Social Order in the Domain of *Ina Ama Beli Darlari*', in A. McWilliam and E. Traube (eds) *Land and Life in Timor-Leste: Ethnographic Essays*, Canberra: ANU E-Press, 24–46.

Bovensiepen, J. (2009) 'Spiritual Landscapes of Life and Death in the Central Highlands of East Timor', *Anthropological Forum* 19(3): 323–338.

Bovensiepen, J. (2014a) 'Installing the Insider "Outside": House Reconstruction and the Transformation of Binary Ideologies in Independent Timor-Leste', *American Ethnologist* 41(2): 209–304.

Bovensiepen, J. (2014b) 'Paying for the Dead: On the Politics of Death in Independent Timor-Leste', *The Asia Pacific Journal of Anthropology* 15(2): 103–122.

Budiardjo, C. and Liem, S.L. (1984) *The War Against East Timor*, London: Zed Books.

Carvalho, D.A. and Palmer, L. (2012) 'Engaging Communities in Resource Development Initiatives in Timor Leste', in M. Langton and J. Longbottom (eds) *Community Futures, Legal Architecture*, London: Routledge, 251–268.

Correia, A. (1935) *Gentio de Timor*, Lisbon: Agência-Geral das Colónias.

Costin, G. and Powell, B. (2006) *Situation Analysis Report Timor Leste*, Brisbane: Australian Water Research Facility, International Water Centre.

da Costa, C., da Costa Guterres, A. and Lopes, J. (eds) (2006) *Exploring Makassae Culture*, Baucau: Publicacoes Matebian-Grafica Diocesana Baucau.

Direccao Nacional de Controlo e Qualidade de Agua (n.d.) *Recurso Bee Rai Okos Distrito Baucau*, Tetun Fact Sheet, available at: http://besik.36-400.com.au/Portals/0/Documents/Pubs_resources/Fact%20Sheet%20Baucau%20TET%20WEB%20VERSION. pdf (accessed 17 September 2014).

Ernstson, H. and Sorlin, S. (2013) 'Ecosystem Services as Technology of Globalization: On Articulating Values in Urban Nature', *Ecological Economics* 86: 274–284.

Fitzpatrick, D., McWilliam, A. and Barnes, S. (2012) *Property and Social Resilience in Times of Conflict: Land, Custom and Law in East Timor*, London: Ashgate.

Furness, L. (2004) A *Preliminary Assessment of the Sustainable Groundwater Yield of Timor-Leste*, Timor-Leste Integrated Water Resource Management Project, Canberra: Asia Development Bank.

Furness, L. (2011) 'Baucau Limestone Dye-Tracing Experiment', Dili: National Directorate of Water Resources, Ministry of Infrastructure.

Furness, L. (2012) 'Baucau Karst Limestone Aquifer Airborne EM Survey', Dili: National Directorate of Water Resources, Ministry of Infrastructure.

Jackson, S. and Palmer, L. (2012) 'Modernising Water: Articulating Custom in Water Governance in Australia and Timor-Leste', *International Journal of Indigenous Policy* 3(3): 1–27.

King, M. (1963) *Eden to Paradise*, London: Camelot Press.

Lansing, J. (2006) *Perfect Order: Recognizing Complexity in Bali*, Princeton: Princeton University Press.

Lavau, S. (2013) 'Going with the Flow: Water Management as Ontological Cleaving', *Environment and Planning D: Society and Space* 31(3): 416–433.

The (re)negotiation of customary relations   179

Loch, A. (2007) *Haus, Handy & Halleluja: psychosoziale Rekonstruktion in Osttimor: eine ethnopsychologische Studie zur postkonfliktuösen Dynamik im Spannungsfeld von Identität, Trauma, Kultur und Entwicklung*, Frankfurt: IKO.

McGregor, A. (2007) 'Development, Foreign Aid and Post-Development in Timor-Leste', *Third Word Quarterly* 28(1): 155–170.

McWilliam, A. and Traube, E. (eds) (2011) *Land and Life in Timor-Leste: Ethnographic Essays*, Canberra: ANU E-Press.

McWilliam A., Palmer, L. and Shepherd, C. (2014) '*Lulik* Encounters and Cultural Frictions in East Timor: Past and Present', *The Australian Journal of Anthropology* 25: 304–320.

Meitzner-Yoder, L. (2005) 'Custom, Codification, Collaboration: Integrating the Legacies of Land and Forest Authorities in Oecusse Enclave, East Timor', unpublished PhD thesis, Yale University.

Ministry of Infrastructure (2012) 'Draft Water Resources Law'.

National Statistics Directorate (NSD) and United National Population Fund (UNFPA) (2011) 'Population and Housing Census of Timor-Leste: Population Distribution by Administrative Areas', Dili: NSD and UNFPA.

Office of the United Nations High Commissioner for Human Rights (UNHCR) (2006) 'Report of the United Nations Independent Special Commission of Inquiry for Timor Leste', Geneva: UNHCR.

Pacific Climate Change Science Program Partners (2011) *Current and Future Climate of Timor-Leste*, International Climate Change Adaptation Initiative. Timor Leste Directorate of Meteorology, Australian Bureau of Meteorology and CSIRO. Available at: www.pacificclimatechangescience.org/wp-content/uploads/2013/06/5_PCCSP_East_Timor_8pp.pdf (accessed 8 October 2014).

Palmer, L. (2007) 'Developing Timor Leste: Recognising the Role of Custom and Tradition', *SSEE Working Papers in Development* 1: 35–40.

Palmer, L. (2010) 'Enlivening Development: Water Management in the Post Conflict Baucau City, Timor-Leste', *Singapore Journal of Tropical Geography* 31: 357–370.

Palmer, L. (2011) 'Water Relations', in A. McWilliam and E. Traube (eds) *Land and Life in Timor-Leste: Ethnographic Essays*, Canberra: ANU E-Press, 141–162.

Palmer, L. and Carvalho, D.A. (2008) 'Nation Building and Resource Management: The Politics of "Nature" in Timor Leste', *Geoforum* 39(3): 1321–1332.

Peake, G. (2013) *Beloved Land*, Melbourne: Scribe.

Rede Ba Rai (2013) *Land Registration and Justice in Timor-Leste: Culture, Power and Justice*, Dili: Haburas Foundation.

Schoffel, P. (2006) 'Timor-Leste: Community-Managed Water Supply and Sanitation: A Case Study from the 2004 Project Performance Audit Phase I and II', Asian Development Bank.

Shepherd, C. (2013) *Development and Environmental Politics Unmasked: Authority, Participation and Equity in East Timor*, London and New York: Routledge.

Shoesmith, D. (ed.) (2007) *The Crisis in Timor-Leste: Understanding the Past, Imagining the Future*, Darwin: Charles Darwin University Press.

Stead, V. (2014) 'Homeland, Territory, Property: Contesting Land, State, and Nation in Urban Timor-Leste', *Political Geography*, in press.

Strang, V. (2004) *The Meaning of* Water, Oxford: Berg Publishers.

Tsing, A. (2005) *Friction: An Ethnography of Global Connection*, Princeton: Princeton University Press.

Viveiros de Castro, E. (2004) 'Exchanging Perspectives: The Transformation of Objects into Subjects in Amerindian Ontologies', *Common Knowledge* 10(3): 463–484.

Wallace, L., Sundaram, B., Brodie, R.S., Marshall, S., Dawson, S., Jaycock J., Stewart G. and Furness, L. (2012) *Vulnerability Assessment of Climate Change Impacts on Groundwater Resources in Timor-Leste – Summary Report*, Record 2012/55. Canberra: Geoscience Australia.

Wilcock, D., Brierley, G. and Howitt, R. (2013) 'Ethnogeomorphology', *Progress in Physical Geography* 37(5): 573–600.

Zerner, C. (1994) 'Through a Green Lens: The Construction of Customary Environmental Law and Community in Indonesia's Maluku Islands', *Law & Society Review* 28(5): 1079–1122.

Conclusion

This book has fleshed out a long-standing regional vitalist philosophy of relations underpinned by an appreciation of complex systems of transgenerational immanence and spiritual ecology. As we have traced this hydrosocial cycle and the storied movement of bodies through water, space and time, we have come to understand water's relational effects across space–time intervals, as well as the material imaginations which elaborate on 'water's active, agential, affective roles' (Bear and Bull 2011: 2262). We have examined the productive frictions which both 'locate particular bodies in particular places' (Bull 2011: 2279) and reconfigure ontological relations (Tsing 2005). At the same time, rather than shifting focus away from 'how water is socialized' (Bear and Bull 2011: 2262; Lavau 2013), we have activated an understanding of water's agency to interrogate the co-production of sociality shared between water and other beings and elaborate the multiplicity of ways that the social may be understood and engaged. In understanding this philosophy we have come to understand its attendant context-specific forms of ethical and cosmo-political interaction across human and non-human realms. We have also seen how this vitalist politics and philosophy is being reconfigured in a society very much in transition. Rather than interrogating the effects of an imperializing 'other' politics and power, we have focused on the refashioning of such ontological assemblages from within the logics and realities of indigenous lifeworlds.

Characterized by spiralling patterns of horizontal and vertical relations, these worlds of more-than-human kin-based relations are made through multiple space–time contingencies, contexts and possibilities. In this world where possible relations are always multiple, actual relations must be continually negotiated as propositions to be confirmed through ritual and exchange. Relations with non-human nature are central to the pursuit of intergenerational well-being. Meanwhile inter-group and inter-familial disagreements, tensions, competition and jealousies are equally present realities, always threatening to create disunity and/or sever relations. This ever transforming web of intergenerational inheritance, sociality, responsibility, exchange, obligation and dispute are the reality from which all else follows. While actual 'bodies' and their ancestral lineage are critical to these relations, the effect is not a reification of descent but an activation of a world 'alive and in movement' (Gombay 2014: 9). In this

182   *Conclusion*

world 'structure is secondary to function' and bodies are not given (Gombay 2014: 9). Rather life is formed 'in motion' (Gombay 2014: 9). As Anderson and Wylie write:

> The flesh is a *process*, not a 'substance', in the sense of something that is simply *there*. This process, an ongoing, originary, process of intertwining and separation, is the very condition of emergence of distinctive, beheld and apprehended matters and sensibilities: horizons, objects, perceptions. It is the fissuring and the braiding in which these register as a 'patterning out', a ceaseless refraction and differentiation.
>
> (2009: 324–325)

It is through this relational materiality of 'patterning out' that we can best understand the dynamics of this region's hydrosocial cycle, a cycle which is dependent on complex socio-cosmic inter-relations.

The hydrosocial cycle revisited

In its specific ethnographic context much of this study has explicated the ways in which the domain of two intermarried ethno-linguistic groups, the Waima'a and the Makasae, have fashioned critical relationships between inland swidden farmers and coastal wet rice cultivators. Whereas swidden farmers control the underground water, they themselves have limited access to it. Underpinned by a metaphysics of inclusive sociality and marriage exchange relations, a ritual relationship has emerged to ensure respect for each other's capabilities and shared resource base and to enable the exchange and circulation of fertility and wellbeing.

Below I explore the way that this exchange between the inland dry farming communities and coastal wet farming communities has traditionally been complemented by rainmaking rituals carried out at a sacred cave on the coastal fringe.[1] This site is intimately connected to the narrative of Joao Lere which we encountered in Chapter 5 (see also dos Santos 1967: 133–135; Correia 1935: 108–110, 132–136) and is likewise embedded in regional socio-cosmic conceptualizations of the hydrosocial cycle. Its rituals and associated practices highlight both social heterogeneity and the ways that this sociality is unified by the circularity of water.

While in this book many of the water infused narratives of place-making we have encountered cloud interpretations of where the pre-eminent political and ritual authority for particular springs emanates from, such opacity aligns with the circuitous nature of the water cycle. In the mountains, we encountered a water cycle which prioritizes the flow of water from the storage tanks of central ranges to the sea, from where it recirculates through the earth feeding the rain clouds (cf. Rodemeier 2009). While shared ancestral names, hydronyms and toponyms across the zone suggest a complicated history of population movements and relationships, as we have seen in Chapter 4, these human movements

Conclusion   183

were enabled by water movements and aqueous ancestral connections. As such the regional opacity of political and spiritual ecology serves well the purpose of connectedness without overly dwelling on either ritual or political precedence. In the existential realm, the realm of ultimate origin, there is through ritual a celebrated relationship between people, animals, the spirit world and sacred water sources. In the dynamic metaphysics underpinning socio-ecological relations, what are being celebrated are shared relationships which are circular, not hierarchical (cf. Reuter 1996: 271).

Thus to conclude this account of a hydrosocial cycle thoroughly integrated with the notion of 'inclusive sociality' and associated spirit ecologies, I want to focus on an origin narrative linked to the sea and the generations of beings that emerged from it. First, however, I turn to the account in Correia (1935: 108–110, 132–136) of the sacred house at Baha Kai Lale built in honour of Joao Lere and the ongoing connection of the people of Wani Uma to this house and the nearby cave of Kai Hunu. According to Correia (1935) in the early twentieth century the house known as Oca Ba'i (W: 'sacred cave') was the most important ritual house in all of Baucau. The elders of Wani Uma explain that this house is the true custodian of Joao Lere's sacred possessions (referred to as his *bandira* = flag (W)) comprised his cloth, seven gongs, plates, a bowl, a clam shell spoon and a seashell.[2]

The Kai Hunu cave associated with Joao Lere's house is located near Bundura (see Map 4.1). Sandwiched between the coast and the Caisidu plateau by seven marine terraces it is set amidst an immediate coastline of seven capes (see Figure 5.2). Above the cave of Kai Hunu on the seventh terrace is another cave known as Lie Gere (W: 'writing cave'). This is where Joao Lere wrote his knowledge (*matenek*) on the rock face in languages including Hindi, Arabic, Chinese, Malay and French. He also wrote a book in these various languages.

As we saw in Chapter 5, one of Joao Lere's most significant powers was his ability to control water. According to these various tellings of his story he could call the sea to rise up, the rain to fall, and the underground waters to flow and emerge in springs. The cave of Kai Hunu itself, accessed via a small opening just inland from the coast, is said to contain seven 'weeping' sources of freshwater in a chamber deep beneath the sea. In the past Kai Hunu was the focal point of a regional rainmaking pilgrimage and ceremony (Correia 1935). While the scope of the pilgrimage significantly diminished after the upheaval of the Japanese occupation, other parts of the ceremony remained extant until the Indonesian occupation when the sacred house was destroyed.[3] As the house is yet to be rebuilt (see below), this rainmaking pilgrimage and its associated rituals have not been carried out for some time.

In April 2012, when I visited Kai Hunu in the company of the current Wani Uma ritual leader (W: *kii lia*) and other elders, as well as a large number of young men, our party was not 'allowed' access to the depths of the cave. The bats guarding it signalled that 'the door would not open' and the ritual leader aborted the descent. The subsequent discussion among senior elders determined that a ceremonial sacrifice to enter the cave was necessary after all. Yet the

184 *Conclusion*

inter-relationship between the cave, the ancestors and the house was such that this sacrifice could not take place until the rebuilding of the sacred house at Baha Kai Lale. This site for this house is located some distance above the cave in the north-western edge of Baucau escarpment. The house's custodians, Wai Luo and Wai Hau, share the responsibility for the Kai Hunu cave with the Wani Uma houses of Watu Naru and Rikainena (as we saw in Chapter 4 these clans are *woi-ba'a* or 'parent' houses for the Caisidu and Wani Uma area).

With the house not yet rebuilt, in 2012 our visit to the cave was carried out under the auspices of the senior Wani Uma ritual leader and custodian of the cave. Nevertheless it emerged later that there was a degree of suspicion expressed among a minority of community members about our intentions in visiting the remote Kai Hunu area. We heard that one young man later spread rumours that the *malae* (my husband and I) had been searching for gold. The cave itself is said by Wani Uma elders to contain many snakes (which, as we saw in Chapter 3, are sometimes manifest as gold):

> People who enter the cave must not wear clothes with pockets lest the snakes hide within them. If the cave door opens, the correct descent is to the north eventually reaching a freshwater source beneath the sea (not the other door to the west which leads to the other world beneath the sea [W: *rea selu*] to where you will be lost forever). Inside the cave voices and barking dogs can be heard. At the place where water is drawn, you can find pieces of betel chew and lime [whose juice is used to wash hair]. When water is drawn a voice is heard yelling out 'people have come to steal water'.

The process of descent which they described to me was also recounted in a similar fashion by Correia (1935). In his account, this descent is a central part of the rainmaking ritual and once drawn these sacred waters are carried out of the cave for a final ritual at Joao Lere's house in Baha Kai Lale. People from right across the Baucau sub-district (although Wani Uma elders report that pilgrims also came from as far away as Lautem and Viqueque) were said to participate in the pilgrimage which culminated in these rainmaking ceremonies. The pilgrims, who would bring with them offerings of various cereals (Correia 1935: 136), would wait at the house while the ritual leaders entered the cave, and would then also be blessed by the sacred waters of Kai Hunu. While these pilgrimages are presently dormant, the senior custodian of the cave from Wani Uma (and the present-day custodian of Joao Lere's sacra) goes periodically to the cave entrance to pray for rain. The elders of Wani Uma are also rebuilding their sacred house complex (which is linked to Wai Luo and Wai Hau). In total there are seven sets of houses in this complex and it is not until the sixth set is built that work can start on the reconstruction of the final house of Joao Lere at Baha Kai Lale.

What this last example of the ritual ecology of water in the Baucau region draws our attention to is the complexity of local understandings of the water cycle. During rainmaking rituals at the Kai Hunu cave a key ancestral name called in

Conclusion   185

prayer is Lu Leki, the controller of the sea and ruler of the ritual centre of Luca. As discussed in Chapter 5, Joao Lere was the son of a man who appeared from Luca. In death Joao Lere transformed into *talibere*, the great snake. The emergence and transformations of ancestral beings into the *talibere* is also the narrative at the heart of the regional hydrosocial cycle. While in Chapter 1, we traced the narrative pathway of this cycle beginning with the ancestor, Luka Bui, from Luca to the sea (*meti*), according to Major Ko'o Raku, this and the story of Joao Lere is connected as well to a much longer story. This latter story begins with the emergence of ancestral winds from across the sea.[4] While sometimes the terminology 'across the sea' is linked explicitly to Larantuka in east Flores, it is also contemporaneous with the 'other world' often glossed simply as the sea. With the emergence of these ancestral winds the world came into being, transforming through six named cycles until emerging as the snake ancestor (*Loi Ofo*) who in this seventh and final cycle continued to transform as a snake, procreating to create human beings. Continuing to transform through time, this snake ancestor, in its various names and guises, is known respectfully as *talibere*. Yet the story of Joao Lere (killed by the Portuguese) signalled an end point in the seamless transitions between people and *talibere*. After he was killed, Joao Lere returned to his family in the form of *talibere*, yet upon seeing a snake his wife called out in fear and *talibere* disappeared. Joao Lere's death, contemporaneous with the expansion of the Portuguese presence across the east, signalled the emerging dominance of the era of light (M: *mu'a usa*, W: *namu rema*). While the power of 'nature' (*natureza* or W: *namu degu, namu rema, ria luli*, M. *mu'a gamu, mu'a usa, mu'a falun*) or the dark world of ancestral beings (*dai*) remained ever present, it was now only communicable through ritual.

In mid 2014 the 'barren' drylands of Caisidu and beyond were embroiled in simmering tensions over the proposed development of a cement factory. Announced in late 2013 the proposal included plans to mine the local karst for the next 100 years. Brokered by national-level politicians and bureaucrats the Australian/Korean joint venture promised hundreds of local jobs and economic development. While the local village heads of Bucoli, Triloca, Tirilolo, Caibada, Bahu, Wailili and Gariuai were said to have given their support for the development, the proposal was only at the exploration stage. Yet even before the social, cultural and environmental assessments of the proposal had been carried out (apparently all to be done by different international consultancy firms), community relations were not proceeding well. The two clans with acknowledged traditional authority over the Caisidu region (Wai Luo and Wai Hau) had not been consulted in the initial consultations (which included a visit of village heads to an Australian mine). The relations of these clans with others in the community who supported the development were rapidly deteriorating. There was high sensitivity and threats of violence.

Others from outside of Caisidu, while welcoming the vision of regional economic development, were also concerned about the risks of the venture. It was said that the ritual leaders from all of the villages needed to be brought together to discuss the matter. Yet while they could '*koalia*' (ask for ancestral permission),

186 *Conclusion*

there was no guarantee that they could ameliorate the consequences of digging up the karst. Major Ko'o Raku recalled a time in the 1960s when a small area of karst was quarried to build the Baucau airport and sea had began rising up through the soil (after which time the project was abandoned). Others too remarked on how the removal of rock from the coastal areas around Caisidu would result in the sea rising up to swallow all the agricultural land. Meanwhile, others from the inland areas feared that such quarrying would mean the underground waters connected to *talibere* (in this case the eels known as Marui Masara) would simply dry up (cf. Barber and Jackson 2012).

Bodily ontology

In many places in the world relations between so-called nature and culture are socialized across space and time and mediated by elders through story and ritual. These vital forces which congeal and shape shift co-produce and participate in an 'aliveness' and such social phenomena manifest simultaneously as various types of permeable being (Lévy-Bruhl 1910; Ingold 2011). These landscapes are 'full of danger and serendipity', inscribed 'with the laws of ritual engagement' activated through 'a discourse of power by a hierarchy of Elders' (Langton 2005: 300). This, writes Langton (2005: 300), is 'the mystery at the heart of property relations'. Physical 'beings', 'objects' and 'features' are all in some senses 'bodies' connected through names and storylines linking them together to different times, places and events. In these highly sensitive matters the proper names of sacred beings cannot be spoken, these ancestors, animals, things and places know their names, they hear and they communicate and this is why they have many names and 'circumlocations' (Ingold 2011: 174). These 'beings' are in addition ever sensitive and unpredictable (as they are fallible, getting things wrong and misinterpreting human actions). Constant care and vigilance is required to ensure that they are not advertently or inadvertently angered or offended (cf. Gelles 2000: 83). In the case of springs, as we have seen, angered water 'bodies' might take the decision simply to relocate.

In a world where everything is particularized, concretized and separate, yet interconnected by a larger cosmic force, carefully tended social relations are necessary to activate, build and maintain generative links between invisible and visible forces (cf. Viveiros de Castro 2012). Everything does or can participate in everything else (Lévy-Bruhl 1910). Yet, as noted above, even non-human beings which are simultaneously singular, plural and collective, are not infallible or all-knowing. The inter-subjective relations between humans and these more-than-human others require particular skills, care and attention to multiple times and multiple presences. This is enabled through *lisan* (customary norms and practices) which both is and provides the framework for relationality. In this process 'the imagination is fastened firmly to the body' (Tsintjilonis 2004: 450), which 'more than manifesting life' crucially 'support and facilitate it' (Tsintjilonis 2004: 451). These bodies, as we have seen above, constitute both the 'homogeneity of life' and the 'heterogeneity of its various appearances or manifestations' (Tsintjilonis 2004: 449).

Conclusion   187

It is in the end the 'invisible internal world of beings' (Tsintjilonis 2004) and their capacity to 'exchange properties' (Latour 2004) and forms which enables life to be appropriately shaped, proportioned and shared (Nancy 2000 cited in Hill 2014). Exploring the renaissance in the post-independence ritual exchange of sacred objects in the kingdom of Babulu in Viqueque, Barnes draws on Mauss to argue that such sacra are in fact:

> inalienable because they are 'endowed with a powerful personality … that clings to its owner and holds his soul' (1990: 44). Nevertheless, the contingencies of history are such that some of these things are inevitably drawn into networks of exchange. In fact, it is often in the strategic interests of the giver to do so in order to increase their own authority and esteem.
>
> (2013: 6)

Barnes concludes by observing that '[u]nderpinning these exchanges lies an inherent tension between the need to control and the need to share (that arguably permeates all exchange relationships) characteristic of a political economy based on agriculture' (Barnes 2013: 6). I would also add that underpinning such exchange relationships is the need for the heterogeneity of 'bodily' ancestral signatures to be continually woven through life's processes (cf. Tsintjilonis 2004). While moral order (Rappaport 1999) and power relations (Bourdieu 1979) are critical aspects of ritual exchange and governance, the circulation of property conceived through the relational personhood of ancestral signatures gives a particular order and mutuality to all such relations.

In this vital materialist politics there is then a critical need for political sensitivity to diverse ontological politics, to their intermingling and their 'cleaving' (Lavau 2013) in particular assemblages. It is not only Western science which is averse to such considerations. Holding firm to a distinction between the human and non-humans as an ethical space of action (Plumwood 2002; cf. Lorimer 2012), newer forms of relational or vitalist theory also often have little to say about post-humanist sociality. For example modern environmental thought which seeks to recognize non-human *presences* in a universal nature (Plumwood 1998), relies for the most part on a continued de-localization of human and non-human relations. This is a conceptualization at odds with the particularized socio-cosmic configurations of 'nature' and property linked to a sense of spatialized self (Langton 2002; Palmer 2004). In the latter's politics of presence there is already a clearly defined ethical and spiritual pathway for communicating with non-human nature. Such pathways are based in localized customary laws, institutions, protocols and decision-making processes.

For the people of Wai Riu on Mundu Perdido, the body of the world (M: *mu'a tane*) is spatialized by the cardinal points of the male sea, the female sea, the head of the land and the feet of the land (M: *meti tufu, meti namu, mu'a gidae, mu'a gi-iti*). In this understanding of being, the head is Mount Matebian, the legs Mount Ramelau, the left arm Mount Boile, and the right arm, Mount Ossuala (see Map 2.1). The heart or navel (M: *mu'a gi-illu*) of this body is

188 *Conclusion*

Mundo Perdido (Wai Nete Watu Ba'i) distributing blood (water) throughout the body (in Makasae *wai* can mean both river and blood). In ritual ceremonies carried out at the centre, these cardinal points of the body and other significant sites and springs must all be called. Other ritual communities have their own spatialized notions of the land as being. For the kingdom of Luca, the land is the body of a buffalo with its head at Mundo Perdido, its horns reaching to the male and female sea, and its heart at Luca. This ritual heart connects the world (ET: *rai klaran*) with the wealth of underworld (or alternatively 'other world' = ET: *rai seluk*). In the narratives attached to many of Luca's powerful water sources, herds of buffalo emerge from the underground waters.[5] Perpetually connecting those living in the light to the darkness of the other world, water is the pathway to an original unity where the earth, sky and underworld were one (cf. Kehi and Palmer 2012). This is the 'original cosmic situation that eternally centers collective life' (Traube 1986: 243).

In a configuration of space and time based on a (shape shifting) bodily ontology, the spiritual ecology of water in the region is reproduced through the circular and inter-subjective intertwining of place, materiality and ritual practice. Ritual practice that traces the connections between the internal world of bodies and place is always framed in connection to other places. Meanwhile springs and their flows (of blood) are understood in connection to other springs and the sea across multiple time scales. The landscape embodied in this way 'draws together time-space notions into a responsive and sentient collective' (Wilcock *et al.* 2013: 585).

While this ontology may seem far from the world conceptualized by natural science there are, according to Wilcock *et al.* (2013: 595), 'common threads of emergent and contingent perspectives of landscape and connection'. For example in both geomorphology and many indigenous ontologies '[t]alking about particular places – as sites with multiple times – reimagines the landscape and [water] bodies as mutually evolving and emergent entities [and is] an articulation of the contingent and mutually constituted relations occurring in connected sites' (Wilcock *et al.* 2013: 582). Similarly in Baucau, Wallace *et al.* (2012: 49) write that:

> The fissured aquifer of the Baucau area is composed of multiple generations of limestone that have risen out of the ocean over time. The complex interconnection of cave systems through the multiple limestone layers, combined with topography, result in the heterogeneous distribution of springs. Additionally, all aquifers appear to have prominent seasonal variations of groundwater levels associated with seasonal rainfall and strong groundwatersurface water relationships.[6]

Hence both the indigenous ontology of the Baucau Viqueque region and scientific hydrogeological understandings of it focus on the mutual constitution of landscapes across space–time wherein 'each physical site is spoken about in multiple times' (Wilcock *et al.* 2013: 582). Yet in contrast to the largely technical

Conclusion 189

concerns of the earth sciences, indigenous narratives about springs give greater context to these emergent relationships and weave them through the landscape (Wilcock *et al.* 2013: 582; cf. Ingold 2011). As Wilcock *et al.* write:

> Tacit knowledge passed down through stories and narratives provides a sophisticated methodology that is itself emergent – it breaks down notions of linear time and human/nature binaries ... teachings about relationality and thinking about the connectivity of time-space.
>
> (2013: 594)

As Urich (1989) has argued about karst agricultural landscapes, we must be ever wary of the capacity of science to silo its thinking according to particular variables, despite the ever present possibilities of alternate readings. Moreover, for local peoples these readings may include the notion of a social catchment or social groundwater flow that transcends naturalized boundaries. These intensely socialized flows are directly linked to an individual and community's social, physical and psychological health, insight into which is always read according to the long-term cumulative impacts of particular courses of action (cf. Barber and Jackson 2012). This raises important questions about the scale at which resources are governed and about what is considered admissible (by whom) as governance regimes seek to emulate the ways in which people are connected to particular water territories. As Barber and Jackson write:

> [w]ater shapes and reflects boundaries between people.... The separation, mixing and flow of waters reflect social groupings and relationships; people are related in particular ways because of water, and water in turn flows according to the relationships between people.
>
> (2012: 40)

As with all other landscapes, the karst landscapes of the Baucau Viqueque zone are not passive physical spaces waiting to be inscribed with meaning, but agential and relational landscapes which connect people and place through multiple and context dependent time–space narratives. Transformations of ancestors into other agential forms (be they permanent landscape features or moving forms such as water) 'break down the binaries between living and non living natures of landscapes' (Wilcock *et al.* 2013: 587). In this moral economy, water and landscapes have 'their own agency to change people, and themselves change in response to people' (Wilcock *et al.* 2013: 592). Across Timor Leste these notions of inclusive sociality and the *lulik* complex are mediated by *lisan* and remain 'the preeminent philosophical, religious, moral and epistemic order guiding relations among the Timorese themselves' (McWilliam *et al.* 2014; Trindade 2011). Sensing and appreciating the immanent force embedded in the continuous multiplicity of the regional hydrosocial cycle, the political and ethical challenge remains to pluralistically think through such alternative waterworlds and 'the ends that people seek in "managing" them' (Gombay 2014: 1).

190   *Conclusion*

In a world of co-being and co-becoming, the cosmopolitics of *lulik* is enchanted, lively, intense and dangerous. Mediating the boundaries of the permissible and the forbidden is a high stakes politics which takes great skill and courage. In their negotiations ritual-political leaders are always guided by the heterogeneous *lisan* and ancestral 'bodies' relevant to their particular houses. For those whom *lulik* is an everyday part of life, it is also an inter-subjective and intensely relational fact of life which must be constantly mediated. Yet if we accept that matter is political (Braun and Whatmore 2010) and that nothing exists outside its relations with others (Rose 2005, 2011; Ingold 2011; Bawaka Country *et al.* 2013), we can also recognize all human and non-human encounters as characterized by such relational politics. In this sense, despite clinging to the (mythic) cosmology and modality of ahistorical global governance technology, even the ostensibly apolitical world of water resource governance is characterized by relational processes of continual 'co-becoming' (Jackson and Palmer 2014; cf. Ernstson and Sorlin 2013). Recognizing this across the Baucau Viqueque zone, ritual leaders insist that 'culture' or *lisan* must be a central component of the governance of the new nation. In the words of one *lia na'in*: 'We achieved independence, but we became stupid (*beik*), *lulik* is running wild.' Left untamed, it is unchecked and in such a world of co-being and co-becoming the fear is that it will wreak devastation on all. While customary practices are undergoing something of a renaissance in many areas, as we saw in Chapter 7, also pervading these haltingly re-emergent relations and exchanges in the independence era is, in many cases, fear. The fear of local people themselves who are unsure about re-instigating communications with ancestors so long neglected (cf. Rodemeier 2009: 480).

Whatever the constraints, according to Wilcock *et al.* (2013; cf. Iovina and Oppermann 2012) there is an urgent need to begin multiple place-based conversations about the overlapping materiality, agency and narrativity of particular landscapes as well as relations of power and dominance. In Timor Leste, the people of Mundo Perdido are already beginning this task. In 2012 they explained to me that scientists from Australia had recently been carrying out geological research on Mundo Perdido and had found fossils of sea fish in the rocky peaks: 'They told us that in the past this area was all sea.' After these scientists had spoken, the elders present confirmed this view: 'They [the elders] also said that there is a close connection between the land and sea, the rain, the wind, the sun, all are connected to each other.' Other scientists told them that Mundo Perdido has unique trees and birds and because of this the Secretariat of State for the Environment encouraged them to carry out a *tara bandu* to ritually regulate resource use and protect the area (see Figure 2.1). The community agreed that it was important to halt indiscriminate (*arbiru*) felling of timber, burning and hunting of animals. The state, in contrast, prioritized a ban on these activities in their entirety. Clearly while both agreed on the need for the *tara bandu*, in the first instance there is a local prioritization of respectful relations, in the latter this relation is now illegitimate (cf. Gombay 2014). Hence while the latter seeks to protect what is there by a blanket ban on certain activities, in the former people and 'nature' are instead recalibrating relations. As a former Liurai from the region, Fransisco da Costa Guterres, explained:

> Lisan and the nation need to walk together. In the future custom needs to be stronger, we need to let our stories about nature flourish and teach them to our future generations. In Portuguese times we learnt other people's stories in school. Now those educated people have returned to the source and seek out the roots of the stories that we ourselves know to be important.

Just as these storied land- and water-scapes enable communication with the 'other world' of natureza (which as we have seen is constituted by the inter-relationships between particular spirit beings), they simultaneously cultivate an awareness of the ebb and flow of vibrant life forces inhabiting multiple times, forms and spaces. Yet as the natural sciences have 'come to think of – and not with – water in more channeled and specialized ways' (Strang 2013: 192), this relational ethic has been displaced by one where human culture is 'somehow *separate from* the material world' (Strang 2013: 205). In a world where there is increased competition over resources, human agency is given primacy and time and space are fixed in a search for certainty (Strang 2013: 205). In contrast, in a world underscored by spiritual ecologies of inclusive sociality it is the nuances of subject–subject relations which define the inter-connections between the human and non-human, the living, the dead and the not-yet-born. The continuing import of these socio-cosmic under-pinnings in the everyday practices and memoryscapes of this region's hydrosocial cycle suggests 'that other relationships to time, to the past, to water and to one another may be possible' (MacLeod 2013: 57). We need to listen.

Notes

1 Small springs on the Baucau plateau are highly sensitive to changes in rainfall and show distinct seasonal variations, while there are more permanent (if variable) flows at the larger springs of the marine terrace zone (Wallace et al. 2012: 58).
2 At present these objects are being taken care of by another sacred house connected to the Wani Uma house complex.
3 However, in the 1930s Correia (1935: 51) wrote that 'Indigenous people need transit licenses if they want to go anywhere'. This suggests that these pilgrimages may have been disrupted somewhat earlier than the Second World War (most probably after the era of the Manufahi rebellions circa 1912).
4 This narrative was first relayed to me by Major Ko'o Raku, interwoven with his more Catholic inflected telling of the earth's origin story involving birds, Christ, the first humans, the python and the kuda resa (see Chapter 2).
5 Boelens (2014: 10) writes that in the Andes, underworld water is now associated with the bull rather than the snake (the bull as a symbol of wealth replacing in myth in the post-Spanish era the indigenous symbolism of a winged serpent and monsters (see Arguedas 1956)).
6 All of which will be impacted by future climate change to rainfall patterns and (at lower topographies) sea level rise. Elsewhere Wallace et al. note that the future of Timor's hydrogeology 'will be dependent on the interaction between geology and climate, both of which have been shown to be complex and variable' (2012: 24).

192   *Conclusion*

References

Anderson, B. and Wylie J. (2009) 'On Geography and Materiality', *Environment and Planning* 41(2): 318–335.

Arguedas, J.M. (1956) 'Puquio, una Cultura en Proceso de Cambio', *Revista del Museo Nacional* 25: 184–232.

Barber, M. and Jackson, S. (2012) 'Aboriginal Water Values and Resource Development Pressures in the Pilbara Region of North-West Australia', *Australian Aboriginal Studies* 2: 32–49.

Barnes, S. (2013) 'Gift Giving and Gift Obligations', paper presented at 7th EuroSEAS Conference, Lisbon, July 2013.

Bawaka Country with Suchet-Pearson, S., Wright, S., Lloyd, K. and Burarrwanga, L. (2013) 'Caring as Country: Towards an Ontology of Co-Becoming in Natural Resource Management', *Asia-Pacific Viewpoint* 54: 185–197.

Bear, C. and Bull, J. (2011) 'Water Matters: Agency, Flows and Frictions', *Environment and Planning A* 43(10): 2261–2266.

Boelens, R. (2014) 'Cultural Politics and the Hydrosocial Cycle: Water, Power and Identity in the Andean Highlands', *Geoforum* 57: 234–237.

Bourdieu, P. (1979) *Outline of a Theory of Practice*, Cambridge: Cambridge University Press.

Braun, B. and Whatmore, S. (eds) (2010) *Political Matter: Technoscience, Democracy and Public Life*, Minnesota: University of Minnesota Press.

Bull, J. (2011) 'Encountering Fish, Flows, and Waterscapes through Angling', *Environment and Planning A* 43(10): 2267–2284.

Correia, A. (1935) *Gentio de Timor*, Lisbon: Agência-Geral das Colónias.

dos Santos, E. (1967) *Kanoik: Mitos e Lendas de Timor*, Lisboa: Ultramar.

Ernstson, H. and Sorlin S. (2013) 'Ecosystem Services as Technology of Globalization: On Articulating Values in Urban Nature', *Ecological Economics* 86: 274–284.

Gelles, P. (2000) *Water and Power in Highland Peru: The Cultural Politics of Irrigation and Development*, New Brunswick: Rutgers University Press.

Gombay, N. (2014) '"Poaching" – What's in a Name? Debates about Law, Property, and Protection in the Context of Settler Colonialism', *Geoforum* 55: 1–12.

Hill, A. (2014) 'Becoming "More-than-Subjects" of Community Economies', paper presented at the 'Institute of Australian Geographers' conference, Melbourne, 30 June–2 July.

Ingold, T. (2011) *Being Alive: Essays on Movement, Knowledge and Description*, London: Routledge.

Iovina, S. and Oppermann, S. (2012) 'Material Ecocriticism: Materiality, Agency and Models of Narrativity', *Interdisciplinary Studies in Literature and Environment* 19(3): 448–475.

Jackson, S. and Palmer, L. (2014) 'Reconceptualising Ecosystem Services: Possibilities for Cultivating and Valuing the Ethics and Practices of Care', *Progress in Human Geography*.

Kehi, B. and Palmer, L. (2012) 'Hamatak Halirin: The Cosmological and Socio-Ecological Roles of Water in Koba Lima, Timor', *Bijdragen tot de Taal-, Land- en Volkenkunde* 168: 445–471.

Langton, M. (2002) 'The Edge of the Sacred, the Edge of Death: Sensual Inscriptions', in B. David and M. Wilson (eds) *Inscribed Landscapes*, Honolulu: University of Hawaii Press, 427–455.

Langton, M. (2005) 'An Aboriginal Ontology of Being and Place: The Performance of Aboriginal Property Relations in the Princess Charlotte Bay Area of Eastern Cape York Peninsula, Australia', unpublished PhD thesis, Macquarie University.

Latour, B. (2004) *Politics of Nature: How to Bring the Sciences into Democracy*, Cambridge, MA: Harvard University Press.

Lavau, S. (2013) 'Going with the Flow: Water Management as Ontological Cleaving', *Environment and Planning D: Society and Space* 31(3): 416–433.

Lévy-Bruhl, L. (1910) *How Natives Think*, translation by L. Clare (1985), Princeton: Princeton University Press.

Lorimer, J. (2012) 'Multinatural Geographies for the Anthropocene', *Progress in Human Geography* 36(5): 593–612.

MacLeod, J. (2013) 'Water and Material Imagination', in C. Chen, J. MacLeod and A. Neimanis (eds) *Thinking with Water*, Montreal: McGill-Queen's University Press, 55–75.

McWilliam A., Palmer, L. and Shepherd, C. (2014) '*Lulik* Encounters and Cultural Frictions in East Timor: Past and Present', *The Australian Journal of Anthropology* 25: 304–320.

Mauss, M. (1990) [1922] *The Gift: Forms and Functions of Exchange in Archaic Societies*, London: Routledge.

Palmer, L. (2004) 'Bushwalking in Kakadu: A Study of Cultural Borderlands', *Social and Cultural Geography* 5(1): 109–128.

Plumwood, V. (1998) 'Wilderness Skepticism and Wilderness Dualism', in J.B. Calicott and M.P. Nelson (eds) *The Great New Wilderness Debate*, Athens and London: The University of Georgia Press, 652–690.

Plumwood, V. (2002) *Environmental Culture: The Ecological Crisis of Reason*, London: Routledge.

Rappaport, R. (1999) *Ritual and Religion in the Making of Humanity*, Cambridge: Cambridge University Press.

Reuter, T. (1996) 'Custodians of the Sacred Mountains: The Ritual Domains of Highland Bali', unpublished PhD thesis, Australian National University.

Rodemeier, S. (2009) 'Bui Hangi–The Deity's Human Wife: Analysis of a Myth from Pura, Eastern Indonesia', *Anthropos* 104: 469–482.

Rose, D. (2005) 'An Indigenous Philosophical Ecology: Situating the Human', *The Australian Journal of Anthropology* 16(3): 294–305.

Rose, D. (2011) *Wild Dog Dreaming: Love and Extinction*, Charlottesville: University of Virginia Press.

Strang, V. (2013) 'Conceptual Relations: Water, Ideologies, and Theoretical Subversions', in C. Chen, J. MacLeod and A. Neimanis (eds) *Thinking with Water*, Montreal: McGill-Queen's University Press, 200–226.

Traube, E. (1986) *Cosmology and Social Life: Ritual Exchange among the Mambai of East Timor*, Chicago: University of Chicago Press.

Trindade, J. (2011) 'Lulik: The Core of Timorese Values', paper presented at *Communicating New Research on Timor-Leste, 3rd Timor-Leste Study Association (TLSA) Conference*, June, Dili, Timor-Leste.

Tsing, A. (2005) *Friction: An Ethnography of Global Connection*, Princeton: Princeton University Press.

Tsintjilonis, D. (2004) 'The Flow of Life in Buntao: Southeast Asian Animism Reconsidered', *Bijdragen tot de Taal-, Land- en Volkenkunde* 160(4): 425–455.

Urich, P. (1989) 'Tropical Karst Management and Agricultural Development: Example from Bohol, Phillipines', *Geografiska Annaler Series B, Human Geography* 71(2): 95–108.

Viveiros de Castro E. (2012) 'Cosmological Perspectivism in Amazonia and Elsewhere', *Master Class Series 1*, Manchester: HAU Network of Ethnographic Theory.

194 Conclusion

Wallace, L., Sundaram, B., Brodie, R.S., Marshall, S., Dawson, S., Jaycock, J., Stewart, G. and Furness, L. (2012) *Vulnerability Assessment of Climate Change Impacts on Groundwater Resources in Timor-Leste – Summary Report*, Record 2012/55. Canberra: Geoscience Australia.

Wilcock, D., Brierley, G. and Howitt, R (2013) 'Ethnogeomorphology', *Progress in Physical Geography* 37(5): 573–600.

Appendix 1

Key research participants (by village of residence)

Video stories and other digital materials recorded in local languages and told by the people below will be published in 2015 in an online Timor Leste Water Archive.

Bahu

Antonio da Costa Gusmao (Major Ko'o Raku)
Joao Baptista, Chefe Ana Ulu
Jose da Costa, Kabu Bee Boile
Mariano da Costa (Mari Kai Wai Mata Bu)
Manuel da Costa (Nai Da)
Igidio da Costa (Kii Da)
Julio da Costa, Chefe Ro'ulu
Julio da Costa
Kabu Bee of Boile, Macadai and Caibada
Cipriano Graz Belo (Bale Rubi)
Jose Maria Mok Kingsang
Agustinho Gusmao

Wani Uma (Caibada Waima'a)

Christiano de Sa (Sau Rai), Chefe Wani Uma
Moses Nai Usu
Joao Ximenes (Ossu Watu)
Delfin de Cha (Bi Raku)
Daniel de Cha (Loi Raku)
Ernesto de Cha (Susu Anu)

Buibau

Armando Nicolau Ornai
Ilesario Sarmento (Anubadu)
Antonio Ximenes (Alawa'a)

Buruma

Paulo Freitas (Bada Kai)

Caibada Makasae

Domingos Defa Nawa (Bee Matan Wai Kinari)

Darasula (Gariuai)

Mariano Gusmao (Wono Loi)
Chefe Virgilio Domingos Freitas (Wai Usa)
Alfonso Freitas Matebian (Ko'o Ala)
Cesaltinu Da Silva Freitas (Ko'o Lai)

Aubaca (Triloca)

Alexandro Da Costa (Loi Osa) and son Armindo da Costa
Mariano da Costa (son of Me Osa)

Tirilolo

Joao Graciano Simoes (Tetu Noko)
Duarte Da Silva
Ricardo Ernesto Belo, Chefe Tirilolo
Carlos Belo
Luis Antonio Belo
Kordai Metan
Domingos Dos Reis

Wailili

Augosto do Rosario Xavier (Anu Watu)
Armindo Siqeira Ornai (Sa Ko'o)
Placido Rosario (Sege Wai)
Adriano Amaral Freitas (Anu Rai)
Luciana Bete Rai
Abilio de Fatima (Usa Kai)

Bucoli

Fransisco Lemos

Berecoli

Elidio da Costa (Loi Bosi)
Vicente da Costa (Modo Leki)

Wai Oli (Venilale)

Hermengildo Amaral and Katuas Loime (Bee Matan Bui Lewa)
Chefe Leonicio Enrique Guterres

Ossu

Salvador Monteiro (Rai Olo)
Fransisco da Costa Guterres (Keu Lai)
Andre Da Costa (Gari Modo) and son Domingos
Manuel da Costa Alves
Filomeno da Camara
Cipriano Ornai (Modo Gari)
Amaro Melo Cabral Ornai (Modo Gari)
Filomeno Monteiro (Sina Loi)
Joaquim dos Reis (Gamu Tuo)

Lacluta

Jose Andre dos Santos
Caitanu Da Luz

Luca

Nai Fransisco Amaral Guterres (Liurai Luca)
David Amaral
Xavio Gomes Guterres (Bai Loi)
Jacinta Pinto Gomes (Lihu Loik)

Irabi

Armindo da Silva

Appendix 2

Luca and We Hali (Lia Dadolin = Poetic Verse)

(Narrator: David Amaral (*lia na'in*), Uma Kan Lor, Luca)

Loro tolu babulu[1] *tolu ba Loro Saen*	Three dominions, three kingdoms are to the East
Loro tolu babulu tolu ba Loro Toban	Three dominions, three kingdoms are to the West
Loro tolu babulu tolu Loro Saen	Three dominions, three kingdoms of the East
Too Tutuala	Extends to Tutuala
Loro tolu babulu tolu Loro Toban	Three dominions, three kingdoms of the West
Too Loro Suai ba sai Kupang	Extends to Suai dominion down to Kupang
Loro tolu babulu tolu Loro Saen	Three dominions, three kingdoms of the East
Loro tolu babulu tolu Loro Toban.	Three dominions, three kingdoms of the West.
Neebe loron ida ferik ida ema uma kain Omain. Ferik nee katak: Emi dadoko liurai oan nee hau mak katak. Katak kantiga. Neebe sia dadoki, ferik katak	(One day an old lady from the house of Omain said: You rock the king's child, I sing the lullaby):
Dadoko ta beik la nonok	Rocking fails to stop the royal child crying
Dadeta ta beik la nano	Swinging fails to stop royal child crying
La na no kaer	The child can not be comforted [does not want to be held]
O Nain We Hali	O the Guardian of We Hali
La na no kaer	The child can not be comforted [does not want to be held]

Appendix 2   199

Nain We Biku	O the Guardian of We Biku
Loron tolu fuik atu fuik liu liu.	During three days the child turned wild, wild and wild.
Neebe ferik katak liurai oan nee para ona tanis, ferik katak fali ida	(After the royal child stop crying, the old lady said):
Bone Bauk sa Bone Bauk modi ami oin ee lae	Bone Bauk, oh you, Bone Bauk, do you uplift us or not
Bone Bauk sa Bone Bauk tias ami oin ee lae.	Bone Bauk, oh you, Bone Bauk, do you protect us or not.
Liurai Bone Bauk nee dudu taha ba fatuk leten nee, nia rona netik dei. Neebe ferik nee katak	(While the king Bone Bauk was sharpening his machete on the stone, he was listening to the lullaby sung by the old lady):
Bone Bauk sa Bone Bauk ee modi ami oin ee lae	Bone Bauk, oh you, Bone Bauk, do you uplift us or not
Bone Bauk sa Bone Bauk tias ami oin ee lae.	Bone Bauk, oh you, Bone Bauk, do you protect us or not.
Liurai Bone Bauk dehan	(King Bone Bauk then spoke):
Se nalo sa kaer sa nodi emi oin ba sa?	Who did what, held what, uplift you for what?
Nalo sa kaer sa tias emi oin ba sa?	Who did what, held what, protect you for what?
Anin lor tabasar, Loro Sae tabasar	The south scatters, the east scatters
Murak hau la kodi, karau hau la kodi	I brought neither silver nor buffalo.
Kodi ba ko'i We Hali, ba hotu We Biku.	I brought them to We Hali, I took them all to We Biku.
Murak liu rai murak,	Silver goes to the land of silver,
mamuk liu rai mamuk.	emptiness goes to the land of emptiness.
Tahan emin nadiki rai la lian.	While your leaves shoot, the land turns noiseless.
Ferik aa katak tan	(The old lady further said):
Hanesan tur iha Labunar We We Biku	Like residing in Labunar of We We Biku
Tur iha Labunar We We Hali	Like residing in Labunar of We We Hali
Nare We Hali rai Kakoli	Seeing We Hali the land of Kakoli
Nare We Biku rai Nakduka	Seeing We Biku the land of Nakduka
Kakoli atu ba koli tan netik	Kakoli is going for a walk
Nakduka atu ba duka tan netik	Naduka is going for a stroll

200 *Appendix 2*

Koli tia lor uma kain nen tolu	Walking around three of the six houses
Duka tia lor uma kain nen tolu	Strolling around three of the six houses
Loro uma kain nen niit ain hat	The lords of the six houses raise their four feet
Dato uma kain nen daet ain hat.[2]	The guardians of the six houses move their four feet.
Miit ain ba makur liu We Haban	Raising their feet to cross We Haban
Niit ain ba makur liu We Haban	Lifting their feet to cross We Haban
Makur liu We Haban Bone Bauk fohon	Crossing over We Haban above Bone Bauk
Daet liu We Haban Bone Bauk fohon.	Trespassing We Haban above Bone Bauk.
Biti nain liu Resi, Resi Bai Afani	The owner of mat Liu Resi, Resi Bai Afani
Naak atu tau lakon, naak atu fo lakon	Said to be hidden away, said to be given away
La tau ba balu, la fo ba balu	It was hidden from others, not being given to others
Fo fali fo basu liu ba Makasar fuik nia rain.	It was given instead to Makasar, the land of the wild.
Mota Masin Babulu nia ain sai ba Tasi Mane (The River Masin Babulu flows down to the South Sea).	
Neebe ba Don ida Lu Leki too ba, ba Don Taek Aman tiha ona we iha Salele, iha namon Hahuduk (When Don Lu Leki arrived there, Don Taek Aman had already fetched the water in Salele, in Hahuduk beach). *Neeba Don Lu Leki nee koa lia husu ona ida Taek Aman tan ba Taek Aman tiha we nee tiha uluk* (Arriving there Don Lu Leki asked first Taek Aman because Taek Aman had been the first one to fetch this water). *Neebe Don Lu Leki ba koalia dadolin:*	(Therefore Don Lu Leki said the following poetic verse):
Be se hakari rai nee rai nee	But he who breaks up this land, this land becomes his land
Se hatir rai nee rai nee,	He who divides this land, this land becomes his land

Nee nia alin maun Taek Ama koalia — (Then his brother Taek Aman responded in a well-versed form):

Be o ida musu hau o se los? — But who are you to ask about me?

O ida seti hau o se los? — Who are you to ask for my name?

Neebe Lu Leki koalia fila fali — (Lu Leki then replied also in a poetical verse):

Hau naran Lu Leki meti oan hau — I am Lu Leki, the son of the tides

Hau naran Lu Leki tasi oan hau — I am Lu Leki, the son of the sea

Hau katak ba tasi, tasi sei nakduka nuu lor ba — I command the sea to recede, it obeys me

Katak fali ba meti, meti sei nakduka nuu lor ba. — I command the tide to recede, it obeys me.

Neebe Don Lu Leki nusu fali ba Taek Ama — (Don Lu Leki asked Taek Aman):

Be o ida seti hau o se los? — But who are you to ask for my name?

O ida musu hau o se los? — Who are you to ask about me?

Nee ida be We Hali nee koalia fali — (The one from We Hali, that is Taek Aman, then spoke in similar poetic tones):

Hau naran Taek Aman fulan oan hau — I am Taek Aman, the son of the moon

Hau naran Taek Aman loro oan hau — I am Taek Aman, the son of the sun

Hau katak ba loro, loro sei nakduka nuu rae ba, — I command the sun to rise, it obeys me,

Hau katak ba fulan, fulan sei nakduka nuu rae ba. — I command the moon to rise, it obeys me.

Neebe ida be Lu Leki lian naaka We Biku nian nee koa lia fali — (Then Lu Leki, the king of We Biku,[3] said the following stanza):

Biit tolu biit, biit nanesa — The strength of three is equal

Beran tolu beran, beran nanesa. — The power of the three is equal.[4]

Hotu tia Don Kupang nee, We Hali nee koalia fali — (Then Don Kupang, the king of We Hali, responded):

Ita rua sei keta rai ba malu — We both have to border this land

Ita rua sei taka rai ba malu. — We both have to divide this land.

Lu Leki koalia fali — (Lu Leki, the king of We Biku, responded):

Ook tuka ba mota, Mota Masin Babulu — Yours extends to River Masin Babulu

Too hodi ba loro e toban los ona. — From the other side of the river to the west.

Hauk tuka ba mota, Mota Masin Babulu — Mine extends to River Masin Babulu

Too hodi ba loro e saen los ona. — From the other side of the river to the east.

202   *Appendix 2*

Notes

1 *Babulu* = *rai* = kingdom.
2 The six lords have six sacred houses called *uma mane nen* (*uma manen*). These *uma mane nen* were then divided into two, each of which called *uma kain nen tolu*. The first *nen tolu* are called We Hali = Rai Kakoli, the second *nen tolu* are called We Biku = Rai Nakduka.
3 We Biku is paired with and here refers to Luca.
4 *Loro tolu, babulu tolu, Loro Saen* and *Loro tolu, babulu tolu, Loro Toban*. Six lords (*mane nen*) with their six sacred houses (*uma mane nen*) which was then divided into two (*uma kain nen tolu*). Three in *Loro Saen* (We Biku) and three in *Loro Toban* (We Hali).

Appendix 3

The custodian of the *tais*

(A 'plain tale' from Boleha, retold by Louisa Freitas)

Once long ago when people had only goat skin and tree bark to wear as clothes there was a hunter who would go to the forest each day to hunt birds with his bamboo hunting pipe. One day when he was returning home he became lost. In the distance he saw a big snake which looked like a python but as he got closer to the snake it turned into a beautiful woman wearing exquisitely coloured cloth and weaving *tais* (woven cloth). She called out to the hunter 'do you want to take me as your wife?' The hunter replied, 'I already have a home with a wife and children'. However, he did like this beautiful woman. The woman liked him too and asked again, 'do you want to take me as your wife?' The man replied again 'No, I already have a wife and children', and with that he continued on his way.

The next day the hunter went to the forest again and once more when he was returning home he saw the snake which again became a woman weaving *tais*. The woman asked again, 'do you want to take me as your wife?' Again he replied 'No, I already have a wife and children' and went on his way.

The same thing happened to the hunter for seven days. Each day he saw the 'snakewoman' and each day she asked the same question. On the seventh day the woman followed the hunter out of the forest. He stopped and turned around to her when they reached the boundary between the forest and the fields. He said to the snakewoman, 'if you cross this boundary and come with me into the fields, do you realize you can never return and never again can you become a snake'. The snakewoman listened carefully and accepted the bargain. She crossed the boundary from the forest to the fields and went with the hunter to become his wife. From that day, she never became a snake again, rather she spent her days weaving *tais* and teaching the other women how to do likewise. The weaving patterns they followed were the same as those of a python's skin.

Glossary of selected Tetum, Waima'a (W) and Makasae (M) terms

Barlake	marriage exchange gifts
Bee (W: *wai*, M: *ira*)	water
Bee na'in (W: *wai buu*, M: *ira gauhaa*)	custodian of the water
Bin-alin (W: *wa'i-wari*, M: *tufu-noko*)	older sister younger sister
Dai (W. and M.)	ancestors, outsiders
Fetosaa umane (W: *w'aa-sae lila*, M: *tufumata omarahe*)	fertility-takers fertility-givers
Kabu Bee (W: *Wai Kabu*, M. *Ira Kabu*)	water controller
Lia na'in (W: *kii lia*, M: *anu sobu*)	custodian of the words
Lisan (W: *lisan*, M: *lisan*)	customary norms/practices
Liurai (W: *liurai*, M: *liurai/rata*)	ruler, local 'king'
Lulik (W: *luli/ba'i*, M: *falunu*)	sacred, forbidden, taboo
Malae (W: *dai*, M: *dai*)	ancestors, outsiders
Malae mutin	Portuguese
Maun-alin (W: *wa'i-wari*, M: *kaka-noko*)	older brother younger brother
Meti	tide
Natureza	'nature' spirit world
Rai klaran (W: *ria tena*, M: *mu'a tane*)	this world
Rai na'in (W: *ria buu*, M: *mu'a gauhaa*)	custodian of the land
Rai nakukun (W: *namu degu*, M: *mu'a gamu*)	dark earth
Rai naroman (W: *namu rema*, M: *mu'a usa*)	light earth
Rai seluk (W: *ria selu*, M: *mu'a gi seluk*)	the other world
Talibere (M)	great snake
Tasi (W: *tasi*, M: *meti*)	sea
Uma lulik (W: *umo luli/ba'i*, M: *oma falun*)	sacred house
Wai (M)	blood, river
Wai (W)	water

Index

Page numbers in *italics* denote tables.

Abercrombie, T. 125
acequia 8, 140
Ade 126n2, n13
Adnan, A. 126n3
Afalokai 73–4, 86
Agama Tirtha, Bali 10
agency 15, 43, 54, 57, 63, 181, 190, 191;
and hydrosocial cycle 17–19, 19–20, 21
agricultural economy 131–3
Ai Sahe 54
Allerton, C. 13, 14–15, 160
alliances 10, 29n4, n9; with Chinese 119;
colonial 107, 109, 116, 118; house-
based 106, 157; wife-taker and wife-
giver 29n9; *see also* fertility-takers
fertility-givers; marriage exchange
relations
Almeida, de A. 16, 68, 70, 78, 79, 104n15
Alor 13, 115
Altman, J. 7, 14
Altman, N. 1
Amaral, D. 53
Amaral, X. 126n11
Ambon 68, 76, 77
Ana Ulu 120
Anderson, B. 7, 19, 20, 21, 63, 182
Andes 8–9, 191n5
animism 14, 43, 159
Apodeti 106, 126n5
Araujo, Fernando 'La Sama' de 172
areca nuts xviii, 26, 56, 116, 131, 170,
176n10, 184
Arguedas, J.M. 191n5
ash trails 83, 84, 93
Asian Development Bank 6, 163, 166
Association in Rural Development (ARD)
154
Atauru (Atauro) 58n17, 86, 87

Atoni 149n4
Attwood, B. 62
Aubaca 70, 71, 102, 177n21
Audley-Charles, M. 3, 164
Australian Aid 164, 165
Austronesian languages 3, 29n3, n6, 63,
68, 78, 80n6
Austronesian societies 3, 10, 14, 29n6, 68,
70

Babo Soares, D. 5
Bachelard, G. 7, 39
Baguia 73, 76, 86, 117, 122, 127n25
Baha Kai Lale 109, 111, 115, 183–4
Bahu 26, 47, 89, 90, 95, 101, 138–9, 143,
145, 146, 157, 169, 170, 185
Bakker, K. 7
Bali 9, 10; *Agama Tirtha* ('religion of
water') 10; bamboo as water carrier 16;
irrigation co-operatives 10, 15; Pura
Batur temple 15; sprinkling of holy
water 16
bamboo 13, 16, 131
Banibere (seven-headed bee) 47, 51
Banister, J. 17, 19
banyan tree 13, 14
Barber, M. 7, 9, 13, 186, 189
barlake xviii, 12, 24, 29n9, 30n15; *see also*
marriage exchange relations
Barnes, S. 132, 140, 149n5, 172, 187
Barad, K. 20
bats 43, 132–3, 183
Baucau 3, 15, 24, 29n3, 70, 77, 78, 80n1,
89–90, 100, 116, 117–24, 125, 153, 188;
airport 156, 175n3, 186; Catholic
Church in 157–61; hospital water
supply 162–3; independence-era water
supply 161–3, 164–6, 167; irrigated rice

206 *Index*

Baucau *continued*
  production 73–6, 136, 137–43; land and
  property disputes 154, 161; late colonial
  development in 154–7; marine terrace
  zone 71, 72–3, 80n7, 96, 98, 102,
  138–9, 141–2; 'new town' 156, 161;
  rainfall 175n6; spiritual ecology of
  spring water in 49–51
Baucau plateau 3, 49, 71, 71–2, 100, 103,
  137, 177n17; groundwater research
  163–5, 174; *see also* savanna
Bear, C. 17, 19, 181
bee na'in see custodians of the water
bees 43, 58n12; seven-headed 47, 51
beeswax 106, 116, 131
bellows 112
Belo, C. 58n16, 80n4, n11, 106, 117,
  118–19, 119, 120, 126n2, n10, 127n18,
  n21
Belu 68
Belu Mau 101
Bennett, J. 19
Berecoli 26, 119, 122, 139–40
Berkes, F. 29n7
betel leaves xviii, 26, 56, 88, 116, 170,
  176n10, 184; *see also bua malus*
birds 43, 63, 73, 74, 110–11, 131, 190,
  191n4
birth 40, 77
bishops 112, 114, 117, 126n9
black (colour) 57n4, 94, 104n8, 134, 136
blood 14, 16, 175n5, 188
Blust, R. 131
boar 131
bodily ontology 186–91
Boelens, R. 7, 8–9, 10, 14, 18, 19, 191n5
Boile 90, 120, 187
Boile Komu 90, 101, 139, 175n7
Boile Mauduku 85, 87
Boleha 73, 75
*Boletím de Comercio, Agricultura e Fomento
  da Provincia de Timor* (BCAeF) 136,
  137, 141, 150n14
Bo'o Dai 167
books 43, 65, 67, 110, 115, 127n27, 140,
  149n12, 183
Boucher, G. 30n13, 62
Boulan Smit, M. 13, 14, 29n10
boundaries 47, 51, 66, 189
Bourdieu, P. 23, 187
Bovensiepen, J. 24, 42, 62, 147–8, 160, 174
Brady, J. 14
Braun, B. 19, 20, 24, 190
breadfruit 73, 77, 124
bride logs 129

Brightman, R. 45
bua malus 116; *see also* betel leaves
Bucoli 101, 120, 170, 185
Budds, J. 17–18, 19
Budiardjo, C. 156
buffalo 24, 58n15, 72, 74, 77, 96, 100, 133,
  136, 141, 142, 146, 167, 172, 188
Bui Leme 81n15
Bui Lua 134, 136
Buibau 104n14, 120, 176n10
Bull, J. 17, 19, 181
Bunak 80n6
Bundura 73, 87, 101, 109, 112–14, 120,
  183; *see also* Ponte Bondura
Burchi, S. 7
Buru 13
Buruma 73, 89, 90, 95, 101, 120, 138, 139,
  145, 157
Butu 71, 73, 96, 101

Cabalaki 63, 121
Caibada 84, 89, 90, 95, 101, 120, 138, 157,
  185
Cairiri 104n6, n12
Caisidu 101–2, 120, 184, 185
capitalism 23
Cardoso, L. 127n23
Carvalho, D.A. 23, 50, 130, 172, 177n19
cassava 132, 133
Castree, N. 21
Catholic Church 30n11, 100, 106, 109,
  126n13, 157–61, 167, 173
Catholicism 42, 45, 64, 114, 157, 173,
  174, 176n11
Caton, S. 18
caves 3, 14, 15, 29n4, 49, 71, 93–4, 95,
  109, 158, 175n4; Kai Hunu 109, 112,
  115, 125, 183–5; Lie Gere 183; Wai Lia
  Bere 49–50, 96–8, 100, 104n14, 155–6,
  157, 164, 168, 172, 176n10; Wai Lia
  Mata 97–8, 164
Celebes (Sulawesi) 68, 70
Ceram 70
ceremonies *see* rituals
Chakrabaty, D. 62
Chefe de suco see village heads
Chen, C. 21
chickens xviii, 133, 135, 136, 149n7
Chinese xvii–xviii, 115, 119, 123, 126n12,
  140, 183
Christu 63
church 174; *see also* Catholic Church
civet cats 43, 49, 91, 92, 104n10, 131
clans 43, 46, 86, 87; *see also* mother-father
  clans

Index 207

climate change 191n6
cloth 24, 64, 77, 116, 131, 183
clothing 66, 67
clouds 14
CNRT 172
cockfighting 156
coconut plantations 131
coconut water 15
coffee plantations 131
colonial administrators 109, 116
colonial period 16, 23, 24–5, 61, 100, 106–28, 129, 136–7, 140, 154–7
colours: black 57n4, 104n8; red 57n4; white 57n4, 104n8; yellow 104n8
Comaroff, J. and Comaroff, J. 25
community managed water supply systems 166–7
Companhia Loidua 120, 121
Conklin, H. 8, 9
conquest narratives 89–90
coral necklaces 77, 106, 168
Coronel Dala Hitu 76, 77
Correia, A. 29n4, 77, 80n2, n4, 81n13, 83, 89, 103n2, 106, 109, 114, 118, 122, 123, 124, 127n20, n22, 127n24, 137, 149n2, 150n14, 150n22, 155, 182, 183, 184, 191n3
cosmopolitics 21
Costin, G. 6, 154, 166, 167
cotton 67, 119
critical ecology 16, 21
crocodiles 15, 43, 49, 68, 79, 81n15, 91, 133
CSIRO Australia 164
'culture' (*lisan*) 43, 56, 64, 190
custodians of the land 50, 101; *see also* spirits
custodians of the water 49, 50–1, 95, 97, 133, 138, 146, 148, 159–60, 165, 167, 168, 175n4, 176n14, 177n16; *see also* spirits
custodians of the words 12; *see also lia na'in*
customary economy 23–5, 30n14, 154, 166–7
customary norms and practices 25, 43, 56, 57, 72, 80n1, 174, 186, 189, 190, 191; *see also lisan*
customary rights 7

Da Camara, F. 135–6, 149n8
da Castro, A. 116
da Costa, C. 27, 29n4, 119, 157
da Costa Guterres, F. 133–4, 191
da Silva, A. 132
da Silva, J.C. 117

dai 42–5, 46, 50, 58n11, 148, 159, 175n5; *see also* spirits
Dai Kele Fatin 114
Dala Hitu 71, 76
Darasula 26, 93, 98
darkness, era of 1, 27, 39, 42–3, 47, 67, 73, 114, 115, 185, 188
Dávila, G. 8
De Josselin de Jong, J. 12
death/death rituals xvii–xviii, 9, 12, 13, 24, 26, 40, 44, 46, 47, 115
deer 131
deforestation 131
development intervention 6, 154
Dili 116, 175n2, n6
Diwake 120
Doel, M. 63
dogs 83, 84, 133, 135, 136, 149n7
Dom see liurai; and headings under Dom *below*
Dom Bastiau 116
Dom Boa Ventura 107, 117–22, 125, 127n23
Dom Fransisco Da Costa Freitas 117, 135
Dom Joao Vicente Paulo 76, 119
Dom Jose dos Reis da Costa 127n21
Dom Manuel dos Reis da Costa 118
Dom Ximenes 117
Domes, J. 81n14
Dores, R. 117–18
dos Santos, E. 79, 104n15, 182
dry season 3, 154–5, 164, 175n6
Duarte, J. 16, 137, 150n14
Dutch 23, 106, 114, 115, 116, 126n2

Eastern Tetum 3, 29n3, 49, 70
Edan (Ade) 126n13
education 106, 110
eels 15, 43, 48, 49, 50, 51, 54, 57–8n8, 79, 83, 88, 91, 92, 94, 104n10, 134, 136, 137–8, 154, 155, 186; *see also tuna*
elections, national 171–2
Ellen, R. 25
empowerment 6
Ernston, H. 20, 173, 190
ethnogeomorphology 174, 188–9
exchange relations 13, 25, 84, 187; colonial 116, 131; marriage 12, 24, 29n4, n9, 73, 77, 93, 106, 109, 129–30, 182

Falintil fighters 172
Fataluku 68, 70, 80n6
Fatumaka 100, 168, 169
fertility 12, 13, 14
fertility-takers fertility-givers 12, 24, 29n9, 77, 93, 99, 100, 102–3, 118, 129; *see also* marriage exchange relations

208 *Index*

fetosaa omane 29n9; *see also* marriage
  exchange relations
Figueiredo, F. 123
fire 13, 39, 43, 57, 62, 63, 66, 67, 79, 100
fish 15, 49, 133
fishing 131
Fitzpatrick, D. 153
floods 14, 70
Flores 13, 14–15, 285
foraging 131
forced labour 106
Forman, S. 14, 16, 26, 29n4, 116, 131,
  132, 150n16
Forth, G. 13, 14
Fox, J. 5, 10, 12, 13, 30n14, 62, 84, 92
França, B. 117
Francillon, G. 29n9, 52, 58n17
Fretilin 106, 126n5, 172, 177n26
Friedberg, C. 131
Furness, L. 3, 6, 29n2, 163, 164, 175n6

Gachenko, E. 7
Galoli 80n3
Gari Arvo 135
Gariuai 168, 170, 185
Gelles, P. 8, 9, 18, 186
Gibson-Graham, J.-K. 5, 17, 19, 24
gituba ginana 48, 57n7, 120–1; *see also* portals
Glover, I. 80n7
goats 24, 96, 100, 141, 143
gold 58n17, 78–9, 88, 100, 101, 104n15,
  109, 124, 127n25, 150n17, 184
gold discs 24, 43, 60, 77, 106, 116,
Gombay, N. 181, 182, 189, 190
gongs 168, 183
Gow, P. 22, 61, 62, 63, 71, 78, 84, 103, 125
Graham, P. 16
Grimes, B. 13, 14, 16
groundwater research 163–5, 174
Gunn, G. 5, 23, 52, 107, 118, 119, 126n2,
  n10, 127n18
Gusmao, X. 61, 110, 172
Guterres, J.L. 172
Guterres J.M. 29n4

Hägerdal, H. 52, 58n16, 61, 81n12, 107,
  118, 126n2, n10, 127n18
Hare Lai Duro 118
head dress 116
healers 43–5
health 13, 15, 16, 43–5, 189
hearths 63
Hera 126n12
Hicks, D. 3, 10, 13, 14, 16, 29n3, 4, n9,
  49, 50, 56, 58n17, n19, 63, 126n9, 133,
  146, 147, 150n17

Hill, A. 187
Hill, H. 5
Hinduism 10, 176n11
Hobsbawm, E. 25
Hohe, T. 24, 130
holy water 14, 15–16; sprinkling of 16,
  30n11
horses 24, 43, 77, 136, 141, 142
Howitt, R. 19
Hull, G. 29n3, 68, 70, 78, 80n5, n6, 103n4
hunter-gathering 131, 149n1
hydro-cosmological cycle 18
hydrogeology 3, 163–5
hydrological cycle 7
hydrosocial cycle 1, 7, 9, 79, 107, 138,
  165, 182–6, 189, 191; agency and
  17–19, 19–20, 21; narratives of 45–8,
  51–7; and ritual centre of Luca 51–6

Illi Manu 86
Incas 9
inclusive sociality 17, 20–3, 25, 42, 45, 56,
  79, 153, 154, 182, 183, 191
independence era 24, 153–4; Baucau town
  water supply 161–3, 164–6, 167;
  community managed water supply
  systems 166–7; development intervention
  6, 154; groundwater research 163–5, 174;
  land and property laws 153–4, 161;
  national politics 170–2; ritual dynamism
  in 167–70, 172–3; sacred house
  reconstruction 157, 173; water laws and
  policies 6, 153, 165–6
India 110, 112
indigene/newcomer dualism 12
Indonesian occupation 5, 23, 106, 134–5,
  156, 167, 183
Ingold, T. 19, 21, 23, 45, 56, 186, 189, 190
Integrated Water Resources Management
  (IWRM) 6, 7
inter-subjectivity 21, 42
Iovina, S. 190
ira kabu see water controllers
Ira Luca 92
Irabi 132–3
iron 142; *see also* metalwork
irrigation 90, 95, 129–50
irrigation channels 95, 129–30, 136, 137,
  138–9, 142, 144, 150n14, 162
irrigation co-operatives 143–5; Andean 9;
  Balinese 10, 15
Iskander, J. 137, 150n16

Jackson, S. 6, 7, 9, 13, 153, 169, 186, 189,
  190

Jennaway, M. 95
Jiménez, A. 6
Joao Graciano Simoes 102
Joao Lere 107, 109–15, 124, 125, 126n11, 127n27, 182, 183
Joao Paulo Vicente 120
Joao Ximenes 85
Johnstone, B.R. 7, 25
Jones, O. 57

kabu bee see water controllers
Kai 74; *see also* Kei
Kai Hunu 109, 112, 115, 125, 183–5
Kai Leki 71
Kai Oli Lale 67
Kai Tui 66
kaiko 8
Kairui 29n3, 54, 63, 70, 80n3
karst 1, 3, 14, 15, 174, 189
Kasa Loi 65, 66, 67
Kawamina 3, 29n3, 63, 68, 70, 78, 80n1, n6
Kehi, B. 12, 13, 14, 16, 26, 39, 49, 50, 63, 81n15, 176n11, 188
Kei 70
kingdoms 13, 115–16, 122
kings *see liurai; and headings under* Dom
Kisar 70, 76–7, 115, 118
Koba Lima 13, 16, 81n15
Kota 126n5
kuda resa 64, 191n4
Kulu Kai 74–5
Kulu Roma 74
Kupang 115, 198–201

La Nina 175n6
labour: division of 103; forced 106
Lacluta 104n6
Laga 77, 79, 122, 133
Lakudarabaha 104n14
Laleia 78, 109, 126n12, 136, 139
land laws 153–4, 161
Langton, M. 7, 13, 14, 22, 186, 187
language 3, 29n3, 63, 68, 70–1, 78, 80n1, n6
Lansing, J. 7, 8, 9, 10, 14, 15, 16, 17, 18, 137, 174
Larantuka 185
Latour, B. 7, 8, 21, 70, 187
Lavau, S. 17, 20, 153, 181, 187
laws: land and property 153–4; water 6, 153, 165–6
Lazarowitz, T. 29n4, 132
Lebalaku Fofa 104n14
Lecomte-Finiger, R. 58n8, 104n8

Ledatame 49–50
Ledatame Ikun 98, 100, 145, 146, 156, 157
Leki Loi 83, 89, 90, 95, 138, 139, 143, 146
Leki Loi Watu 111
Leki Roma 74
Leki Ruo 135
Leki Sae 138
Leti 115
Levi-Strauss, C. 61, 62, 70, 71
Lévy-Bruhl, L. 17, 22, 186
lia na'in 12, 171, 177n24
Lie Gere 183
Liem, S.L. 156
Lifao 114, 115, 116, 117
life 9, 12, 13, 39, 40, 46, 47, 48, 63, 115
lightness, era of 1, 27, 39, 42–3, 46–7, 67, 73, 79, 85, 115, 125, 126n11, 185, 188
lineage house *see* sacred houses (*uma lulik*)
Linton, J. 7, 17–18, 19
Liquica 115, 127n16
lisan 25, 43, 56, 57, 72, 80n1, 174, 186, 189, 190, 191; *see also* customary norms and practices
literacy 5
liurai 109, 122, 127n15, 140; *see also* local rulers; village heads
livelihoods 5–6, 154
local rulers 114, 117; *see also liurai*; village heads
Loch, A. 157
Loi Hunu 133–6
Loi Leki 91–2, 100, 101, 116, 117, 168, 169
Loi Roma 74
Loidua 120
Lorimer, J. 19, 21, 24, 187
Lu Leki (Luu Leki) 52, 58n17, 185, 198–201
Luang 71
Luca 46, 51–6, 57, 58n15, n16, n17, 81n15, 88–91, 92, 101, 107, 109, 115, 116, 125, 127n18, 138, 139, 185, 188, 198–202
Luka Bui 51, 185
lulik 23–4, 25, 26, 42, 88, 171, 173, 190

Maat, H. 137
Macadai 120, 139, 146
Macau 123, 124
McGregor, A. 166
machine cultivation 136, 137, 142
MacLeod, J. 7, 21, 39, 191
McWilliam, A. 1, 23, 24, 26, 50, 70, 80n4, 81n12, 107, 114, 126n1, n9, 130, 131, 135, 155, 156, 169, 174, 189

210 Index

Madaleno, I. 7
maize 116, 131, 132, 133, 137, 145
Major Carlos da Costa *see* Nai Leki
Major Ko'o Raku 27, 46–7, 48, 51, 54, 63, 65, 67, 71, 74, 75, 80n11, 93, 96, 101, 106, 118, 119, 120–1, 122, 124, 126n4, n5, 127n25, 171, 172, 185, 186
Makasae 3, 29n3, n4, n9, 30n19, 54, 63, 68, 70, 80n1, n6, 91, 100, 133, 182
Makassar 71, 77, 80n4
malae 184; *see also* outsiders
malae mutin see Portuguese
Malaku 74
male/female dualism 12
Mambai 49, 57n5, 80n5, 126n11, *130*
Manatuto 109, 114, 126n12, 136, 137, 147, 149n11
Mangili 129
Manufahi (Same) 120–1; rebellions 119, 120, 125
marine terrace zone 71, 72–3, 80n7, 96, 98, 102, 138–9, 141–2
market gardens 142
Maromak 63, 70
marriage 12
marriage exchange relations 12, 24, 29n4, n9, 73, 77, 93, 106, 109, 129–30, 141, 147, 148, 157, 182
marui masara 138, 186
Masin Babulu river 115
matak malarin (positive life force) 12–13
Matebian 63, 71, 77, 87, 90–1, 187
matenek 52, 109–10, 112, 114, 115, 116, 124, 125, 126n11, 146, 183
materiality 20, 21, 190
Mau Ba'i 73, 74, 75
Mau Lau 54–5
Maubara 115
Maukali 120
Mauss, M. 187
Meganck, R. 10
Meitzner Yoder, L. 23, 30n14, 169
Merleau-Ponty, M. 22
meshwork 45
metalwork 71–4, 76, 109, 137, 150n17
metaphysics 18
meti 47, 52, 185, 201; *see also* sea; tides
Metzner, J. 3, 80n7, 129, 131, 140–1, 150n22
Midiki 29n3, 63, 70
military 5, 106, 117, 156, 157, 176n10
milk 14
missionary activity 109, 110, 114
modernity 22, 23
Mol, A. 19

Moluccas 13; *see also* Malaku
Mongolia 23
monkeys 43
moon 13
Moon-Sun deity 22, 52, 63
moradores 119, 120; *see also* warriors
moral economy 8
Moses Nai Usu 110
Mosse, D. 18
mother-father clans 92, 101–2, 184
mother water 87–8
Mount Boile 188
Mu'a Gamu 42
Mullin, M. 56
Mundo Perdido 3, 39, 46, 51, 54, 57n1, 65–7, 70, 84, 87, 137, 164, 188, 190
Myers, F. 22
myths *see* narratives

Nai Leki 107, 119, 122–4, 125, 127n24
Namu Degu 42
narratives 61–7, 189; conquest 89–90; of hydrosocial cycle 45–8, 51–7; origin 63–7, 68, 70, 89–90, 183–4; of return 71–3; Wai Lia spring 92–6; Wai Lili-Wai Wa and Wai Husu Wai spring groves 99–101; Wani Uma 84–8; wet rice production 73–6, 133–6
National Directorate for Water Control and Quality (DNCQA) 163, 164, 165
nationalism 119
nature spirits *see* spirits
natureza 42, 46, 57n3, 66, 114, 125, 135, 185, 191
Naueti 29n3, 63, 68
navel 28, 49, 187
necklaces 24, 77, 106, 168
neoliberalism 20, 23, 24
Neonbasu, G. 16
Nevins, J. 5
Niner, S. 30n15, 110
Noko Loi 127n25
Non-Austronesian languages 70, 78; *see also* Papuan languages
Nossa Senora project 159–60

obligation 12
Oca Ba'i 109, 183
O'Connor, S. 29n4, 71, 78
octopus 15, 49, 74
older sibling younger sibling relations 12, 93, 121, 132
Oliveria, N. 78, 129
Ono Loko 76–7, 80n11
ontological frictions 19–20

Index 211

ontology, bodily 186–91
Onvlee, L. 129–30, 148
open the door ritual 26
Oppermann, S. 190
origin myths 63–7, 68, 70, 89–90, 183–4
Orlove, B. 18
Ormeling, F. 131
Ospina, S. 24, 130
Osso Rua 135
Ossu 26
Ossuala 187
other world 87, 88, 94, 125, 185, 188
outsiders 6, 46, 64, 107, 125; *see also malae*

palm fibres 116, 131
Palmer, L. 6, 7, 12, 13, 14, 16, 20n14, 23,
    26, 39, 49, 50, 63, 81n15, 93, 130, 153,
    165, 169, 172, 177n19, 187, 188, 190
pandanus 13
Pannell, S. 13, 29n4, 131
Papua 68, 70
Papua New Guinea 8
Papuan languages 29, 63, 80n6; *see also*
    Non-Austronesian languages
Partido Democratico 172
Pasquale, V. 5
path clearing ritual 12
peacemaking 107
Peake, G. 6, 154
peanuts 132
Peck, J. 20, 24
Pederson, M. 21, 22, 23, 25, 56
Pélissier, R. 118, 119
personhood 21, 22, 62
pests 10, 136–7
Peterson, J. 103
Philippines 9
Philpott, S. 5
pigs 8, 24, 77, 100, 102, 133, 135, 149n7
Pintupi 22
piped water 134, 155, 161–3, 166, 167,
    177n21
place and place-making 1, 4, 10, 61, 62, 95
plantations 131
plates 183
ploughs 136, 137, 142
Plumwood, V. 187
political authority/ritual authority dualism
    12
political ecology 17, 20, 183
political parties: Apodeti 106, 126n5;
    CNRT 172; Fretilin 106, 126n5, 172,
    177n26; Kota 126n5; Partido
    Democratico 172; Travalista 126n5;
    UDT 106

politics, national 170–2
Ponte Bondura 78, 109; *see also* Bundura
portals 46, 48, 49, 57n5, 79
ports 107, 109
Portugal 57n5, 110, 122, 123, 149n13
Portuguese 5, 23, 42, 46, 100, 106, 107,
    109, 114, 115–16, 117, 119, 122–3, 124,
    127n18, 131–2, 140
positive life force (*matak malarin*) 12–13
post-humanism 16, 19
Posto Wai Lewa 124
poverty 5
Powell, B. 6, 154, 166, 167
power 4, 174
power relations 116, 131, 187, 190
priests 112, 114, 126n9, 159
prohibition ceremonies (tara bandu) 23, 100,
    168–70, 172, 173, 190–1
property, laws and sanctions 153–4, 161,
    166
property relations 21, 22
Prufer, K. 14
pumpkins 132
Pura Batur, Bali 15
pythons 15, 47, 48, 50, 51, 63, 79, 83, 97,
    134; *see also* snakes

Quelicai 29n4, 118–19, 122, 149n12

rai seluk see other world
rainfall 175n6, 191n1, n6
rainmaking 14, 109, 182, 183, 184
Ramelau 57n5, 63, 187
Ramos-Horta, J. 118, 119
Ranger, T. 25
Rappaport, R. 8, 131, 187
rats 43, 136–7
reciprocity 12, 13, 25
red (colour) 57n4
Rede Ba Rai 153
Reis, Vicente *see* Sahe
RENETIL 177n26
resistance, anti-colonial/outsider 6, 107,
    110, 119–20
resistance forces 5
respectful relations 76–7, 109
Reuter, T. 10, 14, 15, 56, 183
rice 24, 66–7, 77, 100, 109, 116; imports
    142; *see also* wet rice
Rikainena 76, 184
rituals xvii–xviii, 8, 15–16, 23, 129–31,
    145–7, 154–5, 167–70, 172–3, 183, 188;
    death xvii–xviii, 12, 24; life xviii, 12;
    marriage xviii, 12; path clearing xviii,
    12; path making 12; rainmaking 14,

212 Index

rituals *continued*
109, 182, 183, 184; sacrifice xviii, 13, 14, 45, 95, 96–7, 102, 133, 134–6, 143, 149n7, 170, 177n21; seven-yearly 95–6, 100, 154, 157, 167; *tara bandu* (prohibition ceremony) 23, 100, 168–70, 172, 173, 190–1; water increase 14, 49–50, 96–8, 160; water 'opening' 143; water sharing/dividing 143–4, 150n20; and wet rice production xviii, 129–31, 133, 134–6, 137, 142, 143–5
Rodemeier, S. 13, 14, 16, 182, 190
Rodriguez, S. 7, 8, 140
Roelvink, G. 17
Roma 70, 73
Rose, D. 19, 23, 190
rota (sceptre) 54, 104n12, 116, 117, 119, 139
Roti 62, 84
Ro'ulu 120, 123
Rubi Lai 70

Sa'a Dahu 75
sacra 79, 88, 101, 117, 132, 134, 135, 148, 167–8, 176n12, 187
sacred 14; Balinese concept of 10; *see also lulik*
sacred houses (*uma lulik*) 10, 12, 16, 24, 63, 93, 95, 148, 169; Baha Kai Lale 109, 115; Boile Komu 90, 101, 139, 146, 175n7; destruction of 154, 156; independence-era reconstruction of 157, 173; Ledatame Ikun 98, 100, 145, 146, 156, 157; Macadai 139; Oca Ba'i 109, 183; Uma Liurai 123; Uma Loi Leki 123; Wabubo 139, 175n7; Wai Mata Buu 146, 147, 177n22
sacrifice 13, 14, 45, 95, 96–7, 102, 133, 134–6, 143, 149n7, 170, 177n21
Sahe (Vicente Reis) 110, 115, 125, 127n27
Saldanha, J. 5
salt production 131
Samalari 120
Same *see* Manufahi
sanctions 166
sandalwood 106, 126n3, 131
sanitation 6, 166
savanna 3, 71, 96–8
sceptre (*rota*) 116, 117, 139
Schapper, A. 80n1
Schefold, R. 57
Scheiner, C. 5
Schoffel, P. 6, 166

Schulte Nordolt, H.G. 52, 61, 149n4
sea 10, 13, 14, 47, 52, 57, 112, 185–6, 201; *see also* meti; *tasi*
seasonal cycle 164
semen 14
Seram 13, 29n10
Seu Baru 54, 55, 66
seven (number) 146
seven-yearly ceremonies 95–6, 100, 154, 157, 167
Shaw, K. 24
Shepherd, C. 16, 132, 135, 154
Sherbondy, J. 9
Shoesmith, D. 171
shrimps 15, 49
Silva, H.L. 149n9
sinkholes 3
'skin changing' 42, 46
sky 14, 188
Smith, N. 7
snakes 43, 49, 50, 78–9, 88, 92, 101, 114, 138, 184, 185; in Andean mythology 9; *see also* pythons
Soares, A.V.M. 52, 54, 80n10, 104n6, 115, 116, 119, 126n2, n13, 127n18, 149n9, 176n9
sociality 21; *see also* inclusive sociality
Soibada 115
Sombai 115
Sorlin, S. 20, 173, 190
space 1
spears 168, 177n22
Spillett, P. 53, 54, 80n4, 81n12, 83, 89–90, 103n2, 126n2, n9, 127n18
spirits 1, 13, 15, 42–5, 46, 49, 57n3, 64, 83, 91, 102, 134, 142, 143, 170; *see also dai*
spiritual ecology 8–16, 183
Sponsel, L. 8, 14, 56
springs 3, 4, 12–13, 14, 15, 29n10, 48, 49–51, 54–6, 61, 63, 65, 83, 84, 87, 88, 121, 137, 186; Aubaca 71, 80n10, 102, 177n21; Bui Lua 134, 136; Caibada 102; Ho'o Oli 102; Irabi 132–3; Ira Luca 92; Loi Hunu 133–6; Mau Lau 54–5; and national politics 170–2; Wai Daba xvii–xviii, 104n12, 139–40; Wai Haulale 102; Wai Husu 51, 102, 137–8, 139, 141, 142; Wai Kinari 104n16; Wai Lakulo 92, 100, 167–9; Wai Lesu 55–6; Wai Lewa 51, 84, 90, 92, 95, 101, 102, 122, 123, 124; Wailili 55, 92, 167–9, 176n15; Wai Lobi 98; Wai Lotu 116–17, 127n19; Wai Lua 176n14; Wai Luca 86; Wai

Index   213

Mata Me 74; Wai Mata Oli 74; Wai
    Mori Bere 104n14, 176n10; Wai Naha
    76; Wai Taka 46, 48, 65; Watabo
    177n16; We Krang 87; We Liurai 53;
    We Lolo 53; We Tasi 104; *see also*
    Wai Lia
Stanner, W. 22
stars 13
Stead, V. 153
Strang, V. 8, 9, 13, 18, 21, 173, 177n29,
    191
Strathern, M. 21
subaks 10, 15
subsistence economy 131
Suchet-Pearson, S. 19
Sulawesi (Celebes) 68, 70
Sullivan, S. 6, 17, 21, 22
Sumba 129–30, 148
sun 9, 13, 39, 46, 47, 52, 57, 79
Sun-Moon deity 70; *see also* Moon-Sun
    deity
supernatural 8
sustainability 24
sweet potatoes 132
swords 24, 43, 73, 76, 77, 106, 168,
    177n22
Swyngedouw, E. 7, 17

Tai Loi 83, 89, 90, 95, 138, 139, 143
tais 16, 64, 67, 77, 94, 111, 131, 203; *see
    also* cloth
talibere 49, 51, 63, 114, 138, 185–6; *see also*
    eels; snakes
Tamisari, F. 22
Tanter, R. 5
tara bandu 23, 100, 168–70, 172, 173,
    190–1
tasi 52, 74, 201
Taur Matan Ruak 172
Tavares, Antonio 107, 113–14, 126n9
tax 106, 119, 136, 140, 155
teak 131
termites 43, 71, 80n9
Tetum 3, 23, 29n3, 68, 81n15
Tetum Terik 29n9, 81n15
Teulale 51, 101, 102, 141
Therik, T. 16, 52
Thu, P. 143
tides 52, 57, 59n22, 201
Tirilolo 26, 89, 90, 95, 101, 120, 138, 139,
    157, 169, 170, 185
Titicaca, Lake 9
totemism 43
trade 68, 73, 80n4, 106, 109, 126n1, n3,
    n12

Traube, E. 1, 13, 14, 49, 57n5, 62, 103,
    126n11, 130, 147, 148, 156, 188
Travalista 126n5
tribute system 116, 131, 145
tricksters 83, 84
Triloca 170, 185
Trindale, J. 189
trunk/tips dualism 12
Tsembaga 8
Tsing, A. 16, 19, 173, 181
Tsintjilonis, D. 148, 186, 187
Tuana, N. 19
Tukung Besi 68
tuna 58n19
Tutuala 112, 114, 198

UDT 106
Uma Lari 117
Uma Liurai 123
Uma Loi Leki 123
uma lulik see sacred houses
Uma Medai 92
Uma Meti 117
underworld 52, 65, 72, 188
UNESCO 10
United Nations 5, 6
United Nations Transitional
    Administration (UNTAET) 161, 163
Urich, P. 131, 137, 189

Vemasse 79, 90, 104n6, n15, 109, 114,
    116–17, 126n12, n13, 139
Venilale 104n6
Vessoru (We Soru) 58n15, 104n6, 133
village heads 140, 143, 144, 154, 156, 157,
    165, 185
Viqueque 54, 58n17, 81n15, 115
Vischer, M. 12, 14
vital materialism 16, 19
Viveiros de Castro, E. 20, 148, 173, 186

Wabubo 139, 175n7
Wai Badu 65
Wai Bobo 52, 58n15,
Wai Daba xvii–xviii, 104n12, 139–40
Wai Hau 86, 87, 101, 102, 184, 185
Wai Husu 51, 102, 137–8, 139, 141, 142
Wai Husu-Wai Lewa 99–101, 103,
    104n14, 117, 121, 169, 170
Wai Kinari 104n16
Wai Lakulo 92, 100, 167–8
Wai Lesu 55–6
Wai Lewa 51, 80n11, 84, 90, 92, 95, 101,
    102, 122, 123, 124

214   *Index*

Wai Lia xvii, 80n10, 92–6, 99, 100, 101, 103, 104n12, 137–9, 141, 142, 145–7, 154–7, 164, 165, 167, 172, 176–7n15, n16, n19, n22; and Catholic Church 158–60; flow cycle 3; pump station system 161
Wai Lia Bere 49–50, 96–8, 100, 104n14, 155–6, 157, 164, 168, 172, 176n10
Wai Lia Mata 97–8, 164
Wai Lia Wai Lobi 87
Wai Lili-Wai Wa 99–101, 103, 117, 121, 169, 170
Wai Lotu 116–17, 127n19
Wai Luca 86
Wai Luo 86, 87, 101, 102, 184, 185
Wai Mata Buu 146, 147, 156, 177n22
Wai Mata Me 74
Wai Mata Oli 74
Wai Mori Bere 104n14, 176n10
Wai Naha 86
Wai Nete Watu Ba'i 39, 54, 65, 188; *see also* Mundo Perdido
Wai Riu 54, 65–6, 67, 187–8
Wai Taka 46, 48, 65, 102
Wai Wono 73, 74
Wailili 26, 91, 92, 100, 104n6, 116, 117, 137, 167–9, 185
Waima'a 3, 29n3, n4, n9, 30n19, 63, 68, 70, 73, 103n4, 126n2, 182
Wali Sae 138
Wallace, L. 3, 29n1, 164, 177n17, 188, 191n1, n6
Wani Uma 26, 73, 74, 76, 84–8, 90, 113, 114, 120, 139, 145, 146, 183, 184, 191n2
'War of the Madmen' 127n18
warriors 89, 103, 120
wars 89, 101, 107, 116, 117, 126n11, 149n1, 155; Manufahi 119, 120, 125
Watabo 177n16
water channels 95, 101, 129, 136, 139, 141, 143
water controllers (*kabu bee/ira kabu/wai kabu*) 133, 136, 138, 140, 141, 142–3, 143, 144, 145
water increase rituals 14, 49–50, 96–8, 160
water laws and policy 6, 153, 165–6
water rights 6, 7
water sharing/dividing 143–4, 150n20

Waterson, R. 57
Watson, J. 10
Watu Naru 85, 87, 184
Waukau 124
we ai balun 53
We Biku 115, 198–202
We Biku We Hali 54, 115, 198–202
We Hali 52, 57, 115, 116, 198–202
We Krang 87
We Lewa 90
We Soru (Vessoru) 58n15, 104n6, 133
We Tasi 104n6
Weibel, P. 21
wet rice production 5, 14–15, 71, 73–6, 98, 103, 129–50, 182; Baucau and 73–6, 136, 137–43; colonial records of 129, 136–7; irrigation co-operatives 143–5; machine cultivation 136, 137, 142; pests 136–7; rituals xviii, 129–31, 133, 134–6, 137, 142, 143–5; spring creation narratives and 133–6
wet season 3, 162, 175n6
Wetar 68, 115
whales 74
Whatmore, S. 19, 190
white (colour) 57n4, 104n8
wife-giver wife-taker relations 29n9, 129
Wilcock, D. 174, 188, 189, 190
Williams, N. 22, 56
Winarto, Y. 137
wind 57n6, 79, 113, 185, 190
Wittfogel, K. 17
Wittgenstein, L. 1, 39–42, 64
women 26, 30n15, 30n16, 149n3
Wono Loi 83, 89, 90, 95, 138, 139, 143, 146
Wono Sae 138
World Heritage 10
Wurm, S. 70
Wylie, J. 7, 19, 20, 21, 63, 182

Xanana *see* Gusmao, X.

yams 93, 133
Yang, M. 23
yellow (colour) 104n8
Young, D. 14

Zerner, C. 173